LOST AND FOUND

Finding Self-Reliance After the Loss of a Spouse

LOST AND FOUND

Finding Self-Reliance After the Loss of a Spouse

LOST AND FOUND

Finding Self-Reliance After the Loss of a Spouse

P. Mark Accettura, Esq.

Steven J. Case

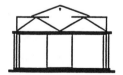

Collinwood Press,
Farmington Hills, Michigan

P. Mark Accettura, Esq.
Steven J. Case

Collinwood Press
35055 W. 12 Mile Road, Suite 132
Farmington Hills, MI 48331

The information contained in this book is not intended to be comprehensive and should not be construed by readers as individual legal advice. The laws pertaining to estate planning are inherently complex and constantly changing. Therefore, readers should consult an experienced estate planning attorney for specific legal advice regarding their individual estate planning needs.

Cover Design and Page Layout: JBGraphics, Jillian Blume, JBlumeG@aol.com

Cover Photo: © 1999 Wesley R. Hitt c/o Mira

Interior Photography: © Keith Tishken

Library of Congress Catalog Number: 2001117500

Printed in the United States

International Standard Book Number: 0-9669278-1-8

Table of Contents

CHAPTER THREE

NAVIGATING SOCIAL SECURITY
Doreen Benson

CHAPTER FOUR

INSURANCE: CLAIMS, LIFE, HEALTH AND LONG TERM CARE
James M. Knaus, CLU, ChFC, CFP

CHAPTER FIVE
PUTTING YOUR FINANCIAL HOUSE IN ORDER
Steven J. Case, CLU, ChFC, CFP, CDP

CHAPTER SIX

IRA AND RETIREMENT DISTRIBUTIONS
P. Mark Accettura, Esq.

CHAPTER SEVEN
SETTLING THE ESTATE:
PROBATE AND TRUST ADMINISTRATION
P. Mark Accettura, Esq. and Samuel A. Hurwitz, Esq.

CHAPTER EIGHT

TAX REPORTING

P. Mark Accettura, Esq.

CHAPTER NINE

Basic Estate Planning
P. Mark Accettura, Esq.

CHAPTER TEN

Advanced Estate Planning
P. Mark Accettura, Esq.

CHAPTER ELEVEN
PRENUPTIAL AGREEMENTS
P. Mark Accettura, Esq.

CHAPTER TWELVE
LOSING INDEPENDENCE
P. Mark Accettura, Esq.

CHAPTER THIRTEEN
MAKING FUNERAL ARRANGEMENTS
P. Mark Accettura, Esq.

About the Authors

P. MARK ACCETTURA, ESQ.

P. MARK ACCETTURA is a practicing attorney specializing in the areas of estate planning and taxation. He is the author of The *Michigan Estate Planning Guide*, Collinwood Press, 1999, and is a frequent lecturer on estate planning topics. Mark received his Bachelor of Arts degree from Oakland University in 1977, his law degree in 1981 from the University of Detroit/Mercy School of Law, and his Master of Laws Degree (LL.M. in taxation) in 1982 from New York University School of Law.

Mark was an adjunct professor at the University of Detroit/Mercy School of Law from 1984 to 1994, where he taught courses on income taxation, estate and gift tax and pension and employee benefits.

Mark hosted Law Talk, a one-hour public access television show seen in 37 cities in southeastern Michigan. Mark's guests include judges, legislators and other legal policy makers. Mark has been on sabbatical while writing The *Michigan Estate Planning Guide*, and *Lost and Found*. You can contact Mark either through his link on www.lostandfoundspouse.com or directly at maccettura@agplc.com.

STEVEN J. CASE,
CLU, ChFC, CFP, CDP

STEVEN J. CASE graduated from Cornell University with a B.S. in business administration and applied economics. He is also a Certified Financial Planner (CFP), a Chartered Life Underwriter (CLU), a Chartered Financial Consultant (ChFC), and a Certified Divorce Planner (CDP).

Steve lives in Michigan with his wife Cheryl and two daughters: Isabella and Alexandra. He is a co-founder and senior partner of Financial Independence, Inc., an independent financial planning firm. He works one-on-one with clients to help them understand their income needs, priorities, and goals, in order to design relevant, achievable financial plans for personal wealth enhancement and asset protection. He plans and conducts financial planning seminars aimed at helping participants reduce taxes, increase wealth and protect their wealth for retirement.

Steve founded a non-profit organization that sponsors outreach programs for widows. The programs included seminars, support groups and a weekly radio program covering topics relating to the loss of a spouse.

Steve is securities licensed with Washington Square Securities to sell stocks, bonds, and mutual funds. He is a Registered Investment Advisor Affiliate of Washington Square's Corporate Registered Investment Advisor. He is licensed in the State of Michigan to sell life insurance and annuities.

You may contact Steve through his link on www.lostandfoundspouse.com.

DOROTHY E. DEREMO

Dorothy E. Deremo, RN, MSN, MHSA, CNAA, CHE, is the President and Chief Executive Officer of Hospice of Michigan (HOM). HOM is the largest statewide not-for-profit end-of-life care company in the nation and provides compassionate palliative care to 900 patients a day.

Ms. Deremo has held key nursing administration and hospital executive positions. She has published numerous articles and was a contributing author to two books prior to *Lost and Found*.

Ms. Deremo graduated from Henry Ford Hospital School of Nursing in 1969, received her Bachelor of Science in Nursing from Wayne State University in 1974 and her Master's Degree in Nursing from Wayne State University in 1976. She completed her Master's Degree in Health Services Administration Program at the University of Michigan in October 1994.

Ms. Deremo is a member of Sigma Theta Tau, the National Honor Society for Nursing, and has been active in many professional organizations: The American College of Health Care Executives, National Organization of Nurse Executives, the Michigan Organization of Nurse Executives, and the American Nurses' Association.

In 1986, Ms. Deremo was a Johnson & Johnson/Wharton Fellow at the University of Pennsylvania. Ms. Deremo also was a Health Trust Fellow at the King's Fund College studying the British National Health Service 1995. She is a Diplomat of the American College of Health Care Executives and certified in Advanced Nursing Administration through the American Nurses' Association.

THOMAS LYNCH

Thomas Lynch is the author of *Bodies in Motion and at Rest* and *The Undertaking: Life Studies from the Dismal Trade*, winner of an American Book Award and finalist for the National Book Award, and three collections of poetry: *Skating with Heather Grace*, *Grimalkin & Other Poems*, and *Still Life in Milford*. His poems and essays have appeared in the Los Angeles Times, the New York Times, Esquire, Newsweek, Harper's, The New Yorker, The Paris Review, the London Review of Books, and elsewhere. Mr. Lynch lives in Milford, Michigan, where he is the funeral director.

DOREEN BENSON

In Doreen Benson's 26-year career with the Social Security Administration, she held numerous positions including service representative, claims representative, operations analyst, field representative, and public affairs specialist. She served as the official agency spokesperson co-hosting a call-in radio program answering Social Security questions from listeners, and wrote a weekly column in *The Detroit News* from January 1995 through the summer of 2000.

JAMES M. KNAUS,
CLU, ChFC, CFP

James M. Knaus is a Certified Financial Planner as well as a Chartered Life Underwriter, Chartered Financial Consultant, and Licensed Life Insurance Counselor. He has over 31 years of financial planning experience, concentrating in the areas of estate, tax, insurance and investment planning. He serves on the board of the Certified Financial Planner Board of Examiners, Denver, Colorado, and is the board chair for 2001. Mr. Knaus is a member of the Society of Financial Service Professionals as well as an adjunct faculty member in the Oakland University Personal Financial Planning Program.

LYNN GROSS, ESQ.

Lynn Gross received her Bachelor of Science Degree in Economics from Oakland University in 1987, and her law degree from Detroit College of Law in 1993. Since 1993, Lynn has been admitted to practice in all Michigan Courts, as well as the United States District Court, Eastern District of Michigan, and the United States Court of Appeals for the Sixth Circuit. Lynn's practice focuses on estate planning, estate administration, trust administration, estate, trust and gift taxation, and probate. A frequent lecturer on estate planning, Lynn's years as a litigator lend to her probate court and dispute resolution practice.

SAMUEL A. HURWITZ, ESQ.

Samuel A. Hurwitz practices in the areas of estate planning, trust and estate administration and Medicaid planning. He received his Bachelor of Arts degree in Economics from Oberlin College in 1978, and graduated from the University of Illinois College of Law in 1981. Sam became a Certified Public Accountant (Illinois) in 1990, and has earned a Certificate in Financial Planning. Sam has been admitted to practice in all Michigan Courts since 1981, The United States District Court, Eastern District of Michigan since 1982 and the United States Tax Court since 1984.

Introduction

I MET ANN when I was a young attorney. She was in her late sixties, and at the time I was barely thirty. I knew her husband, but only met Ann after his death. Ann was a good woman, a mother of two. Her late husband had been self-employed. He had handled most of their financial affairs. Ann's role was that of a traditional homemaker, not at all involved in family finances. Ann was a recovering alcoholic who had overcome her disease with the help of her minister, God, and Virginia Slims. Although her late husband had left her well off, Ann was plagued by the fear that she would run out of money, a fear I would come to learn is experienced by most widows irrespective of their actual net worth. Her fears were compounded by what she perceived to be mounting funeral, accounting, and legal bills. Not having worked with professionals before, all such fees seemed exorbitant to Ann. During the settlement of her late husband's affairs, Ann became increasingly anxious.

Initially, Ann relied on me, not just for legal advice, but also for emotional support. I was a little uncomfortable with what I observed to be a growing emotional attachment, but wasn't alarmed. Contrary to the public portrayal of attorneys as sharks, snakes, or worse, a natural bond often occurs between attorneys and their clients. This is especially true for clients, such as Ann, who are in distress.

Ann's growing dependence began to interfere with my ability to represent her. As time went on, she became hurt, disillusioned, and angry. How could I charge her so much knowing of her pain and precarious financial condition? Despite her growing anxiety and mistrust, I pressed on in the administration of her husband's estate, hoping her anxiety would subside with time.

Ann's plight worsened when she learned, soon after her husband's death, that her son was terminally ill. Tragically, within months of her husband's death, we were attending her son's funeral.

After her son's death, we resumed our work. She seemed to be coping reasonably well, so it came as a surprise when she told me that she had become so discouraged by her new responsibilities that she had considered suicide. I now know, what regrettably I did not understand at the time, that not even a single utterance of the word "suicide" can be allowed without immediate intervention. Within two weeks, Ann had taken her life.

Obviously, Ann needed professional psychiatric help. I don't know that I could have prevented her death, but I vowed that in the future I would intervene at the slightest hint of trouble. I also had a new appreciation for the pain and trouble experienced by recently widowed clients.

This book is my attempt to give surviving spouses the resources they need to grieve, learn, and even to prosper. Perhaps, if Ann had had such a book, her tragic death could have been avoided.

Having had twenty years' experience as a lawyer, I have witnessed the struggles of scores of widows and widowers. I now understand that only those who have lost a spouse know the pain of such a loss. While the emotions are most acute in the first few months after death, feelings of sorrow, grief, guilt and even anger often linger. It is a time of great insecurity and uncertainty.

Although each spouse reacts differently, they all suffer. The depth of grief and the length of the recovery vary greatly and derive from an impossibly complex set of factors including the length of the marriage, whether or not the couple had children, and the level of the survivor's dependence on his or her spouse. The ability of the surviving spouse to recover to a happy, healthy and financially secure life is more predictable. Experience indicates that the more independent and self-sufficient the survivor, the faster the recovery. However, many put up a good front. They are not always as independent as they would want you to believe, so it is important that each takes the careful and measured steps necessary to recovery.

The mission of our book is to provide surviving spouses, of all backgrounds and experience, with the tools necessary to facilitate a speedy recovery to a happy, healthy life.

The loss of a spouse is, in the truest sense, a rude awakening. The survivor must not only deal with his or her grief, but also must step into circumstances for which he or she may be ill equipped. The survivor must find emotional and financial stability, as well as a new purpose, and life plan. It is a dizzying process. Well-meaning friends and relatives offer advice, sometimes good, sometimes not. Quick decisions are often made without proper guidance and forethought because of pressures brought to bear by the immediacy of the situation.

While Ann may not be the typical case, her story illustrates the wide-ranging needs of the recently widowed, including emotional, financial, legal and accounting help. No one professional can fully advise the widow or widower, and shouldn't try. Professionals should avoid giving advice outside their area of expertise.

Lost and Found is a reference for professionals and laypersons alike, to provide the most expert advice available to surviving spouses. We have assembled leading authorities in the fields of grief counseling, funeral planning, law, social security, investing and insurance to provide their learned insight and direction. I am aware of no other resource, written or electronic, that brings such wide-ranging expertise under a single umbrella. I am honored and pleased to have assembled such an informed group.

To supplement the good counsel provided by our authors, the book has a separate Directory of Resources. The Directory is a compilation of telephone numbers, addresses, web sites, and a bibliography, that offer additional information pertaining to the topics discussed in the book. Each author has helped our Directory staff to identify the most comprehensive and useful assistance in his or her field. The Directory will aid the reader in finding more information on personal grief counseling, Social Security, government benefits, insurance, financial planning, estate planning, and funeral arrangements.

Steven J. Case created www.lostandfoundspouse.com to continuously update the Directory. The Website is a summary of the Directory, and will evolve as the resources change. New resources will be added as they become available and those that become obsolete will be deleted. Through internet links, www.lostandfoundspouse.com will also allow the reader to directly contact the contributing authors, outside service providers, and government agencies.

The first chapter of the book addresses grief, since the journey to self-reliance cannot begin without proper grieving. For some, dealing with their new duties distracts them from their loss. Others are paralyzed by their grief and unable to cope. Just as airline passengers are instructed to apply their own oxygen masks before attending to their children, in times of grief, take care of yourself first! You cannot help anyone, especially yourself, if you are suffocating under the weight of your own grief. In Chapter One, Dorothy E. Deremo, President and CEO of Hospice of Michigan, provides an inside look into the grieving process, and shares some inspiring stories of surviving spouses who have recaptured the joy of living.

Some things can't wait, however. Various receipts, papers and documents must be saved and tagged. Chapter Two, "Getting Organized," identifies important documents to locate and save. For example, date of death values are extremely important for income and estate tax purposes, so it is advisable to save the newspaper stock page on the date of death (and both Friday and Monday's paper for weekend deaths). Chapter Two identifies the tasks that require immediate attention and important documents to save. Comprehensive charts and checklists aid the effort to get organized.

Doreen Benson, a longtime employee of the Social Security Administration and columnist for The Detroit News, explains Social Security benefits in Chapter Three. Dealing with the Social Security Administration is one of the first "to-do" items for surviving spouses. Ms. Benson explains Social Security benefit programs in simple, understandable terms.

Proper insurance coverage is important for a secure future. While some coverages may carry over from your late spouse, others need to be purchased. To avoid gaps in coverage, health, life, and long term care insurance should be evaluated as soon as possible after the death of a spouse. In Chapter Four, insurance expert James M. Knaus discusses the essentials of health, life and long term care insurance, including options which may be available under your late spouse's insurance programs.

Surviving spouses are perhaps most vulnerable in the investment area. Unfortunately, the road to grandma's house is rife with foxes wanting to eat grandma's nest egg. Unscrupulous characters, motivated by their own interests, abound. Adding to the problem, a number of sociological and demographic studies indicate that today's typical surviving spouse is a woman who is not knowlegeable about the world of investments. The combination can be unfortunate, even tragic. This is not to say that surviving spouses shouldn't use the services of investment counselors. To the contrary, a qualified impartial investment advisor is essential for the novice and experienced investor alike. The key is to be knowledgeable enough to evaluate the investment counselor's credentials and performance. In Chapter Five, Steven J. Case educates the reader in the fundamentals of investing, and the qualities to look for in choosing a professional investment advisor.

The nature and extent of legal intervention at the death of a spouse depends on a number of factors including whether or not probate is involved, the size of the estate, whether your late spouse had a trust or trusts, and whether there was a family business. Each estate requires different settlement procedures. Chapter Seven discusses various estate settlement procedures required for different estates, as well as the rules pertaining to post mortem trust administration.

Most married couples file a joint income tax return while both spouses are living. What impact does the death of one spouse have on the filing status of the surviving spouse? Do special rules apply in the year of death? These and other questions are answered in Chapter Eight. Revocable trusts that continue after the death of the grantor, which would be the case on the death of the first spouse, require special care. Such trusts become irrevocable upon the grantor's death, and thus become separate taxable entities requiring their own tax identification number and separate annual income tax return (Form 1041). Larger estates may require the filing of a federal estate tax return (Form 706) within nine months of death. Chapter Eight discusses all such tax filings and is essential reading to understand and to supplement the advice of a professional accountant.

Time tarries for no one, and the big wheel of life continues to revolve. Each of us will pass one day. There are lessons to be learned from a spouse's death. Their death can and should inspire us to plan our own estate and legacy. The amount of estate planning you require will depend on how well you and your late spouse planned. Well-laid plans reviewed and revised immediately prior to death may require little or no modification. Conversely, there may be an urgent need for estate planning if no planning was ever done. In such cases, you may have to play "catch-up" to avoid unwanted income and estate tax consequences at your death. Special planning is necessary if you are the default caretaker of children from prior marriages, handicapped children, or a family business.

Chapter Nine is an introduction to basic estate planning concepts that allow you to avoid probate and to generally put your estate planning house in order. Chapter Ten discusses more advanced estate planning concepts for surviving spouses with larger estates which would otherwise be subject to estate tax.

Funerals, burials, and cremations are an integral part of the grieving process. They provide closure, finality, and living proof that our mate will not be home when we return. In burying our dead, we often ponder our own lives and mortality. In a sweet yet sorrowful way, contemplating our life, legacy, and death adds to our life experience. Chapter Thirteen, "Making Funeral Arrangements," contains helpful information on funerals, burial, and cremation. Funerals are for the living. At the end of Chapter Thirteen we are fortunate to have reproduced the final chapter of renowned author, poet, and funeral director Thomas Lynch's book *The Undertaking: Life Studies from the Dismal Trade.* In Mr. Lynch's chapter entitled "Tract," he muses about his own life and death; it is a must read. If your spouse is still alive, you may want to skip to Chapter Thirteen and read it first. If your spouse is gone, Chapter Thirteen will be useful in contemplating your own final plans.

Lost and Found was written to help you ask the questions. There is much to do upon the death of a spouse. The chapters of this book will help you understand the issues and learn the jargon. You will gain from the information whether you tackle a particular job yourself or seek professional help. Aside from knowledge, it is my wish that *Lost and Found* gives you hope. These may be difficult times, but time heals and painful memories fade. Your task is to move forward, administer to yourself and your deceased spouse's affairs, then make a new life for yourself. I wish you well.

P. Mark Accettura

Acknowledgement

This book would not have been possible without the help, support, ideas, research and editing of my family, friends and colleagues. With love and gratitude to my wife Amy, who helped me pull the whole thing together. Many thanks to our graphic artist, Jillian Blume who is the inspiration and perspiration behind the layout and design of the book. Thank you, Keith Tishken, my old college friend for the interior photography. Thank you, James Jenkins, CPA and staff for your help with Chapter Eight, Tax Reporting. I thank my clients for their patience over the last several months of writing, and to Kimberly Rapp, Lynn Gross and Samuel Hurwitz for their input and help while I wandered around in a daze trying to juggle home, practice and *Lost and Found*. I thank the many people who lent their professional expertise and insight including: Margaret Cotter (Grief), Mark Ziegler (Funerals), Peg Reimer (Funerals), and Gregory Stock.

P. Mark Accettura

To my parents, my wife, Cheryl, and my daughters Isabella and Alexandra.

Steven J. Case

Chapter One

Grieving the Loss of a Spouse

Dorothy E. Deremo, Hospice of Michigan

Introduction

DEATH CHANGES EVERYTHING, especially when it's the death of your spouse. You may experience confusion, doubt, fear, abandonment, insecurity, anger, sorrow and a host of other feelings. The ground is shaking and everything seems to be in flux, including your finances, your social life and even your own health.

Suddenly there is no plan or pattern in place. All of your images of the past are displaced by the fuzzy realization that fate has dealt you a blow that has changed your life. Waves of strong emotion threaten to engulf your ability to think, make decisions and properly care for yourself. Strong, even overpowering emotions are a normal and expected consequence of your loss. Once you come to accept that your primary source of love, happiness and security is gone, the grieving process can begin.

We are much more knowledgeable about physical injuries than injuries of the spirit. If we have a physical injury like a cut, we bleed, and a scab forms over the wound. We protect the area from infection by keeping it clean and shielding it from re-injury. The scab may break open delaying the healing process, but eventually the tenderness lessens, the wound heals and normal function returns. We know with time our cut will heal and we will be restored to health.

The same healing principles apply to injuries of the spirit. Losing a spouse can be an emotional assault that hurts deeply. If you're scared, confused and hurting, you are not crazy. You would not be human if you were not struggling to cope. Your emotional and physical reactions are part of the normal grieving process that follows a profound loss.

Grieving is a normal process that contributes to emotional healing. With time, your wounds will mend and your life, though changed, will continue. It is important that you not deny your grief, but feel it fully. Enlist the help of those around you. Don't be alone. As Thomas Lynch says in "Tract," reproduced in Chapter Thirteen, "The only way around these things is through them."

The stories of the surviving spouses that we share in this chapter illustrate how people react differently to the loss of a spouse and how their reactions can contribute to, or hinder the healing process. We will make specific recommendations to help you on your journey of healing and discovery. Those of us who have made this journey can attest to the fact that there is hope, and you will again experience joy.

The death of a spouse propels us on a difficult journey that is unique to each. During life, we experience many kinds of loss. Some are small and relatively easy to bear, like losing a favorite piece of jewelry or misplacing your driver's license. Others cause us to question our abilities and our self-worth, like the loss of a job or the failure of a business. Some force us to accept that life changes, such as when our children leave for college or when we divorce. Loss is a part of life.

Because you share so much of your life with your spouse, it is only natural that his or her death shakes you to the core. Together, you may have raised a family, laughed, cried and celebrated every special event you can remember. You may have been married so long that the time before you were married seems like someone else's life. You expect your spouse to be at your side. Losing your spouse is like losing a part of you.

You may feel buffeted about and may lose confidence in yourself. You may feel confused, unable to make even minor decisions or feel as though you lack the strength to carry on. Many widows and widowers alike find it difficult to make important decisions without the advice or direction of their spouse. As a result, they often fail to make time sensitive decisions.

To complicate matters, you may not know how to act while grieving. We learn how to behave in school, at the movies and work, but not how to act while grieving. You may worry that friends and family will think you are not grieving enough, trapping yourself in the grieving stage just to prove your love for your spouse. Healing and moving on with your life neither proves nor disproves your love for your spouse. Being "okay" simply means that you choose to live in spite of fate's blow. It is your right to be happy, live your life and even remarry. Some survivors emerge from their late spouse's shadow to resume a career, become a family leader or a public crusader.

Stages of Grief

It has been said that we never get over the loss of a loved one, but instead we slowly integrate the loss into our lives. In his book, "*The Journey Through Grief*," author and grief counselor Alan Wolfelt, Ph.D. identifies six stages of grieving.

1. **Acknowledging the reality of the death** – it can take weeks or months to accept that our loved one is really gone.
2. **Embracing the pain of the loss** – although we may rather hide our pain, we need to confront it and express it with caring people.
3. **Remembering the person who died** – our loved one might have died but our relationship continues. We need to remember and cherish our time together.
4. **Developing a new self-identity** – discovering who we are without our loved one. We are changed by love and by grief. Reinvesting in life—developing a new life plan.
5. **Searching for meaning** – we ask "why" and we look for new meaning to life.
6. **Receiving ongoing support from others** – seeking out people who will allow us to mourn, to cry, to remember and to realize our own value. It helps to share our burden.

We do not march through the stages of grief in a linear fashion as was previously thought by experts. Rather, each person has his or her own way of moving through the stages, often cycling back and forth among them. With time, emotions become less intense, shorter in duration and the time between grief cycles lengthens.

My mother, with whom I was very close, died several years ago. As a professional nurse and CEO of a hospice company, I "knew" intellectually about grieving. But, "knowing" intellectually about grieving and experiencing the loss of a loved one first hand are different. Early on, I was consumed with the memory of her last days. I thought of things that I could have done or said. I cried a great deal. Eventually, I found peace and acceptance of her passing. One morning while showering, I remembered being at her bedside just before her death. I burst into tears and sobbed for several minutes. I was caught off guard by the intensity of my feelings, but unlike previous months I quickly recovered to go on and enjoy the day. My grieving period was slowly coming to an end.

Acknowledging the death of your spouse can be the most difficult step in the grieving process. Your spouse's passing may seem unreal or temporary and you may have the lingering sense that he will appear at any moment. You may even look for him at the time that he normally came home, or you may expect him to be there when you return. Gradually, you will accept that your spouse's passing is real and permanent.

Grieving, like all feelings and emotions, is also physical. You may feel sick, tired or listless. You may not have the energy to get out of bed or get dressed. You may lose your appetite. All of these physical reactions are normal. Expect to experience any number of the common reactions to grief described below.

Common Reactions to Grief

PHYSICAL AND EMOTIONAL REACTIONS	BEHAVIOR REACTIONS
Sleep disturbances/dreams	Crying
Weight and appetite changes	Preoccupation
Weakness and fatigue	Apathy regarding activities
Deep sighing	Decreased activity
Decreased resistance to illness	Detachment from surroundings

Restlessness/impatience Rapid heart beat Increased blood pressure Tightness in chest Difficulty swallowing Pit in the stomach Impaired decision-making ability Concentration difficulties Forgetfulness	Disorientation to time and place Withdrawal from friends Seeking of solitude
	EMOTIONAL REACTIONS
EMOTIONAL REACTIONS	Re-evaluation of beliefs Anger at God Distance/closeness with God Difficulty attending place of worship
Shock Disbelief Numbness Confusion Sadness and depression Guilt Yearning/loneliness Fears/anxiety Feelings of being lost Anger	

It is Healthy to Grieve

Allow yourself to grieve fully and openly. Do not fear the painful emotions that seem to be rocking your foundation. You may cry, moan or even yell in anger. Crying is nature's way of soothing you when you are in distress. Crying releases proteins and hormones, such as prolactin, that comfort the body and purge toxins.

If you are lost in your grief, confused by the cacophony of competing feelings, emotions and physical manifestations of your loss, get help! Individual therapy and grief support groups have helped many grieving spouses. Help is available through your local hospice, your funeral home, your priest, minister or rabbi. You would not hesitate getting professional help if you were in a car accident. Don't be ashamed to seek professional help if you are bleeding emotionally. Failing to attend to your real emotional and psychological needs will only result in continued emotional and physical dysfunction. This advice is most true for men, who would often rather "gut it out" than admit that they are hurting.

The following stories of Beth, Norman, Susan, and John illustrate how various surviving spouses grieved the loss of their spouse.

Acknowledge the Loss

Beth

Brian went to the emergency room when his headache did not respond to his normal course of aspirin and bed rest. Physically fit at 63, Brian adhered to a fitness plan that included daily five-mile runs. He was rarely ill, so he considered the Saturday evening visit to the hospital an inconvenience. In fact, Brian and his wife, Beth had plans later that evening.

Brian soon realized that he and Beth would not make either dinner or their movie. When the doctor entered the room, Brian was not prepared for what he was about to hear. He listened to the news calmly while intently watching Beth's face. Beth sat perfectly still as the doctors delivered the news: Brian had a brain tumor.

As they talked about their medical options, the need for a second opinion and further tests, Beth drifted off. She remembered their home on the lake, and kayak paddling along the shore. As if looking through a scrapbook, she pictured their children setting the table for Brian's birthday dinner, wrapping presents, and packing for holidays at the cottage. As she listened to the doctor, Beth slumped into the chair next to her husband. The room and voices grew hazy. Her hands felt clammy and she could hear her heart beating loudly. Beth's grieving had begun.

When your spouse is terminally ill, the first noticeable loss is the cadence of your former life. Before the impossible news sinks in that death is a possibility, you begin to grieve the life you had as two healthy people. The sense of loss becomes part of the fabric of your life with each visit to the doctor, each prescription, each sleepless night spent caring for the person that shares your life. In a way, your changing life helps prepare you for the more staggering reality of your spouse's death.

Up to the moment that Brian took his last breath, one year after his visit to the emergency room, Beth believed and desperately hoped that he would recover. Her denial allowed her to forestall acceptance of his pending death and gave her enough hope to be an effective caregiver. Perhaps nature knows that we cannot endure the pain of complete acceptance all at once. Denial is a slow-drip acceptance of death, preventing a jarring downpour of grief.

Complete denial, on the other hand, would prevent you from experiencing the loving intimacy of your spouse's last days. Knowing that the end is near and accepting death allows you and your spouse to have meaningful conversations, reunite with distant relatives, make peace with God and make final plans. One of the roles of hospice is to facilitate such end of life involvement with family, friends and clergy. Although painful, saying goodbye and making peace with loved ones allows for a level of intimacy that you may have never before experienced.

Beth deeply grieved the loss of her husband. She replayed their life together in her mind like an old movie. During their thirty-six years of marriage, they had idealized each other and rarely disagreed. His income provided a comfortable lifestyle. She raised four children and relied on Brian to handle their finances.

In the months following the funeral Beth walked around their big house like a lost child, looking for signs of Brian. Her heart leapt every time the phone rang, hoping to hear his voice. At 5:30 in the evening, she anticipated his arrival from work, her body aching with loss. Her best friend was gone forever. She thought she would never feel secure again without him.

To help her cope with her loss, Beth relied on grief support services offered by the hospice that had provided care to Brian in the last few months of his life. Like many hospices, her hospice offered bereavement support for thirteen months following the death of a loved one. Beth joined a grief group with others like her. At first she cried each time she told her story, but as time went on her grief diminished. Talking openly with other widows and widowers made her feel less alone. In fact, over time she found herself mentoring newly widowed group members, adding to her growing sense of balance and competence.

Beth was intimidated making decisions without Brian. She had little or no experience filing tax returns, managing investments or administering an estate such as Brian's. She felt a fresh stab of grief with each decision she faced as it reminded her of the calm, matter-of-fact way Brian had managed their affairs.

Gradually, Beth tackled her responsibilities with growing competence and strength. Through her efforts and the passage of time, she was able to accept her new life without Brian. By acknowledging the loss of her husband and openly addressing her grief she was free to take control of her life.

The Story of Norman

Norman was in his late 70's when his wife, Edie, died. When Edie was alive, she and Norman enjoyed taking long, leisurely Sunday afternoon drives. They would embark with neither a plan nor a particular destination in mind. During the summer months, they stopped at roadside stands to purchase vegetables, fruits and fresh-baked pies. For Halloween, they bought pumpkins and corn stalks to decorate their porch. In the spring they filled their trunk with annuals to be planted in the large clay pots of their garden.

They stopped for dinner on each return trip. After forty years of Sunday drives, they had a favorite restaurant in every direction. Their Sunday ritual was one of the things that Norman most missed after Edie's death. To keep her near, Norman had Edie cremated and kept her ashes with him saying: "I keep her with me, I'm comforted by that."

Norman reeled when Edie died. Her death plunged him into a confused and listless state. He felt that his life had no meaning. Norman was the financial provider while Edie took care of hearth and home. Months after her death, Norman revealed: "Now I understand what my wife did; everything."

As a couple, they had a small, but active social circle. They had one child, a son, Michael. Edie was the family's social director. She organized dinners, get-togethers and holiday celebrations. She was also Norman's link to his son, calling him weekly to invite him and his family for dinner. Norman was a stoic working man typical of his era, but he enthusiastically took part in everything his wife arranged and was grateful for her making their house a home.

The dinner parties stopped at Edie's death. Norman struggled to make phone calls and maintain contact with friends and family. While Edie was dying, Norman often talked to the hospice workers about his connection to his son, and how awkward he felt phoning him. He said, "Edie always did that, so it feels strange, even though I love my son. I'd better call him or I may never see him again."

Norman's daughter-in-law, Ann, tried to help father and son stay in touch. She made weekly calls to Norman to see how he was doing and often invited him to their home for dinner. Michael visited his father on his way home from work once a week to help him with home repairs and to chat. While Norman loved his son, and admired Ann, he didn't want them to feel responsible for him. He believed he was still able to take care of himself.

Norman was in pain. Michael and Ann, realizing that Norman was too private to accept their help, suggested that he participate in a grief support group. They told him that it would be good for him to get out of the house and talk to other people who were also grieving. At first, Norman felt uncomfortable in a group of strangers and questioned how the group could help him cope with his loss. It was especially hard in the beginning because he was the only man in the group.

Unfortunately, men commonly shun help from others and actively avoid participating in support groups. They are often embarrassed to talk about their feelings or to openly admit their grief. Norman also suffered from this misguided belief, but was surprised when he began to find comfort in talking with others about his experience.

After six months in a support group, Norman no longer felt the need to keep Edie's ashes. He called his son to discuss the best place for Edie and agreed to spread her cremains at a beautiful, unspoiled place that Norman and Edie passed on their Sunday drives. On the agreed upon day, Norman, with Michael and Ann spread Edie's ashes in a green field beneath a lovely tree.

Helping Others Help You Grieve

Death can make the most socially skilled among us feel awkward and uncertain. We often don't know how to adequately express our condolences. You can help your friends and family by letting them know how they can help. For example, you might tell them that you look forward to their phone calls, or that they should stop by regularly to check on you. In the beginning, you may feel reluctant to express your needs, but it will get easier. Friends and family want to help you through this time, but don't want to interfere. Give them direction. Accept their love and kindness. All will benefit.

The Story of Susan

Susan was conflicted by Joe's death. A handsome, outgoing man, Joe was the life of the party. But out of the sight of friends, Joe drank and was abusive. After years of being deeply unhappy in her marriage, Susan began seeing a counselor. It took her months to muster the courage to leave Joe, but she steadfastly made her plans. She heard Joe crying as she gathered the children and left him. Joe was devastated. After Joe pleaded for months for her to come back, she agreed to see him provided he got help with his drinking. He was angry at Susan, but realized that complying with her demands was the only way to keep his family. He joined Alcoholics Anonymous, found a therapist and began to change his life.

Joe found a new job and stopped drinking. Susan moved back home and together they began seeing a marriage counselor. They committed to repair the damage to their marriage and move on. There were many happy days after they got back together. Rather than attending parties and group gatherings, Susan and Joe focused on family outings with their children.

Four years later Joe was diagnosed with terminal cancer. That night Susan cried in Joe's arms. She noted with irony that he was finally being strong for her as they were facing the end. Because they needed the emotional and physical support Susan and Joe decided that they would ask for hospice care.

Despite her love for Joe, Susan was also angry at him for getting sick when things were finally going right for them. She loved her husband and he loved her. Their financial problems were behind them and he had just celebrated four years of sobriety. His illness was a violent blow that neither of them was prepared to handle. As Susan overcame the initial shock of the news, she became increasingly preoccupied with life's unfairness, blaming Joe for how difficult things had become.

A hospice social worker suggested that Susan keep a daily journal. Susan doubted that writing would help, but began writing about her feelings of sorrow and rage. Before long, she found comfort in writing and began to make room for her love, anger and guilt. She decided to talk with a therapist to help her work through her feelings.

With the help of the social worker, her therapist and Joe, Susan made a conscious decision to put her anger aside and enjoy the limited time she and Joe had left to them. They spent Joe's final weeks together. Susan stroked Joe's forehead and promised him that their children would grow up to be adults that would make him proud. Joe began to plan his funeral, selecting songs, readings from the Bible and some favorite poems. They cherished their family time talking to the kids about what was ahead.

When Joe died Susan was lost. After devoting so much of her energy to caring for Joe, she now had a difficult time focusing on everyday tasks. Susan's family became alarmed when, months after Joe's death she had not regained her appetite. She ate only chicken broth and tea, and had dropped to 100 pounds on her 5'5" frame. She had stopped seeing her therapist and appeared to have given up.

One night she was awakened to the sound of her daughter crying. Susan tried to get up but was dizzy and disoriented. She was unable to discern whether her daughter was truly crying or if she was imagining the noise. She climbed into bed with her daughter, and held her sobbing body, as she cried for daddy. Susan had fallen so deeply into her own grief that she could not see her children's suffering. In the morning, Susan called her doctor and her therapist. She was confused and barely functioning, but knew something had to be done.

Susan's initial reaction to Joe's death was normal. After the repair of their marriage, she was angry at the unfairness of Joe's illness. Remembering from their separation what life had been like without him she was afraid to continue alone. Unfortunately, Susan became lost in her sorrow neglecting herself physically, leaving her children confused and alone. Startled into reality by her daughter's night terrors, Susan was able to solve her self-destructive behavior and provide the necessary support and comfort to her children.

The Importance of Self-Care

Caring for yourself is neither selfish nor self-indulgent. Neglecting your physical or mental health is harmful to you and your family. The death of a spouse is a significant risk factor for developing serious illness. Proper rest, healthy meals and light exercise will nurture your body and mind. Deep breathing and relaxation techniques will calm you and create a place for healthy thoughts.

If the people that love you are worried about you, hear them. Although it may seem that they are interfering, they mean well. They may be more objective about your health than you are during this period. Seek help and advice from your family and friends, grief support professionals or from your clergyman. If it is difficult to share your feelings with those closest to you, seek out a neutral counselor.

Beginning a New Life

If you are like most married couples, your spouse was an integral part of your identity. You were seen as a "couple" by your friends and neighbors. Your hobbies, vacations and entertainment choices were influenced by things your spouse liked doing or you enjoyed doing together. Without your spouse you may feel like a "fish out of water."

You begin a new life the day your spouse dies. Assess your hobbies, friendships, where you live. Are they right for you? If not, replace them with new activities and rituals. Perhaps you want to get your college degree, write a book, make jewelry or travel? Make a plan now for the rest of your life. On the other hand, avoid rash decisions. Often, strong emotions interfere with clear thinking. Carefully consider major changes. Seek the advice of others.

The Story of John

Twice a week John played tennis with the guys from work. He loved his work and the camaraderie of his co-workers. No matter how crazy the workload, he made sure that tennis was on his calendar. But in the two years since his wife, Julia felt the lump in her breast he found no joy in either tennis or his friendships.

John and Julia had been married 10 years when she was diagnosed with terminal breast cancer throwing them into what became a frantic and failed medical journey. They had a two-year-old daughter, a beautiful new home and a happy life built on love.

Julia loved Christmas and passionately decorated for the holiday. They hosted numerous holiday parties inviting his co-workers, family and friends. Julia, an architect, liked to create beautiful environments and Christmas was the holiday that most inspired her. They enjoyed shopping for their daughter. John was proud of his wife, her beauty and quick mind. He liked to buy her one special gift at Christmas, usually a piece of jewelry or something for the house. John shopped with a heavy heart the Christmas Julie was ill knowing that he could not buy her the only gift she wanted; life.

When they talked about their daughter, tears streamed down Julia's face. John wanted to save Julia, and he wanted their life to be like it was before the illness. Chemotherapy treatments made party planning, decorating and shopping impossible tasks for Julia. John could not muster the energy to do it for her. He hired someone to decorate their tree and hang lights. Even if it did not feel like Christmas, it would look like Christmas at their house.

When Julia died, one year after her diagnosis, John felt that he had also died. Routine chores like going to the grocery store or making dinner became burdensome. While his sister and mother helped, he lay in bed and stared at the ceiling. Oddly, he was relieved by Julia's death. It pained him to watch her suffer, to see her sadness when she held their daughter and to watch her beauty fade. John was learning that the anguish of grief could be as intense as the joy of love.

John did not return to work for a month after her death. He avoided all conversations about his wife and their ordeal. Although he tried hard to focus, John found it difficult to concentrate on work.

His employer and his clients were understanding, and temporarily shifted his responsibilities.

After several months, he began to play tennis once a week. He didn't play well, but it felt good to use his muscles. One day in the locker room after a match, his friend Mike asked about Julia. John found it too painful to talk about her. He hurried to pack his things and left the club. Alone, John cried in the car.

The first Christmas after Julia's death, John thought that decorating their tree would be too painful. His mother and sister insisted that he celebrate the holiday for his daughter's sake. Relenting, John agreed to let them decorate their tree. Although the lovely tree and festive room evoked painful memories of Julia's passion for the season, he was buoyed by his daughter's joy.

Holidays and Special Occasions

Holidays and special occasions may be especially difficult for you. We expect special occasions to be a time of joy and togetherness. Your spouse's absence at such times is a painful reminder of your loss. You may dread the approaching month of your spouse's birthday, your wedding anniversary or your first Thanksgiving alone. The first year can be especially difficult, filled with "firsts" without your loved one. As time passes, your grief, even at holidays and special occasions, will subside.

Give yourself the freedom to change or replace your old traditions. You may decide to forego mailing holiday cards in favor of writing a few intimate letters to special friends or family. Plan a special outing with a friend or relative, like going to a movie, visiting an art museum or trying a new restaurant. Once you decide what is best for you, communicate your wishes to your friends and family.

Keeping the Memory of Your Spouse Alive

John didn't remember exactly when the pain began to lift. Soon he was playing tennis regularly at or near his former level of play. John was reluctant to talk openly about Julia believing that it would make his friends uncomfortable. However, in the locker room one day John told his friend Mike that he had decided to wear a small gold medal that he had given Julia. "She really liked this medal and it reminds me of her," he said.

Despite bringing tears to his eyes, John also began talking to his daughter about Julia. He told her, "Mommy would love the way you look in this dress. I wish she could see you." But as time went by, Julia became a normal part of their conversation and this was a way of keeping her spirit alive.

He placed a picture of Julia in his daughter's room. They talked about her in the quiet moments before she went to bed. He was careful to recall specific memories of Julia's laugh or her favorite sayings so that his daughter would never forget her.

He was shocked the first time someone mentioned dating. John thought: "Are you kidding? No way!" Yet, as time passed, John longed for the intimacy he shared with Julia. One day he noticed a pretty woman at the grocery store. He stopped short, feeling disloyal to Julia. To avoid eye contact, he focused his attention on his groceries and picked up a magazine to avoid eye contact. John felt awkward. It was the first time that he had noticed another woman since Julia's death. At that moment he realized that he did not want to continue his life alone. One day, when the time was right, he would meet someone to share a laugh, his love and his life.

You need not forsake your love for your spouse. You couldn't if you tried. Your spouse is a part of your life's fabric, woven into your soul by years of living and loving. Cherish the memory of your spouse. Maintain the memory of your spouse as an integral part of your history. Don't allow mention of your spouse to disappear from conversation. Share a story, a laugh about a funny incident and display photos where you will see them during the day.

In the End, This is Your Journey

Allow yourself to grieve fully. Surround yourself with friends and family who love you. Talk to them and let them help. Become involved in the bereavement program of your local church, hospice or funeral home. Take time to nourish your body and spirit. Eat well, get adequate sleep and exercise. If you are stuck in unhealthy grief that jeopardizes your long-term physical or emotional health seek the help of a professional therapist. You may not recognize that you are in physical or emotional danger. Rely on the "eyes" of family and friends who may be better able to objectively assess your coping skills.

Gradually, the intensity of your grief will subside. Holidays, a song on the radio or special occasions may trigger unexpected tears or feelings. With time, you will recover more quickly from these episodes.

We are never the same after the death of a loved one. As we grieve our loss, we are also reminded of our own mortality. We may wonder and reflect about how we will use the balance of our time on this earth. Nothing defines life more than death. It is a time to examine our relationships and our personal, professional, financial and spiritual objectives. Your spouse's death may ignite a healthy sense of urgency about your life.

There is much to do in the weeks and months that follow your spouse's death. Your duties may temporarily distract you from your grief, but don't "lose" yourself in them. Move at your own speed. Enlist the help of family, friends and professionals. When you sense that you are racing, becoming frantic and losing touch, stop, breathe and make time for yourself.

> *Sometimes, amid the cacophony, I stop*
> *and feel the cool breeze on my face.*
> *I draw a long deep breath,*
> *filling my lungs with moist fresh air.*
> *I pause and savor a complete exhale.*
> *I linger, I wonder, I think, that for at least this moment*
> *It is good to be alive.*

Franco Bollo *(The Healing)*

Chapter Two

Getting Organized

P. Mark Accettura, Esq. and Lynn Gross, Esq.

YOUR MORTGAGE COMPANY, your daughter's college, and the gas company don't care that you've just lost a spouse. For these and other creditors, it's business as usual. Clients are often hurt and angry that they must answer to uncaring credit department employees when, after the funeral, their monthly note is overdue. They cry, "Don't you understand that I've just lost my spouse?" Unfortunately, the reality of day-to-day living isn't suspended by your spouse's death.

The death of a spouse can be a rude awakening. Not only must you now manage your household alone-a responsibility for which you may not have been well prepared even under the best of circumstances-you must also address the myriad of new responsibilities resulting from your spouse's death.

Ready or not, important tasks must be attended to. Get help, get counseling, but get things done. Pay professionals if you're not able, literally or emotionally, to take care of business! The cost of professional help pales in comparison to costly mistakes. The sooner you get started, the better. This work will not only avoid problems down the road, but also may momentarily distract you from your grief and sense of helplessness during this difficult period. Too much to do is better than too much time to ruminate.

Getting Started

Getting started is more important than where or how to start. That said, as a matter of pure necessity, you're going to need cash, cash and more cash. You will quickly discover that much of your net worth, no matter how substantial, isn't readily accessible. Real estate, IRAs, mutual funds, and retirement accounts may not be readily convertible to cash. Life insurance typically takes at least thirty days to process, so you won't have immediate access to the proceeds. You might rely on credit cards to fly your kids in for the funeral and to pay the caterer, but you're probably going to need to convert other assets to cash to satisfy your other short term needs. Investigate the following potential sources of immediate cash:

- Cash in bank, brokerage, or credit union accounts in your own name or held jointly with your late spouse.
- Certificates of deposit (CDs) can be liquidated without penalty for early withdrawal at the death of an owner.
- Borrow against your brokerage account. Because such loans are secured by your account there is minimal paperwork and therefore little delay. Borrowing is tax-free and is therefore preferable to selling investments.
- The pre-age 591/2 penalty on your spouse's IRA and annuities is waived at the account owner or annuitant's death. However, the distribution is subject to income tax.
- Obtain a cash advance on your credit card from your local bank.

Satisfying short-term cash needs is one of your immediate concerns. Once the storm of the first few months has passed, though, you will need to develop a long-term financial plan. That is, you must identify sources of income and necessary expenditures to begin charting your long-term financial course. Chapter Five discusses how to prepare a detailed analysis of your income, expenses, and assets to determine your available cash flow.

Of course, you have every right to indulge yourself in the weeks following your spouse's death. Weeks, however, shouldn't turn into months and certainly not into years. You may need to discipline your spending habits so that your available cash flow matches your income needs. However, spending too little is just as bad as spending too much. We've seen wealthy widows agonize over even minor expenditures, often depriving themselves of deserved personal pleasures such as recreation, travel, and domestic help. On the spending side, you should develop a budget, separating recurring essential expenses from discretionary expenses. The key is to live a full and thoughtful life within, not above or below, your means.

Whom to Contact

After satisfying your immediate need for cash, you should inform the **Social Security Administration** (1-800-772-1213) of your spouse's death, and begin the Social Security benefits claims process. You may apply by phone, over the internet or at your local Social Security Administration office. The claims process is discussed in greater detail in Chapter Three.

Next, notify your spouse's **employer** of his or her death, and file for any benefits owed you, such as life insurance payments, pension income, and health insurance coverage. Call the Human Resources Department, or similar department, to find out which benefits you are entitled to and how to obtain them. Then, notify relevant **life insurance companies** of your spouse's death. Have the actual policy, or at least the policy number, before calling (see "Claim Procedure" in Chapter Four). Eventually, you will have to write a letter to both the employer and each insurance company to formally request benefits. Your letter should request payment of benefits and contain your spouse's full name, social security number and date of death. Attach a copy of the death certificate to each letter.

Make sure you order at least 15 certified death certificates from the funeral director. You will need to provide a certified copy to claim your spouse's benefits, transfer investments, file tax returns, and sell real estate. Things will go much more smoothly if you don't run short.

Contact the **financial institutions** where you and your spouse have accounts. Find out which accounts you may access (checking and savings) and which accounts you can't. If you and your spouse had joint accounts, transfer them to your name alone or to your revocable trust. You will be asked to produce a copy of the death certificate at the bank to complete these transfers.

Assets owned by your spouse alone (and not owned in trust), that do not name a beneficiary, will be part of his or her **probate estate** (see "Assets Passing Through Probate" in Chapter Seven). Once you have been appointed as the personal representative of your spouse's estate (see "Appointment of Personal Representative in Formal/Informal Probate" in Chapter Seven), you should re-title such accounts to the "Estate of [your spouse]." You will need to present the financial institution with a copy of the letter of authority received from the probate court formally appointing you. You should apply for and obtain a tax identification number for your spouse's estate and use that number to open the account. Your attorney or accountant should apply for the tax identification number using IRS Form SS-4.

If your late spouse has a **revocable trust**, it became irrevocable at death. You will need to present the financial institution with a copy of the trust appointing you as successor trustee (even though they likely already have a copy somewhere in their archives), and establish your authority over the account. Although the name of trust accounts stay the same, you must remove your spouse's social security number and replace it with a new tax identification number received from the IRS from information supplied on Form SS-4 (see Chapter Eight: "Tax Reporting").

Finally, you should assemble a professional team of advisors including an **accountant**, an **attorney**, and a **financial advisor**. If you are already working with professional advisors, simply give them a call as soon as you can (but not more than thirty days) after your spouse's death. If you haven't been working with professional advisors, specific recommendations for locating a qualified accountant, attorney, and financial planner are located at the end of Chapters Eight, Nine, and Five, respectively. Valuable resource materials can also be found in the Directory of Resources. An accountant will help you with your spouse's final income tax return and other tax reporting (see Chapter Eight). The attorney will assist you in administering your spouse's trust or probate estate (if applicable), as well as to evaluate your own estate planning needs (see Chapter Seven and Chapter Nine, respectively). Ask your advisors what you should bring to your first meeting so that your time together can be as productive as possible.

Income Taxation of Inherited Property

As a general rule, inherited assets are received **income tax** free. The *primary exception* is "*income in respect of a decedent,*" or "IRD." Income in respect of a decedent is income **earned** by a decedent **before** death, but not **paid** until **after** death (IRD is discussed in greater detail in Chapter Six: "IRA and Retirement Distributions" and Chapter Eight: "Tax Reporting"). Examples of IRD include bond interest, deferred compensation, your spouse's last pay check, IRAs, 401(k)s, and other retirement plan distributions. Items of IRD are taxed at your personal income tax rate in the year received.

In addition to being tax-free upon receipt, inherited assets receive a "stepped-up" basis. Basis is the mechanism used in tax law to measure gain or loss when an asset is sold. Basis is a person's investment in an asset, usually its purchase price. A step-up in basis is essentially a forgiveness of pre-death appreciation, allowing inherited assets to be sold income tax free. For example, if Harry paid $10,000 for a stock, his basis is $10,000. If he later sells the stock for $20,000, his gain is $10,000 ($20,000 sale price less his $10,000 basis).

If, rather than selling the stock, Harry left it in trust to his wife, Wendy, she can sell the stock immediately after Harry's death and pay no tax. Wendy pays no tax because her basis is the fair market value of the stock on the date of Harry's death. If Wendy waits a year and sells the stock when it has increased in value to $30,000, her gain is $10,000 ($30,000 sales price less $20,000 basis). To substantiate your new basis, it is extremely important that you document the value of your late spouse's assets as of the date of death. The Asset Inventory With Values Worksheet in Appendix A will help you record the date-of-death value of all assets.

A full step-up in basis occurs when an asset is held **solely** in the name of the decedent. Different rules apply where assets are held jointly between a husband and wife. If the joint tenant is the decedent's spouse, the surviving spouse receives a stepped-up basis on only one-half of the value of the asset. For example, if Harry and Wendy paid $10,000 for the stock and owned it jointly at the time of Harry's death, Wendy's new basis would be $15,000 (her $5,000 share of the original purchase price, plus Harry's $10,000 stepped up basis on his half). This rule applies no matter which spouse supplied the funds to acquire the asset.

The Economic Growth and Tax Reconciliation Act of 2001 ("Act") eliminates the federal estate tax effective in the year 2010. The Act eliminates the stepped-up basis effective in 2011. Interestingly, the Act contains a "sunset" provision, requiring Congress to ratify full repeal in 2010. Unless Congress, in 2010, again votes to repeal the estate tax, both the estate tax and the stepped-up basis are **retained**. The delayed effective date of the Act and the sunset provision make it difficult to plan. You cannot be confident that either the estate tax or the stepped-up basis are things of the past. The solution is to keep good records and be prepared for any and all eventualities.

Locating and Organizing Important Papers

Your next task is to locate and organize important documents and records. If you and your late spouse kept good records, this process should be relatively easy. However, if you used the "big box" filing system, you have some work ahead of you. Organizing important documents and records will make the job of concluding your spouse's affairs easier. The information you gather will be used to:

1. Assess your current financial condition;
2. Develop a long term financial plan;
3. File income, gift, and estate tax returns;
4. Administer your late spouse's estate or trust;
5. Help you create your own estate plan; and
6. Allow for the orderly conclusion of your affairs at the time of **your** death.

The information you gather in this Chapter is the starting point for almost every other chapter in *Lost and Found*. In future chapters you will be asked to review documents, categorize and value assets, and determine your net worth. Being organized has another benefit: peace of mind. The greatest fear is the fear of the unknown. You will find that knowing where you stand will put your mind at ease. The process of getting organized in and of itself can be good therapy.

The best way to get started is to open a separate folder for each category of documents or set of records discussed below. Label each folder in pencil until you know how many you will need.

Locate all **life insurance policies** on your spouse's life, and put them in a folder labeled "Life insurance policies."

Next, find your spouse's **original Last Will and Testament** ("Will"). Your attorney may have it in his or her file, or it may be in your home safe or bank safe deposit box. The Will should be filed with the probate court of the county in which your spouse resided at the time of death, even if there are no assets to be probated. Then, look for other estate planning documents such as his **revocable trust**, irrevocable trust, or charitable trust. Your spouse's Will and trust name the people with authority to handle his post-death affairs. You are likely to find that you are the only person with that authority. If you are named with others, however, you should make a list of their names, addresses and phone numbers. You may also find a list disposing of specific personal items, sometimes called a "Personal Property Memorandum," with your spouse's other estate planning documents. Keep all of these items in a folder labeled "Estate Planning Documents."

Make a list of the name, address, telephone number and social security number of each of your spouse's children (if you are not the natural or adoptive parent) and other beneficiaries named in his Will or trust. You may need this information later, especially if any assets must be probated. Keep this list in a separate folder labeled "Beneficiaries."

If your spouse was a veteran, you may be eligible for veterans benefits. To find out, you will need to contact the Department of Veterans Affairs and send a copy of his **military records,** including honorable discharge papers showing his branch of service, dates of service and rank. Keep these papers in a folder labeled "Military Records."

Finally, locate the **last two years' income tax returns** and put them in a folder labeled "Tax Returns," along with any **gift tax returns** (Form 709) you find (see "Record Retention" in Chapter Eight).

Next, gather asset information. When it comes to financial matters, your task is threefold: first, you must create a folder for each asset type (real estate, brokerage account, IRA, etc.). Second, you must enter each asset on the Asset Inventory With Values Worksheet. Finally, you **must** enter the date-of-death **value** of each asset under the column that corresponds to how the asset is owned. A blank worksheet can be found in Appendix A. You should photocopy Appendix A and tailor it to your needs.

Asset Inventory with Values Worksheet

ASSET TYPE	OWNERSHIP					
	Husband	**Husband's Trust**	**Wife**	**Wife's Trust**	**Joint w/ spouse**	**Joint w/ others**
Checking and/or Savings account					$1,000	
Mutual Funds				$100,000		
IRA	$70,000		$30,000			
House		$100,000 (1/2 value)		$100,000 (1/2 value)		
Rental Property		$50,000 (1/2 value)		$50,000 (1/2 value		
Life Insurance On Husband's Life:		$200,000 (Trust is payee on death)	$50,000			
On Wife's Life:						
TOTAL:	$70,000	$350,000	$80,000	$250,000	$1,000	

Assemble the following information with respect to **each** parcel of **real estate** owned by your spouse either individually or with others: a copy of the deed (look for a document called either a "Warranty Deed" or "Quit Claim Deed"), copies of most recent mortgage statements, including balance due, loan number, lender name and address, the property address, and copies of the last property tax bill. Put these items in a separate folder labeled "Real Estate." You should create a separate folder for each parcel.

Next, locate the most recent **bank, savings,** and **credit union account** statements. Put the statements in a folder labeled "Bank Statements." The statements should show the account owner, the name and address of the institution, the type of account, the account number, and the balance.

Find the most recent **investment**, mutual fund, brokerage, or other similar account statements. The statement should contain the exact name of the account, the number of shares, date purchased, purchase price (cost basis), and current value. File each account in a separately labeled folder. It is extremely important that you separate pre-tax investments (such as IRAs and other retirement accounts) from regular (previously taxed) accounts. Pre-taxed savings are subject to an entirely different set of rules when it comes to investing, tax and estate planning (see Chapter Six: "IRA and Retirement Distributions").

If your spouse had any stocks or bonds in "certificate" form (meaning that you have the actual stock certificate or bond), you should put a **photocopy** of the stock or bond in your folder and store the **original** in a secure place. Lost stock certificates and bonds are difficult to replace. If you have not kept records, you could even lose your investment. You should re-register the stock or bond in "street name" with your financial advisor, brokerage house, or bank as soon as possible. Securities held in street name are logged in the books of the financial institution. In exchange, your account at the institution (which should be in the name of your revocable trust) is credited with a corresponding number of shares.

To transfer stocks and bonds held in certificate form into street name, your financial advisor will need an **original** death certificate (and an original probate court letter of authority if the stock or bond was in your spouse's name alone) for **each** company involved (for example, five stock certificates for one company is treated as a single transfer). You will be charged a fee based on the number of companies involved. Allow at least ten days for sales or other transfers in certificate form to clear. If you want to do it yourself, you can contact the "investor relations department" of the company in question and ask them how to go about transferring the shares into the name of the new owner. However, we recommend that you enlist the help of a professional. Having a particular financial institution make the transfer on your behalf does not obligate you to use their financial planning services in the future. Once you go through this process, you will undoubtedly resolve never again to own stocks or bonds in certificate form. Enter the value of the stock or bond on the Asset Inventory With Values Worksheet.

If your spouse had an interest in a **corporation, LLC, partnership,** or other **"closely held"** (meaning not publicly traded on a stock exchange) business, gather all of the information you can find evidencing your late spouse's ownership interest and file it in a separately labeled folder. The folder should contain the name of the business, the names and addresses of all officers or partners, the Articles of Incorporation (for corporations), Partnership Agreement (for Partnerships), or the Operating Agreement (for Limited Liability Companies, or "LCC"). Save business tax returns, if you find any, as they often contain valuable information including the names of all owners and the profitability of the enterprise. Also look for a "buy/ sell agreement," where co-owners contractually agree to buy out the deceased owner's interest at death. Often, buy/sell agreements are "funded" with life insurance to allow the surviving owner to purchase the deceased owner's interest in a single payment. When it comes to closely held business interests, you should contact the company's attorney and accountant as soon as possible to determine your rights and responsibilities.

Save all **life insurance policies.** You may be required to submit the original policy to collect the proceeds. Review Chapter Four for tips on making a claim and the various settlement options available. Each insurance company should send you "Form 712" along with payment of the proceeds. Form 712 indicates the amount of the proceeds (including accrued interest) and the beneficiary to whom they were paid. Form 712 must be attached to the estate tax return (if one is required). Unfortunately, insurance companies often don't send Form 712 unless specifically asked. Life insurance policies and Forms 712 should be filed in the "Life Insurance Policies" folder.

Next, determine the beneficiary of your spouse's IRAs, 401(k) Plan, company **retirement plan,** or any other type of retirement plan. Most likely, you, as surviving spouse, are the sole beneficiary. You must determine when and how to begin taking distributions from these plans (see Chapter Six: "IRA and Retirement Distributions"). Request a copy of the beneficiary designation form from the plan administrator. Your request should be in writing, and should include the date of your spouse's death, social security number, and a copy of the death certificate. Keep all retirement plan documents in a separately labeled folder.

Gather information on outstanding **debts,** such as credit card statements, medical bills, personal loans, vehicle loans, mortgages, etc. Keep these items in a folder labeled "Debts."

Keep records of **expenses** that are deductible on the estate tax return: funeral expenses, accountant and attorney fees, administrative fees, and appraisal expenses (see "Form 706" in Chapter Eight). Put these items in a folder labeled " Estate Expenses."

Finally, read your mail carefully so that you don't throw away important documents or notices. Ferreting out important mail has become more difficult in recent years as junk mail purveyors have mastered the art of making junk mail look important. File incoming mail in the appropriate file folder on a regular basis.

Sift through your **safe deposit box.** Add the name of a trusted family member to the box so that it isn't frozen at your death. States no longer automatically freeze safe deposit boxes at death. However, if the only name on the account is that of the deceased, authority to enter must be obtained from the probate court.

Obtain Date of Death Value of All Assets

Determining the **value** of all assets is important to determine whether estate tax is due (see "Planning to Avoid Estate Tax" in Chapter Nine), and to establish your new basis. Estate tax and basis are determined using the date-of-death value of your spouse's property. To ascertain date-of-death value:

1. Review investment account statements (including IRAs and other retirement accounts) for the date of death value of account assets.

2. For stocks and bonds, the date of death value is the average between the high and low for the date of death. If your spouse died on the weekend, add the high and low for Friday and the high and low for Monday and divide by four.

3. Obtain **certified appraisals** on all real estate. The state equalized value (or other tax value used in your community) and a "market analysis" prepared by a real estate agent are *not* sufficient.

4. Obtain **certified appraisals** on all closely held business interests.

5. Depending on the size of the estate, you may also need to obtain an appraisal of your spouse's personal property, especially if your spouse owned any collectibles of value (art, wine, vintage cars, etc.).

6. The value of life insurance proceeds is reflected on the Form 712, discussed above.

7. Save the stock page from your local daily newspaper (or The Wall Street Journal) for the day of your spouse's death. If the death occurred on a weekend, save Friday and Monday's paper.

8. You may use the sale price as the date-of-death value of any asset sold within nine months of death as long as the purchaser is an unrelated third party and the sale was "arm's length" (i.e., not a below market sale to beat the tax man).

Determine your Expenses

It is important that you keep current with your household bills. By their nature, creditors tend not to be sympathetic. You could ruin your credit rating if you fall behind in your payments. If you have the cash, you should pay all household expenses as well as funeral, cemetery, and burial expenses within thirty days of being invoiced. Save evidence of your payment of all funeral related expenses as they are deductible for estate tax purposes. Also, the fact that you paid your late spouse's funeral bill will count in your favor in the event a dispute arises as to whom should be appointed as your late spouse's personal representative.

Normally, you shouldn't save routine household bills (unless you want to build an addition on your home to house them). However, you will need them after your spouse's death to calculate your average monthly expenses. Look at your checkbook register for the prior twelve months to identify non-recurring expenses such as car repair, un-reimbursed medical, dental, prescription drug expenses, household services, and gifts. Make a list of each household expense and your average monthly payment. Typical expenses include:

1. Mortgage payments.

2. Home equity loan payments.
3. Utilities (including telephone and cable TV).
4. Food and clothing.
5. Car payment.
6. Car maintenance and repairs.
7. Installment loans.
8. Medical expenses.
9. Credit card debt.
10. Taxes (federal, state, property).
11. Insurance premiums (homeowners, life, health, disability, auto, long term care).
12. Miscellaneous expenses (entertainment, education, pets, gifts, charity, club memberships, professional fees, etc.).

Separate your bills, your spouse's bills, and your joint bills. Pay your bills and your joint bills first, so that your own credit history is not adversely affected. Your spouse's individual bills should be paid from the trust or estate checking accounts you opened, as discussed above.

Check your spouse's individual credit card statements (ones where you are not on the account) to determine whether your spouse had a credit life insurance ryder that will pay off the outstanding balance at death. If there is no insurance, contact each creditor directly to inform them of your spouse's death. You may request an extension of time to pay or arrange for a negotiated settlement of the debt. Explain that your spouse's estate is not sufficiently liquid to immediately pay the debt in full. Many credit card companies will accept an immediate reduced payment rather than wait months for payment of the full amount. You will need to provide the creditor with a copy of the death certificate. It is important to confirm any negotiated settlement in writing when sending your final payment.

If you and your late spouse were joint obligors on all of your credit cards, you should establish new credit in your own name. Developing your own credit history is important if you intend to borrow in the future. Don't take your spouse's name off joint credit cards right away; otherwise you will be bombarded with irritating calls from creditors preying on the recently widowed. Use your new line of credit and completely close out the joint credit cards and lines of credit when they are paid off.

Identify Available Sources of Cash Flow

Identify your immediate sources of cash flow, including:

1. Bank, brokerage or other accounts that you owned individually or jointly with your spouse;
2. Salary or other personal income;
3. Social Security;
4. Pension benefits from your spouse;
5. Annuity payments;
6. Rental Income;
7. Insurance income;
8. Investment income (interest and dividends);
9. Alimony and/or Child Support; or
10. Proceeds from the sale of an asset.

Make a list of each item and the monthly amount you expect to receive. The income and expense information you gather is the starting point to creating a financial plan.

SUMMARY CHECKLIST

1. **Whom to contact**
   ❑ Social Security Administration
   ❑ Spouse's employer – Human Resources Department
   ❑ Life insurance companies
   ❑ Financial institutions
   ❑ Attorney
   ❑ Accountant
   ❑ Financial Advisor

2. **Important information to locate and save**

FOLDER NAME	CONTENTS
Death Certificate	15 certified copies

Life Insurance (including any accidental Death policies, if applicable)	Copies of all policies and Forms 712.
Estate Planning Documents	Last Will and Testament, Trust, Memorandum.
Beneficiaries	The name, address, telephone number, and social security number of each family member and beneficiary.
Military Records	All military records including honorable discharge papers showing branch of service, dates of service and rank.
Tax Returns	Last two years income tax returns (federal, state, and local) and all gift tax returns.
Real Estate	Deeds, mortgage statements, lender's name & address, current value, property tax bills, appraisal.
Bank Accounts	Statements containing bank name & address, account number, account type, balance, and title-holder.
Investment Accounts	Statements containing name of fund or brokerage house, stocks in the account, number of shares, date purchased, purchase price, title and current value.

Stocks and Bonds	Actual stock certificates and bonds or bond statements. Closely held business interests: all documents relating to closely held business, such as its name, the names & addresses of all officers or partners, Articles of Incorporation, Partnership Agreement, or Operating Agreement, tax returns, and any buy/sell agreements.
Retirement Plans	All documents relating to any IRAs, 401(k)s, or other qualified or non-qualified retirement plans.
Debts	Credit card statements, medical bills, personal loans, vehicle loans, mortgage loans, or other debt of your spouse.
Expenses	Copies of invoices, bills and receipts relating to funeral expenses, accountant fees, attorney fees, appraisal expenses and other estate administrative expenses.

3. **Determining asset value**
   ❏ Review all bank and investment account statements.
   ❏ Obtain certified appraisals of real property.
   ❏ Obtain certified appraisal of family owned or closely held businesses.
   ❏ Review Forms 712 for value of life insurance policies.

❏ Obtain appraisal of personal property/collectibles.

❏ Determine Date of death value of stocks – review newspaper financial section.

4. **Determine immediate liabilities**

❏ Funeral, cemetery & burial expenses

❏ Mortgage payments

❏ Home equity loan payments

❏ Utilities

❏ Food and clothing

❏ Car payment

❏ Car maintenance and repairs

❏ Installment loans

❏ Medical expenses

❏ Credit card debt

❏ Taxes (federal, state, property)

❏ Insurance premiums (Homeowners, Life, Health, Disability, Car)

❏ Miscellaneous expenses (entertainment, education, pets, gifts, charity, club memberships, professional fees, etc.)

5. **Identify cash flow sources**

❏ Bank, brokerage or other accounts that you owned individually or jointly with your spouse

❏ Salary

❏ Social Security

❏ Pension benefits from your spouse

❏ Annuity payments

❏ Rental income

❏ Insurance income

❏ Investment income (interest and dividends)

❏ Proceeds from the sale of an asset

Chapter Three

Navigating Social Security

Doreen Benson

History

THE NATION'S NEED for a comprehensive plan to address the financial challenges of death, disability, and old age became increasingly apparent during the economic upheaval of the Great Depression. Family life changed dramatically as we moved away from our historically agricultural roots toward a more industrial and urban economy. The economic safety net of the family farm was quickly disappearing.

By executive order of President Franklin D. Roosevelt, the Committee on Economic Security was formed to study the problem of providing economic security to a changing America. Just over a year later, the Social Security Act was signed into law on August 14, 1935. The first Social Security number was assigned in December of 1936, and the first FICA (the well-known acronym for the Federal Insurance Contributions Act) taxes were withheld from worker's paychecks in January 1937. Originally, Social Security covered only the contingency of retirement. Social Security coverage was expanded in 1939 to include dependents and survivors of workers. Payments of monthly benefits began in January 1940. Social

Security was expanded once again in 1960 to include disabled workers and their families. Basic health insurance for senior citizens, called Medicare, was signed into law in 1965.

Notwithstanding recent criticism that Social Security is insolvent and outdated, it endures as one of this country's most successful and essential government programs. Recent projections indicate that even without any changes to the program it will remain financially solvent for at least the next three decades. However, change is inevitable. As it has in the past, Social Security will adjust to changing economic, demographic, and political conditions and continue to meet the needs of current and future generations of American workers.

If you work long enough and meet the earnings requirements discussed in this chapter, you will be eligible for monthly Social Security retirement benefits when you retire. The amount of your benefit is based on your earnings record. You may also be entitled to benefits based on your late spouse's earnings. Our focus will be on this aspect, called survivor benefits. The Social Security benefits available to disabled workers and their families are beyond the scope of this chapter and therefore are not covered. Several other government entitlement programs related to Social Security, namely Medicare, Medicaid and Supplemental Security Income, are covered later in this chapter.

Survivor Benefit Overview

The following family members are eligible for survivor benefits:

- A surviving spouse (of any age) who was married to the worker at the time of his death (or an ex-spouse that has not remarried) that is caring for a child of the deceased (whether natural, adopted, or step) who is under age 16.
- A surviving spouse (or an unmarried ex-spouse) caring for a disabled child of any age, if the child is receiving Social Security benefits
- Unmarried child under age 18, or under age 19 if a full time high school student (can include natural, adopted, or stepchild).
- A child age 18 or older and severely disabled before age 22. The benefits may continue regardless of age as long as the child remains totally disabled.

- Parents of the deceased worker, if they were dependent upon the worker for at least one-half of their support.
- A surviving spouse age 60 or older (can be an ex-spouse).
- A surviving spouse 50 or older who is disabled (can be an ex-spouse).
- A $255 lump sum payment to a surviving spouse (or minor children if no spouse).

Earnings Requirement

To qualify for regular Social Security benefits, or survivor benefits for the worker's family, an individual must have worked and earned sufficient "credits." Workers earn credits based on their earnings. In 2001, every $830 in earnings equals one credit, up to a maximum of four credits per year ($3,320 in annual earnings in 2001 equals the maximum four credits). The amount of money needed to earn one credit increases annually based on the cost of living (in 2000 it was $780). Generally, workers need 40 credits (10 years of work) to qualify for regular benefits. However, fewer than 40 credits are needed to qualify for survivor benefits. For the family of a deceased worker to be eligible for survivor benefits, a worker born in 1930 or later needs one credit for each year after age 21, up to the year of death. For workers born prior to 1930, one credit is needed for each year after 1950, up to the year of death.

> **For example:** a worker born in 1950 who died in 2000 would require 28 credits (seven years of work) for survivor benefits to be payable to family members. (The worker was age 21 in 1971, and needed one credit for each year after age 21 up to the year of death -1972 through 2000 = 28 "credits").

Under any scenario, the family is eligible for a reduced survivor benefit if the deceased worker had at least six credits (one and one-half years of work) in the three years before death.

Benefit Amounts

Earnings are the basis for calculating both eligibility and benefit amount. Relatively small amounts of earnings over a long period allow the worker to accrue credits. As noted above, only $3,320 was needed in 2001 to earn four of the forty credits necessary to be eligible for Social Security (regular Social Security benefits also require the worker to have reached full or early retirement age as described below).

Once **eligibility** is established, the **amount** of the monthly benefit must be determined. Social Security benefits are based on the deceased worker's date of birth, date of death, and earnings. Earnings are adjusted for inflation and then averaged over the worker's lifetime to reflect **average adjusted monthly earnings**. Average adjusted monthly earnings are then multiplied by percentages prescribed by the law. The product is the deceased worker's **base benefit amount**.

The worker's base benefit amount is then multiplied by a percentage determined by the age of the beneficiary and the beneficiary's relationship to the deceased:

- A surviving spouse age 65 or older when entitlement begins: 100 percent.
- A surviving spouse age 60 to 64 when entitlement begins: a sliding scale ranging from 71 to 94 percent.
- A surviving spouse (any age) caring for a child under age 16: 75 percent.
- Children: 75 percent.

The higher the lifetime earnings of the deceased worker, the greater the potential benefits for the family. In 2001, the estimated average monthly Social Security benefit for a surviving spouse and two children is $1,696. For a widow or widower living alone, the average monthly benefit is $811.

There is a limit, called a "family maximum," on the amount of survivor benefits that can be paid to the family of a worker. The limit is generally equal to somewhere between 150 to 180 percent of the deceased worker's base benefit amount. If several family members are eligible for survivor benefits, and their aggregate benefit exceeds the maximum, their individual benefits will be reduced proportionately.

For example, if a worker's base benefit was $500, a 75 percent benefit (generally due a surviving spouse or child) would be $375. However, if the worker was survived by a spouse and four minor children, each family member would not receive the full 75 percent benefit (the adjusted benefit for children and surviving spouses age 60-64), as this would exceed the family maximum of $750 (150% of the base amount). To determine the proper benefit amount in a family maximum case, the maximum benefit payable would be divided equally among the family members. For example, a family of five (surviving spouse and four minor children) would each receive $150 a month, or one-fifth of the $750 family maximum. As the oldest child matures and stops receiving Social Security, his or her benefit will be divided and shared equally by the remaining family members. The family maximum rule generally comes into play in survivor claims of younger families (a surviving spouse with young children) and can become complicated when there are ex-spouses with children of the deceased worker.

The Social Security Administration will make an official determination of the survivor benefit amount when the claim is finally adjudicated, but can provide a benefit **estimate** at the time of application.

Benefits from Two Accounts

You may be eligible for survivor benefits as well as benefits earned from your own work record. The rules that apply when choosing between the two can be confusing.

Both spouses must meet the age requirements to receive a monthly benefit. If a worker elects early retirement benefits at age 62, and his spouse is age 55, she would have to wait until age 62 to begin receiving benefits if both are still living. On the other hand, if one spouse has died, then the survivor could receive benefits at age 60.

As noted above, in the event of a worker's death, the surviving spouse must be at least age 60 to receive survivor's benefits (or earlier if the survivor is disabled or caring for minor children of the deceased). If the surviving spouse is only age 55 at the time of the worker's death (and not disabled or caring for minor children of the deceased), he or she must wait until age 60 to qualify for survivor's benefits (although his children under age 19 may qualify directly). At age 60, the surviving spouse could begin receiving surviving benefits (unless he or she remarried). Such survivor benefits are permanently reduced for age.

To receive the full amount of the deceased spouse's benefit, the survivor would have to wait until she attained full retirement age (age 65 for people born in 1937 or earlier).

If you elect to receive survivor's benefits, you may elect to take your own benefit when you attain early retirement age (62) or full retirement age (age 65 for people born in 1937 or earlier) based on **your own** work and earnings if it would result in a higher monthly benefit.

Where both spouses worked and both are receiving retirement benefits, in the event that one spouse dies, the survivor would be eligible for whichever benefit is greater.

A different set of rules apply when one spouse worked outside the home and the other did not (or on a very limited basis). If both spouses were at least age 65 when the worker spouse began receiving full retirement benefits, the non-working spouse would receive a benefit equal to one-half of the working spouse's benefit even if the other spouse never worked outside their home. If the working spouse then dies, the surviving spouse receives the deceased spouse's full benefit and must relinquish her one-half benefit.

In the event of the death of a spouse where both are older than the full retirement age (65 if born in 1937 or earlier) and each are receiving their own monthly benefit based on their own work history, the survivor is entitled to the higher benefit (not both) upon the death of his or her spouse.

Remarriage

Generally, you will not be eligible for Social Security survivor benefits if you remarry prior to age 60. After age 60, or age 50 if disabled, remarriage will not terminate survivor benefits on your late spouse's record. Keep in mind that if you remarry on or after attaining age 62, you may be eligible for a different, and possibly higher, benefit on the account of your new spouse.

How to Apply for Benefits

You should contact the Social Security Administration and apply for benefits as soon as possible after your spouse's death. You may apply in person (at your local SSA office), by telephone (1-800-772-1213), or via the internet (by visiting their website at www.ssa.gov).   If you call, representatives are available to speak with you weekdays from 7 a.m. to 7 p.m.   The SSA recently unveiled *www.ssa.gov/women*, a website for women, providing basic social security retirement information, survivor's benefits, disability, and Supplemental Security Income benefit information pertinent to women.

The best times to call are later in the day, later in the week, and later in the month. If you don't mind voice mail option menus, there is an after-hours voice mail system to handle a variety of questions and concerns. A word to the wise: keep a record of the name of the Social Security officials you speak with, the dates of your calls, and the subject of your conversations. This information may be useful in the future if your application cannot be located or you receive contradictory information.

The application process generally takes less than 30 minutes. You will be asked several questions, to determine your eligibility for Social Security and other government benefits. You will be required to submit evidence to substantiate your entitlement including:

- Evidence of relationship (marriage certificate, divorce judgment, etc.);
- Birth certificates for all benefit applicants;
- Proof of death (death certificate);
- Recent wage information for the deceased;
- Social Security numbers for all family members applying for benefits; and
- Bank account information to initiate direct payment of your benefits to the financial institution of your choice.

The above list is not inclusive. The evidence required may vary depending on your individual circumstances. Photocopies of requested documents are **not** accepted. Original documents (or certified copies from the official agency that issued the original document) are required. Certified documents are usually available through the city or county clerk where the event occurred, and generally must have a raised seal of the issuing agency for identification purposes. Original documents will be returned to you at the end of the application process. *Do not delay filing your survivor claim simply because you don't have the requested documents. SSA can assist you in obtaining any evidence necessary to process your application for benefits.*

The SSA will usually make a determination as to your eligibility and monthly entitlement within thirty days of receiving your application and supporting documents. When benefits are approved, an award letter will be sent to you. The letter notifies you of your date of entitlement to benefits, payment due date, and benefit amount. The letter is an important document, and should be saved with your other important papers.

As a courtesy, funeral directors often notify the SSA of a worker's death. This contact, however, does not constitute an application for benefits. You must still make application as soon as possible to report your spouse's death and indicate your intent to file a claim. Benefits are not retroactive! If you wait to apply, you may lose out.

Other Programs or Benefits

Lump Sum Death Payment

A lump sum death payment in the amount of $255 is made to the worker's surviving spouse (or his minor child(ren) if there is no surviving spouse). Prior to 1983, this payment was referred to as a "burial benefit," as it was paid directly to the funeral home at the family's request. This is no longer true. For working couples, the lump sum payment is only paid on the death of the first spouse unless there are minor children.

Medicare

Medicare is the federal government health insurance program for seniors (age 65 and older), the disabled (under age 65), and individuals (any age) who have permanent kidney failure. Medicare provides basic health care coverage for approximately 80 percent of allowable medical charges (after specific annual deductible expenses are met). It does not cover every medical expense, or the cost of long-term care (except in limited circumstances described in "Medicare" in Chapter Twelve).

Medicare consists of two parts: Part "A" covers inpatient hospital care as well as a portion of the first 100 days of a patient's stay in a skilled nursing facility (or home health care) following a hospital stay, and hospice care. Part "B" of Medicare covers doctor's services, medical services, supplies, and other services not covered by Part "A." While Part A is free to eligible workers, Part B coverage requires that you pay a monthly premium (for 2001, the basic Part "B" premium is $50 per month), which is automatically deducted from your monthly social security check if you receive benefits. Workers electing to defer retirement beyond age 65 may make quarterly Part B premium payments directly to the SSA. Part B should not be viewed as optional. Although your participation is elective (you must pay premiums), Part B coverage is an essential part of your personal medical plan.

Most seniors are eligible for Medicare, based on their own work record or on their spouse's. Individuals age 65 or older are eligible for Medicare Part "A" if they:

- Receive Social Security or railroad retirement benefits, or
- Are not receiving benefits but have worked long enough to be eligible for them, or
- Would be entitled to Social Security benefits based on a spouse's (or ex-spouse's) work record, or
- Worked long enough in a federal, state, or local government job to be insured for Medicare coverage.

Individuals under the age of 65 are eligible for Medicare Part "A" if they:

- Have been a Social Security disability beneficiary for 24 months, or
- Have permanent kidney failure.

Individuals who do not qualify for Medicare Part "A" under these rules may purchase coverage (in 2001, the Medicare Part "A" premium is $300 per month).

The eligibility requirements for Part "B" are different from Medicare Part "A." Virtually anyone who is 65 or older (or who is under age 65 but eligible for Part "A" as outlined above) is eligible to purchase Medicare Part "B" coverage.

If you are receiving Social Security, you will automatically be contacted a few months before you become eligible for Medicare (either at age 65 or 24 months after disability). If you are not receiving Social Security at the time you become eligible for Medicare, you should contact the Social Security Administration (by phone at 1-800 772-1213) at least three months prior to your 65th birthday to obtain important information and determine your Medicare eligibility. Delaying Medicare enrollment may cause a delay in coverage.

Consult the Directory of Resources ("Social Security and Government Benefits") for additional information on Medicare.

Medigap Insurance

The coverage offered under Medicare Part A and B is somewhat limited. As noted above, Medicare covers only 80 percent of allowable medical charges after annual deductible expenses have been met. Medicare does not cover eye glasses, prescriptions, or dental care. The private sector has responded to fill the gaps in Medicare coverage by offering private health insurance that covers medical costs not covered by Medicare. For obvious reasons, these policies have come to be known as "Medigap" policies. The costs of Medigap policies vary from company to company and according to the coverage chosen. Medigap policies typically cover the 20 percent that Medicare doesn't pay, as well as some of the services excluded under Medicare. You may purchase a policy covering deductibles and even prescriptions. Medigap insurance is often part of the benefit package of a former employer (see "Medigap Coverage" in Chapter Four).

Medicaid

Medicaid is a state-run health care program for low-income individuals. Medicaid also covers the cost of long-term nursing home care for people who have exhausted their assets (see "Medicaid" in Chapter Twelve).

Supplemental Security Income (SSI)

Supplemental Security Income ("SSI") is a federally funded program that provides limited financial security for people with little or no income or resources. SSI is available to individuals who are age 65 or older, and to the blind or disabled of any age (even children). Those eligible for SSI are also eligible for food stamps, Medicaid, and other social services.

SSI benefits are based on need. Eligibility is similar to that of Medicaid. To qualify, an individual must reside in the United States and be a U.S. citizen (or lawfully admitted for permanent residence), have limited income and not have more than $2,000 in resources ($3,000 for a couple), not counting their principal residence, and one car.

Miscellaneous Social Security Issues

Benefit Estimate

There is a special form you can use to get a "Personal Earnings and Benefit Estimate Statement." Contact the Social Security Administration (Toll free at 800 772-1213, in person at the local branch office, or via the internet at www.ssa.gov) for the form that will enable you to receive a free, detailed, personal estimate of Social Security benefits. The estimate is automatically mailed each year to those not receiving benefits.

Direct Deposit

Direct deposit of Social Security checks is the fastest and most secure method of payment delivery. Checks sent through the mail are 10 times more likely to be reported lost or stolen. Direct deposit will be suggested at the time of your initial claims application, but can be elected at any time after payments begin. You must supply your bank account information, including financial institution routing number, to elect direct deposit.

Full Retirement Age Increases

The traditional full retirement age of 65 is changing. For people born in 1938 and later (age 62 in the year 2000 and after), the age at which full, unreduced retirement benefits begin will gradually increase until it reaches the new "full" retirement age of 67. Review this chart to determine how the change affects you.

Year of Birth	Full Retirement Age
1937 or earlier	65
1938	65 & 2 months
1939	65 & 4 months
1940	65 & 6 months
1941	65 & 8 months
1942	65 & 10 months
1943 – 1954	66
1955	66 & 2 months
1956	66 & 4 months
1957	66 & 6 months
1958	66 & 8 months
1959	66 & 10 mos.
1960 and later	67

Early Benefit Option Remains

"Early" reduced benefits continue to be available for workers and spouses at age 62, or as early as 60 for survivors. However, the "early" benefit reduction will be greater in the future. "Early" benefits are permanently reduced based on the number of months benefit checks are received prior to the "full" unreduced retirement age. The scheduled increases in the full retirement age described above will automatically result in additional months between "full" and "early" retirement, and therefore, an increased reduction in early retirement benefits.

Delayed Retirement

If you decide to continue working beyond your Full Retirement Age, your benefit amount on your own work record will increase in two ways. Additional years of work may increase your average lifetime earnings -- the basis for benefit computations. Also, delayed retirement credits added to your record for such work can increase your benefit anywhere from three to eight percent (depending on your year of birth) annually, up to age 70. Work after age 70 will not increase your benefit.

Automatic Cost of Living Adjustment ("COLA")

Social Security benefits are adjusted annually to help keep pace with inflation. The COLA is based on the Consumer Price Index from the third quarter of the previous year through the third quarter of the current year. The percentage of the cost of living increase is announced each fall and benefits are increased the following January. During the last decade (from 1990 through 2000) Social Security benefits increased from a high of 5.4 percent in 1991, to a low of 1.3 percent in 1999, for an average COLA increase of 2.8 percent over the last 10 years.

Annual Earnings Test

Work and earnings after entitlement may reduce your monthly Social Security benefits if you are younger than your Full Retirement Age. If you have earnings as a survivor, only your benefit is reduced, not the benefits of other family members. Work and earnings of disabled individuals and those receiving SSI payments are handled differently. If you are receiving one of these categories of payment and are working, you must report your earnings to the SSA.

Until January 2000, the Social Security retirement benefits of working recipients under the age of 70 were reduced to the extent they had earnings over the allowable limit. Now, only work and earnings **before** your Full Retirement Age are considered. The amount of "allowable" earnings changes annually. In 2001, the allowable earnings limit for anyone younger than "full" retirement age is $10,680. For every $2 earned over this limit, $1 is withheld from your Social Security benefit.

Special rules prorate earnings for the year a worker attains full retirement age, with only those months prior to the worker's birth month being counted against benefits.

Divorced Spouse

If a marriage lasted at least 10 years, a former spouse may be eligible for benefits on a worker's Social Security record. The amount of the benefit paid to the ex-spouse does not reduce the benefit paid to the worker or current spouse. This is true of both "life" cases (retirement or disability) as well as "death" cases (i.e. survivor benefits).

Taxes

Social Security benefits are taxable to the extent that one-half of your benefits when added to your other income (including investment income, dividends, and even tax-exempt interest) exceeds the Internal Revenue Service (IRS) "base amount" of $25,000 ($32,000 if married). If you have substantial income, as much as 85% percent of your benefits could be subject to income tax at your marginal rate. For additional information about taxes, contact the Internal Revenue Service at 1 800 829-3676, or visit the IRS website www.irs.gov.

Government Pension Offset

Receipt of a government pension based on work not covered by Social Security (federal civil service for example) may reduce or offset your Social Security survivor benefit. Additional information is available directly from the SSA. Call and ask for their special fact sheet, "Government Pension Offset." A separate fact sheet, "A Pension from Work Not Covered by Social Security" explains the effect when a government worker is also eligible for his or her own Social Security benefit.

Leaving the United States

If you are a U.S. citizen, extended travel or residency in most foreign countries does not affect your eligibility for Social Security benefits. However, Social Security benefits may not be sent to Cambodia, Cuba, North Korea, Vietnam and some of the former republics of the Soviet Union. The list may change based on world events. You should obtain current country status from Social Security prior to finalizing your plans to move abroad. Generally, Medicare does not cover health care outside of the U.S.

Services are free

Beware of anyone charging a fee for Social Security services. There is no charge to obtain a Social Security card, change a name on a card, replace a lost card, apply for benefits, change an address, report a death, request publications or otherwise obtain information or any other Social Security transactions.

Chapter Four

Insurance: Claims, Life, Health, and Long Term Care

James M. Knaus, CLU, ChFC, CFP

As THE NAME implies, "insurance" protects us from life's risks. Life, disability, health, long-term care, and for that matter, property and casualty insurance, provide safety and comfort if and when our worst fears are realized. Insurance of any kind is a burden when you don't need it and a godsend when you do.

If your late spouse had life insurance, you must make a claim for payment of the proceeds. You must also elect whether to take payment in a lump sum or over a period of years. If others depend on you for their support, you own a business, or you will have substantial income or estate tax liability at your death, you yourself might need life insurance.

Unless you are over the age of 65, handicapped or indigent, you are responsible for your own health insurance. Even if you are 65 or older, you may want to supplement the coverage provided under the Medicare program. Maintaining high quality comprehensive medical coverage for you and your family is of critical importance. Any gap in coverage exposes you to potentially devastating risks.

Health insurance and Medicare provide only minimal coverage in the event you require long-term nursing home care. Medicare provides coverage for a portion of the first one hundred days of nursing home care if you enter the nursing home from the hospital in a related illness (see Chapter Twelve, "Losing Independence"). Medicaid is available for indigent nursing home patients, in a limited number of facilities on a limited-availability basis. If you have substantial assets, long term nursing home care isn't an issue. If you have limited assets, you might consider long-term care insurance to avoid dissipating all of your assets and to insure a stay in a quality facility.

Locating Life Insurance Policies

Finding life insurance isn't always an easy task. Look through important papers at home, at the office, and in your safe deposit box if you have one. Examine your checkbook register for payments to life insurance companies. You may enlist the help of your insurance agent, your late spouse's human resources/employee benefits department, or the Veterans Administration to help you determine if coverage exists. When speaking with your late spouse's employer you might also inquire about other benefits such as accidental death benefits, unused sick time, unused vacation pay, deferred compensation arrangements, and qualified retirement plan benefits. Look for "credit life" insurance on large purchases such as your home and auto. Although we don't recommend you purchase credit life, your spouse may have obtained this coverage to pay off large debts. Typically, credit life insurance premium payments are added to the monthly loan payment on purchase.

You may also use the power of the Internet to locate life insurance policies on your spouse's life. For instance, check http://www.life-search.net.

Even if you find old policies that you know or suspect have lapsed, there may still be value in terms of a death benefit. It will cost you nothing to ask.

Claim Procedure

You should begin the claims process as soon as possible after your spouse's death. The life insurance claims process will take approximately thirty days from the time you make your claim to your receipt of proceeds. The first step is to call your agent, your late spouse's company benefits department, the Veterans Administration or the life insurance company directly.

In recent years, insurance companies have simplified the claims process. Although each company's procedures are different, all that is usually needed is your claim for payment (sometimes required to be in writing on a form sent to you by the company) and a death certificate. Nonetheless, you should have the following information handy:

1. A copy of the policy.
2. Your spouse's last day worked.
3. His date and place of birth.
4. Source of birth information.
5. Date, place and cause of death.
6. Your name, address and Social Security number.

If you choose the lump sum settlement option, the insurance company may require you to surrender the original policy document. If another settlement option is selected (see below), you should keep the policy as evidence of your continuing entitlement to distributions. You may be entitled to additional (sometimes double) benefits if your late spouse's death was accidental.

If your spouse died within 2 years of the policy issue date (the "contestability period"), the insurance company is likely to conduct a routine investigation to determine whether the death was caused by suicide, or if the application contained fraudulent misrepresentations. This procedure may delay the claim process.

Settlement Options

Life insurance companies offer a number of settlement (payout) options at death. This is true for group as well as individual policies. The option you choose will depend on your short-term and long-term income needs, as well as your faith in your ability to manage your finances. We strongly recommend that you elect the lump sum option and integrate the proceeds into the financial plan you develop with the knowledge gained in Chapter Five. The most popular distribution options are summarized below:

Lump Sum

Lump sum distributions are the most common form of life insurance payout. They allow you full and immediate access to proceeds to pay current expenses and invest the money however you see fit. In most cases, a lump sum payment is preferred. The cash proceeds can be invested consistent with your financial plan (see Chapter Five) considering your need for income and future growth.

Life Income

Proceeds from the policy are paid to you over the balance of your life. The monthly benefit depends on your age and gender, and is calculated using standard actuarial tables of life expectancy. The life income option has a number of important drawbacks. Although you are guaranteed a payment for life, the payment is not adjusted for inflation. Once the life income option is chosen, it may not be altered. Finally, your heirs would be adversely affected by your premature death, since payments stop at your death, even if you die after receiving only one payment! For these reasons, life income is the least attractive payment option.

Life Income, Period Certain

The life income, period certain option provides income for the **longer** of your life expectancy or the period certain (usually five or ten years). If you die before the period certain, your beneficiary continues to receive the income amount for the balance of the period. For example, if you choose a "life income, **ten** year certain" option, and die after six years, your beneficiary is entitled to income for four years after your death. The period certain feature eliminates the risk of early death, but will reduce your payment. (See the table below).

Life Income, Installment Refund

This option guarantees the return of your investment. Amounts not paid to you as life income will be paid to your beneficiary in a lump sum. For example, if you placed $100,000 under the life income, installment refund option, and had received $70,000 by the time of your death, your beneficiary would receive $30,000.

Fixed Period

The fixed period option provides income for a specific period of time such as ten or fifteen years. This option may be appropriate when you need income only for a set number of years. Because it is not a life income, the amount will be higher than any of the life income options.

Interest Only

The interest only option pays interest at regular intervals, but you reserve the right at any time to elect another option or a lump sum. The interest only option is best used on a temporary basis while you complete your financial plan.

The following chart illustrates the anticipated monthly payment for the various non-lump sum settlement options based on a $100,000 death benefit:

SETTLEMENT OPTIONS: AN EXAMPLE*

$100,000 DEATH BENEFIT
SURVIVING SPOUSE: FEMALE AGE 62

Life Income	$548/month/life
Life Income, Ten Year Certain	$531/month
Life Income, Installment Refund	$499/month
Fixed Period: Ten Years	$962/month
Interest Only	$500/month

*Income figures are based on guaranteed interest rates. Actual, or "current" rates will likely be higher.

Determining Your Own Life Insurance Need

If you have children who depend on you, college expenses, substantial debts, a family business, or anticipated estate tax liability, you may need life insurance on your own life. Even if you are 60 or even 70 years old, you can still buy life insurance as long as you are reasonably healthy. The "million dollar" question is whether you need life insurance, and if so, how much. The answer depends on your future economic need, balanced against the cost of insurance. Determining your insurance needs requires a detailed analysis of your current and future expenses as well as your sources of income.

Take for example a surviving spouse with three children, ages 12, 10 and 7. Let's assume the following additional facts:

- Annual living expenses are (after tax) $60,000 (food, clothing, auto, insurance, entertainment, and miscellaneous expenses).
- An effective (average) income tax rate of 20%.
- Estimated funeral expenses for the surviving spouse of $10,000.
- A mortgage balance of $80,000.
- College funding needed for all children of $100,000.
- A $20,000 emergency fund.
- Gross income from the survivor's employment of $27,000.
- The family receives $15,000 of Social Security benefits per year.
- Investments in the amount of $325,000.

Let's also assume that the family will earn 8% annually on investments, inflation will be 3% per year, and that income is needed for 15 years, taking the youngest child to age 22.

Although $325,000 of investments sounds like a lot of money, and it is, it would not be enough to provide for the children if the surviving spouse dies prematurely.

Lump Sum Needs: (Last Expenses, College Funding, Mortgage and Emergency Fund)	$210,000
Income needs: $33,000 per year for 15 years, inflation-adjusted	$362,718*

Total Capital Required
(Lump sum plus income needs): $572,718

Less: Existing Capital $325,000

Amount of Life Insurance needed $247,718

*$75,000 needed, less $42,000 ($27,000 income + $15,000 Social Security).
This amount represents the present value of an increasing income for 15 years.

Even with the $325,000 properly invested (earning an 8% average
rate of return), there would be a shortage in the event the surviving
spouse in our example dies prematurely. At the very least, the surviving spouse should purchase term life insurance in the amount of
$250,000 for a fifteen-year period. The annual premium for a
healthy female in her forties would be less than $1,000 per year.
Moreover, a revocable trust should be created to avoid probate and
to manage the spouse's assets until such time as all of the children are
raised and able to manage an outright distribution of their inheritance (see Chapter Nine, "Basic Estate Planning").

Types of Life Insurance

The **type** of insurance appropriate for you depends on a number of factors, including your age, how much you are able to
spend, as well as the length of time and the purpose for which
it is needed. As a general rule, if you are under the age of fifty
and need insurance coverage for a limited period (until children
finish college), term insurance would be the most appropriate
for you. If you are over the age of sixty, and have a permanent
need for life insurance (payment of estate tax, equalization of
your estate among many children, etc.) a permanent product
like whole life, universal life, or variable life would be more
suitable for your needs.

It is extremely difficult to be a smart consumer when it comes to
life insurance. Insurance policies tend to be like snowflakes, with no
two alike. It is impossible to compare them. This is true even for

term policies where the only thing being purchased is a simple promise to pay a death benefit. Compounding the problem is the fact that you cannot blindly rely on the advice of your agent, whose commission depends on the type of policy sold. The key is to obtain the advice of a trusted advisor and to ask the right questions to keep him honest.

There are no absolutes when it comes to buying insurance. You will need sound advice when choosing among the following options:

Term Insurance

Term Insurance is the least expensive form of insurance, since it insures against the loss of life for a specified period of time. Term insurance is preferred if you are under age fifty, need a large death benefit, and cost is an issue. The policy does not build up value from year to year. If you stop making premium payments, the policy simply lapses. As such, term insurance has no "cash surrender value." You can choose the length of time you intend to keep the policy. You have the right to continue the policy during the guarantee period without evidence that you are still insurable. You can elect a one, five, 10, 15, 20, 25, or 30-year term. The longer the guarantee period the higher the annual premium. Most term insurance is convertible to a permanent policy with the same company without evidence of medical insurability.

Whole Life

Whole Life is a form of permanent protection that combines a death benefit and an increasing cash surrender value. Although the premiums are substantially higher than term insurance, whole life can be very economical for those with a long-term or permanent need for life insurance. Over time, premium payments may be paid from the policy's cash reserves. You may also elect to reduce the death benefit if you are unable or unwilling to make future premium payments. If the policy is participating (that is, there are dividends payable), you may be able to use the dividends to help you pay the premiums or to otherwise enhance the benefits of the policy.

Universal Life

Universal Life is a hybrid form of permanent insurance. Basically, universal life is term insurance with a "side-fund." The side fund is an investment account that holds general short-term interest-sensitive assets of the insurance company. Universal life premiums are lower than those for whole life, but higher than term insurance premiums. Universal life offers permanent protection at a cost below that of whole life. As with all permanent products (whole, universal, and variable), the growing value of the side fund is used to offset the higher cost of maintaining the death benefit as you age.

Variable Life

Variable Life is permanent insurance with a side fund invested in mutual funds. Variable life is attractive to people who believe that in the long run stocks will outperform other investments. Many companies have combined the best features of universal and variable life insurance into variable universal life insurance ("VUL").

Tax Aspects

Life insurance death benefits are generally received **income** tax free. Although life insurance is included in the decedent's gross estate for **estate** tax purposes, no estate tax is imposed when the proceeds are paid to the surviving spouse (unless the surviving spouse is not a U.S. citizen) on account of the "unlimited marital deduction." (See Chapter Nine: "Basic Estate Planning"). Large life insurance policies should be owned in an Irrevocable Life Insurance Trust ("ILIT") if they would otherwise cause the insured's estate to be taxable (see Chapter Ten: "Advanced Estate Planning").

If one of the deferred settlement options is chosen, a portion of each payment is an income tax free return of the original proceeds, and the balance is taxable to the beneficiary as interest income. The insurance company will annually provide you with Form 1099 indicating the taxable portion of the distribution (a copy of Form 1099 is also filed with the IRS).

Health Insurance

The loss of a spouse may be accompanied by a loss of health care coverage. Having a gap in coverage for even a single day can be devastating to you and your dependents. If you are eligible for Medicare, no gap in coverage will occur (unless you fail to timely apply for coverage). However, you could experience a gap in **full** coverage if your supplemental "Medigap" coverage (see below) lapses. If you are not at least 65 years of age and thus not eligible for Medicare, one of the first orders of business after your spouse's death is to secure medical insurance. You can secure private health insurance from any number of private health insurance carriers, or from your late spouse's employer, if you are eligible for "COBRA" coverage.

"COBRA" Coverage

If at the time of your late spouse's death, he or she was employed by a company with at least twenty full-time employees, you may be eligible to continue his or her hospitalization and major medical insurance. The right to continuation coverage was created under the Consolidated Omnibus Budget Reconciliation Act, and is commonly known as "COBRA coverage." The insurance is identical to the coverage offered while your spouse was alive. The maximum period that you may continue your late spouse's coverage is 36 months. Both you and your dependent children are eligible. COBRA coverage is not free; you must pay your late spouse's employer 102% of its cost for carrying you. The company's employee benefits department should be able to provide specific information as to the coverage available as well as premium cost. COBRA coverage will likely be cheaper and more comprehensive than coverage you can find on your own, especially if you or a member of your family has serious health problems.

"Medigap" Coverage

If you are eligible for Medicare (age 65+) you should purchase Medicare supplement ("Medigap") insurance to cover medical costs not covered by Medicare. The most significant gaps in Medicare are deductibles, co-payments, and non-covered charges. Adding Medigap coverage assures nearly complete hospitalization and major medical coverage and is therefore recommended. Since Medicare only covers prescription costs associated with a hospital stay, you should also purchase the Medigap prescription option. Medigap can be purchased from many major medical insurance companies. You might consider using the plans suggested by AARP as a way to compare various Medigap policies. Call the AARP Health Care Options toll free number at 1 (800) 245-1212, ext. 99.

Part A of Medicare generally provides reimbursement for hospitalization and miscellaneous services and supplies, plus home health care and limited skilled nursing care. Part B of Medicare covers doctors' services, medical services, and supplies. The charts below summarize the major provisions of Medicare Parts A and B.

MEDICARE PART A

SERVICE	BENEFIT	GAP
Semi-private room & board	All costs for first 60 days, except the first $792	$792
	61st through 90th days, all except $198 per day	$198/day
Post-Hospital skilled *Nursing facility care* [after 3+ days in hospital; within 30 days of discharge from hospital]	First 20 Days All Costs	None
	Next 80 Days All but $99/day	$99/day
Home Health Care	Unlimited, if under physician's treatment plan	20% of amount of durable medical equipment

Medicare Part A is financed through the 1.45% tax on all earned income, with an employer matching amount equal to the employee's tax.

MEDICARE PART B

SERVICE	BENEFIT	GAP
Medical Expense: Doctor's Services, Inpatient and Outpatient medical services, and supplies, Physical and Speech Therapy, Ambulance	80% of approved amount (after $100 deductible)	$100 deductible plus 20% co-insurance

Note: You must also pay for any charges in excess of the Medicare-approved amount.

Medicare Part B is financed through monthly premiums of $50 per person, deducted from your Social Security check.

Important: see the discussion of Medicare in Chapter Three "Navigating Social Security" for a more detailed discussion of Medicare.

Long Term Care

Even if you have adequate medical insurance, you may still be a candidate for long term care ("LTC") insurance. Long term care insurance has become increasingly popular as our population has aged. Statistics show that the older we get, the greater the likelihood that we will experience an extended stay in a nursing home or require full time home health care. Traditional health insurance does not cover long term nursing home care. Medicare covers a small portion of the cost of long term care for a stay of no more than one hundred days (see "Medicare" in Chapter Twelve).

The most important variables in any LTC policy are:

• Daily Benefit Amount.
• Length of coverage for any nursing home stay.

- Waiting (elimination) period.
- Cost of living increases.
- Number of "ADLs" (activities of daily living) included.
- Premium cost.

Ideally, an LTC policy should cover the full daily cost (daily benefit amount) of your stay, and continue (length of coverage) for life. Naturally, if cost is a consideration, you may decide to cover a reasonable portion of the daily cost, and have coverage continue for a shorter period, say three years. Three years of coverage tends to be popular for two reasons: first, the average nursing home stay is less than three years, and second, the Medicaid divestment period is thirty-six months (see Chapter Twelve: "Losing Independence"). The philosophy here is that you can give away ("divest") all of your assets upon entering the nursing home and be eligible for Medicaid when your LTC policy runs out.

The longer the LTC waiting period (also known as the elimination period), the lower the premium cost. A ninety day waiting period is common in part because Medicare covers a portion of the first one hundred days of your stay (if you are entering the nursing home from the hospital for a related condition).

LTC insurance may provide benefits long into the future. For that reason, it is extremely important that the daily benefit amount be indexed for inflation. You have two basic choices: either simple or compounded increases in your daily benefit amount. Although 5% simple increases are common, 5% compounded interest is better. Your selection will depend on your other resources and your premium tolerance.

The Activities of Daily Living usually include the following:

- Bathing
- Toileting
- Continence
- Dressing
- Transferring
- Eating

You are eligible for benefits under your LTC policy if you need substantial assistance with two or more ADLs, and your care is expected to last for at least 90 days, or, if you need supervisory assistance due to a cognitive loss such as Alzheimer's or dementia.

Other important features and benefits to investigate while shopping for LTC insurance include:

- Home health care benefits
- Intermediate and custodial care
- Waiver of premium
- Bed reservation
- Respite care
- Discounts for good health
- Guaranteed renewability

Fortunately, it is easier to compare LTC policies since they have become somewhat standardized. Nonetheless, it is prudent to obtain objective advice from a qualified professional, such as a financial planner with expertise in long term care planning. As always, check out the financial stability of the insurance company through rating services like Best's, Moody's, Standard & Poor's and Weiss.

Long-term care premiums are income tax deductible to the extent that when added to other health care premiums and unreimbursed medical expenses they exceed 7.5% of your adjusted gross income.

Medicaid

If you have substantial liquid assets you may be in a position to self-insure your LTC needs. In the event you require nursing home care and do not have LTC insurance, you will be required to pay for your care out of your own pocket. Medicare provides coverage for a portion of the first one hundred days of nursing home care if you enter the nursing home from the hospital in a related illness. Only when your assets have been sufficiently depleted will you qualify for Medicaid. Medicaid eligibility is discussed in greater detail in Chapter Twelve. However, as a general rule you will be required to exhaust substantially all of your assets (other than your home and your car) before you qualify for Medicaid.

Planes, Trains, and Automobiles

You should contact your property and casualty insurance agent and review your home and automobile coverage. Ask about an "umbrella" policy covering liability over and above your individual home and auto policies. Umbrella coverage is purchased in million dollar increments and tends to be a real bargain. You should sell your late spouse's car (or turn it in to the leasing company). Don't let family members use your cars or recreational vehicles and expose you to unnecessary liability.

Conclusion

First, attempt to locate all life insurance policies on your late spouse's life. Then, begin the claims process as soon as possible in light of the fact that it may take 30 days to receive proceeds. Even though you may be offered a number of settlement options, the lump sum option will almost always be the best choice. Life Insurance proceeds should be integrated into a comprehensive financial plan discussed in Chapter Five. If you have dependent children, or other need for liquidity, you should purchase life insurance on your own life. You should take immediate steps to protect yourself from any gap in health insurance coverage, and evaluate your need for long-term care insurance. You should limit your exposure to property and casualty claims by securing adequate insurance including an umbrella policy. Finally, you will need the assistance of a competent and trusted insurance professional to help you evaluate your insurance needs and the appropriate products.

Chapter Five

Putting Your Financial House in Order

Steven J. Case, CLU, ChFC, CFP, CDP

You may feel the loss of your spouse most acutely when it comes to financial matters. Money is directly tied to our inner sense of security and well-being. Perhaps that is the reason that so many people are "bad" with money. What they are saying is that money scares the hell out of them. They're afraid they won't have enough, afraid someone will steal it, or that their friends will find out how much or how little they have. With so many emotions attached to money, it's not surprising that people fail to properly address their money issues. These same people will blindly turn their money over to near strangers so they don't have to deal with it. They are vulnerable not just because they don't know much about money and finances, but because they don't want to know.

You may have happily relinquished all financial responsibilities to your spouse when you got married only to have it dropped back in your lap at his or her death. It is common to be angry at your late spouse for dying and leaving you to make important decisions alone. If your spouse was in charge of your family finances, you likely have little or no background in financial matters and may only vaguely understand your sources of income and monthly expenditures. Even if you were the financial manager in your household, the death of your spouse dictates that you rethink your financial future.

Your spouse's death may impact your income from wages, Social Security and pensions, leaving many unanswered questions: Do you have enough monthly income? Do you need to work? Will you have to invade principal to maintain your current lifestyle? Are your investments appropriate for your new life plan? These and other questions are answered in a process known as "financial planning."

The objective of this chapter is to give you a greater comfort level in the financial realm, to be able to choose a capable financial planner to assist you, and be able to adequately judge his or her performance. Ultimately, you must take control of your money. You need to know what's going on, not just to avoid getting fleeced, but also to effectively manage your money. You shouldn't spend too much or too little. It would be a shame to deprive yourself of life's pleasures because you (wrongly) feel that you can't afford them. Knowing what you have allows you to live within, not above or below, your means.

The following are the basic elements of financial planning:

1. Determine your net worth.
2. Determine your monthly sources of income and expenditures.
3. Define your future goals.
4. Determine if your current investments are properly suited for your new life plan.
5. Minimize financial risk through diversification.

Unless you have extensive training in financial matters, you will need help developing your financial plan. Although well-meaning friends and family may offer suggestions about the management of your money, investments that have worked for them may not fit your situation. Financial planning isn't about picking winners -- that's called gambling. Financial planning involves the five steps described above and requires that you make a plan that is right for you.

Choosing a financial planner may be one of the most important decisions you will make after your spouse's death. Stories of widows who have been taken advantage of by unscrupulous investment advisors abound. Solicit recommendations from friends and family and interview three candidates. Choose someone who is experienced, licensed and credentialed. Make sure to review "Choosing a Financial Planner" at the end of this chapter.

Without question, money is the number one source of **anxiety** for widows and widowers. What is the fear? The fear is of the unknown, and the antidote is **knowledge**. That is not to say that you need to become a financial planner. You only need to understand what you have, what you need and where you're going. To start, you need to assess your current financial position and develop a written plan.

Determine Your Net Worth

The first step is to determine your "net worth." Net worth is simply the value of your assets less liabilities. The information you gathered on your "Asset Inventory with Values Worksheet" in Chapter Two is your starting point. You should also gather the most recent statements for each asset and liability. Look for bank, brokerage, IRA, 401(k), credit union, as well as mortgage and credit card statements. This information is part of the mosaic of your current financial position. Keep these statements handy, since either you or your financial advisor may need them to contact the financial institutions for more information.

Determine Monthly Income and Expenses

Determining your monthly income and expenses is more difficult than determining your net worth. If you're like most people, you don't know where the money goes each month. No, you probably don't have a hole in your wallet! You probably use the "pay as you go" budget method, hoping that you don't run out of money during the month. Record your cash inflows (income) and outflows (expenses), including non-monthly items. For example, if you pay $2,400 in annual property taxes, divide the cost by 12 to arrive at a monthly property tax expense of $200. If you are computer literate, programs such as Quicken and Microsoft Money are excellent for helping you keep track of your income and expenses. You can even

pay your bills online. For the first few months, keep a detailed journal of your daily expenses to get a clearer picture of where you are
spending your money. If your total income exceeds expenses, you
have a surplus that can be earmarked for savings. If your expenses
exceed your income, you are practicing "deficit spending," and
immediate corrective action is required.

Define Your Goals

What are your personal and financial goals? Although it may
sound like a simple question, very few of us ever take the time to
plan our future, let alone commit our thoughts to writing. Once you
know where you're going, finding the right path is rather straightforward. On the other hand, as the old saying goes, "if you don't
know where you're going, any road will get you there."   If your
future seems cloudy, and you are having difficulty identifying your
personal and financial goals, here's an exercise: Start by dreaming.
Put your dreams in writing. Be specific. What do you want? How
much will the goal cost?   Set a time frame to reach the goal.
Organize your dreams by category (personal life, career, health,
financial standing) and prioritize them. Create a written action plan.
Implement your plan. Review the plan regularly and monitor your
progress. Adjust the specifics of your plan if necessary. And finally,
celebrate your accomplishments!

In order to set financial goals, think about the following:

• When do you want to retire?
• How much money per month do you need?
• What large purchases do you wish to make (college, second home,
  car, vacations)?

The following example illustrates the power of a written plan:

The senior class at Harvard University was surveyed about
their life goals. The results showed that only 3% of the class
actually had clear, established goals and had them in writing.
The other 97% may have had goals, but they were not clear
and were not in writing. Twenty years later, the same group
was resurveyed. The results showed that the 3% who had

clear, written goals had lived happier, healthier, and more fulfilling lives. In addition, the survey also showed that this 3% had a cumulative net worth that exceeded that of the other 97%—combined.

(Source: *Body For Life: 12 Weeks to Mental and Physical Strength* by Bill Phillips and Michael D'Orso).

Can You Get There From Here?

You must determine whether you can maintain your current lifestyle after your spouse's death. In all likelihood, even without planning, you'll be fine for the time being. The question is whether you will continue to enjoy the same lifestyle for the rest of your life. Answering the question of whether you can get there from here requires a detailed analysis of your current assets, your sources of income, your spending habits, the anticipated rate of return on your investments and a projected inflation rate.

Short of going to work (or to continue working), your plan should call for you to "not touch principal." Although the exact definition of "principal" is open to debate, the concept is clear. If you spend more than you take in, you erode your nest egg. Once you start spending savings, you begin a descent that ends with you running out of money. Like a downhill skier, you pick up speed as you go. Less principal means less income. The lower your income, the more you erode principal, and so on and so forth.

Despite your best-laid plans, some factors like inflation, stock market fluctuations, and unforeseen emergencies are outside of your control. The key is to minimize these risks with a diversified investment strategy and adequate insurance.

Diversification, described more fully below, is the process of investing in different investment vehicles (guaranteed investments, stocks, bonds, mutual funds, and real estate), in various sectors of the economy (drugs, industrials, high tech, banking, municipal, utilities) in such a way as to minimize the risk that any one sector will suffer a significant downturn. One only has to remember the fall of high tech stocks in 2000-2001 to be reminded that having all of your eggs in one basket can be a risky practice.

Clients often hold stock of their current or former employer. Whether out of company loyalty or as a result of a company-matching program, these clients may have a significant portion of their net worth invested in a single company. Although they may feel safe, in reality they are exposing themselves to substantial risk. They could be wiped out if their company experiences a severe downturn.

In addition to being diversified among a variety of investment types, sound investing dictates that you monitor the **amount** of your investment in each category. A tried and true paradigm of investing is the "investment pyramid" shown below. Basically, start at the bottom. Only when you have fulfilled your need at a given level should you move up to the next level.

Insurance is at the base of the pyramid because you must first protect yourself from unforeseen events (such as death, disability, illness and an extended nursing home stay) that could threaten your financial security. Estate planning must also be in place to assure your family's well being in the event of your permanent disability or death.

Once your insurance and estate planning needs have been satisfied, you should have sufficient liquid investments and cash reserves to cover your short-term needs in the event of an interruption of your income. The amount of your readily accessible cash will depend on your other sources of income including Social Security, pension, and IRA minimum distributions (see Chapter Six, "IRA and Retirement Distributions").

Next are mutual funds, stocks and bonds owned outside of your IRAs and 401(k)s. Assets in this category are less accessible than cash and passbook savings, and may result in capital gains when liquidated, but are subject to a lower tax rate than distributions from IRAs, 401(k)s and annuities that generate "ordinary" income.

Annuities, IRAs, and 401(k)s follow. With twenty years of IRA and 401(k) savings, this category is the fastest growing category of assets in the United States. Special planning is necessary since distributions from these assets are subject to income tax. We have seen over-saving in this area, with clients afraid to touch their vast retirement savings for fear of paying tax on the distributions. Two important points need to be made about retirement savings: First, retirement savings should be used! They're intended to supplement your Social Security and pensions, so work out a systematic withdrawal program and add the distributions to your monthly income. You'll have to start taking it anyway when you turn age 70 ½ (see Chapter Six). Next, integrate retirement accounts into your overall invest-ment strategy. It's all your money! Make sure that your assets as a whole satisfy your needs.

Once your financial house is in order with insurance, liquid invest-ments and your long-term growth portfolio, you then have the luxury to invest in more speculative investments if you are so inclined. Naturally, speculative investments such as oil and gas, limited partnerships and commodities should constitute a very small portion of your portfolio and should only be invested with money you can afford to lose.

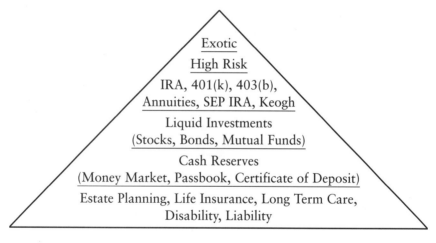

Again, the key is diversification. To protect against inflation (see below), you shouldn't hold only low-risk, low yield invest-ments. Nor should you hold only high-risk investments. The proper mix depends on your risk tolerance, your age and your income needs.

The Impact of Inflation

Inflation is the rise in the price of goods and services over time. Your spending power will erode if you fail to account for inflation in your financial plan. For example, an investment portfolio weighted too heavily in favor of low-growth, low-risk investments is vulnerable to inflation.

To illustrate, if Bev invests $10,000 in a certificate of deposit ("CD") paying 5% interest, compounded annually, she will earn $500 in interest in her first year. If Bev is in the 28% tax bracket and we assume an inflation rate of 5%, she actually lost ground financially. She paid $140 in income taxes ($500 X .28 = $140) resulting in $360 (the original $500 interest less the $140 owed for taxes) of "net investment income." Now consider that Bev's initial investment of $10,000 is not actually worth $10,000 in today's dollars due to inflation. Assuming a 5% inflation rate, Bev would actually need $10,500 to have the same spending power as she did one year earlier. Since her portfolio grew by only $360, Bev actually had a real rate of return of a **negative** 1.40% after taxes and inflation. Her income and portfolio are growing, but the cost of goods and services is growing at a faster rate. Bev is slowly losing ground.

Investment Risk

It is often thought that as risk increases, so does return. Actually, higher risk gives the **potential** for higher returns, but it also creates the potential for higher losses. That is not to say that higher risk investments such as individual stocks do not have a place in your portfolio. Historically, stocks and other "equities" (see below) have out-performed all other investments, earning a rate of return in excess of ten percent. Since low risk investments rarely offer even the potential for high returns, you cannot achieve diversification without some amount of risk. The key is to determine the level of risk you can live with.

Everyone's risk tolerance is different. Your risk sensitivity may be quite different from your late spouse's, and may have changed since your spouse's death. The key is to achieve the rate of return to meet your short-term and long-term goals, without incurring a level of risk that keeps you up at night.

Diversification

The most effective way to minimize investment risk (including the risk of inflation) is to diversify your investments. By combining different investments you can insulate your portfolio from fluctuations within asset types. The benefits of diversification are illustrated by the following comparison of two portfolios. The first is diversified, containing 50% stocks and 50% cash (e.g. CDs and Treasury bills). The second is non-diversified, with the entire 100% invested in stocks. Each portfolio will invest $100,000 for two years. In the first year, the market grows by 20% while the going interest rate is 5%. In the second year, the market declines by 20% while the going interest rate stays constant at 5%. Let's compare the two strategies and see what happens:

DIVERSIFIED

Year 1	Stock investment returns [20% X 50,000] =	$10,000
	Guaranteed investment [5% X 50,000] =	$2,500
	Total Gain	$12,500
	Portfolio Value	$112,500

Assume that the portfolio is then re-balanced to 50% in each category.

Year 2	Stock investment returns [–20% X $56,250] =	($11,250)
	Guaranteed investment [5% X $56,250] =	$2,812.50
	Total Gain (Loss)	($8,437.50)
	Portfolio Value	$104,062.50

NON-DIVERSIFIED

| Year 1 | Stock investment returns [20% X $100,000] = | $20,000 |
| | Portfolio Value | $120,000 |

| Year 2 | Stock investment returns [–20% X $120,000] = | ($24,000) |
| | Portfolio Value | $ 96,000 |

Despite a stock market downturn of 20 percent in year 2, the diversified portfolio lost only 7.5 percent. The non-diversified portfolio lost the full 20 percent.

Tax Considerations

Income tax must be factored into your financial plan. Distributions from IRAs (other than Roth IRAs), and 401(k)s are fully taxable. The interest on municipal bonds is tax-free. Annuity payments are part taxable and part tax-free. The portion of the annuity payment reflecting your "investment in the contract" is tax-free, while the portion representing growth on your investment is taxable as ordinary income (see more about annuities below).

Your Financial Plan

Your financial advisor will develop a financial plan taking into consideration your net worth, income needs, risk tolerance and future goals. The plan should contain specific investment recommendations. Depending on how you are invested, some of your investments will need to be converted to fit with your plan. Life insurance proceeds and any retirement distributions received by you on account of your spouse's death (whether or not they were rolled over into your own IRA) will likewise be invested according to your plan. To implement your plan, you and your advisor will choose a diversified mix of the various investment options described below in "Understanding Investments." Once your plan is in place, you should meet with your investment advisor no less than annually to assess your changing needs as well as changes in the market.

Future investment choices will be made based on the quality of the investment under consideration as well as whether it's consistent with your financial plan. With your financial plan in place, you are the captain of your ship tacking your way to your destination. Following your financial plan will minimize the risk of market downturns and allow you to live the life you have chosen for yourself.

With a plan, you are better able to resist the temptation to purchase the investment *du jour* or "time" the market based on the headlines in the morning paper or a television commentator's financial outlook. The daily news is a snapshot of current events that naturally distorts the long-term view of investing. History has proven that market timing is nearly impossible, and should definitely be avoided. The following chart illustrates the remarkable opportunities lost if you were out of the market on some of the highest-rising market days of the past decade:

STOCK MARKET 1/1/91-12/21/2000	S&P 500 ANNUALIZED RETURNS
In the market all 2,258 trading days:	14.9%
Out of the market the 10 best days:	10.3%
Out of the market the 20 best days	7.0%
Out of the market the 30 best days:	4.3%
Out of the market the 40 best days	1.9%

The message is clear. Chart a course and a plan and stick to it. Review your plan regularly, but not less than annually and adjust your plan as needed to account for changes in the market and your life.

Understanding Investments

Various investments are used to diversify your investment portfolio and to implement your financial plan. It is important to understand your investment choices as well as their role in your financial plan. The following several pages highlight the various major investment categories.

Guaranteed Investments

Generally, guaranteed investments are a good place to put money for the short term, if, for instance, you plan to use the money to make a large purchase in the near future. Common guaranteed investments include money market accounts, passbook accounts, certificates of deposit and treasury bills.

Money Market Account

Money market accounts pay an adjustable interest rate. The funds are readily available all the time without penalty. The FDIC generally insures money market funds but you must check in each case to be sure.

Passbook Account

Like the money market account, this account also pays an adjustable interest rate and the funds are readily available without penalty. The interest rate is generally lower but more stable than a money market account interest rate.

Certificate of Deposit (CD)

A certificate of deposit is a fixed amount invested at a fixed interest rate for a fixed period of time, e.g., 6% annually for 2 years. The funds are not liquid; that is, they are not readily available to you. In exchange for "giving up" ready access to the funds, the interest rate is usually higher than for a money market account. If you liquidate a CD before its maturity date, there will likely be an interest penalty. CD interest rates are more predictable than money market and passbook account interest rates because the rate is fixed at the time you invest. CD deposits also are usually FDIC insured.

Treasury Bill

A treasury bill is a short-term obligation of the United States government, paying a fixed interest rate for a fixed period of time. Treasury bills are often thought to be very safe investments because they are backed by the full faith and credit of the United States government. These fixed income securities have maturities ranging from 30 to 365 days and are free from state income tax.

Bonds

A bond is an "IOU" generated when an investor lends money to the bond issuer. Bonds pay a fixed interest rate and have a fixed maturity date. Bonds are generally low-risk, stable investments that return steady income. Bonds are issued by various companies, or by federal, state and local branches of government. Bonds generally mature anywhere from ten to thirty years from the date of issue. A Note ranges in maturity from one year to ten years. By investing in a bond or note, you receive a fixed interest rate and the return of your original investment (principal).

The interest on most state and local government bonds is tax-free. However, the interest rate paid on such "municipal bonds" is generally lower than that available on corporate bonds and other guaranteed investments such as CDs. Generally, the higher your marginal income tax rate, the more attractive tax-free bonds will be.

There are a number of risks in buying bonds. First, the company issuing the bond could experience a financial hardship that would jeopardize repayment of the bond interest or even the principal. Secondly, as interest rates rise, the value of your bond decreases. However, the reverse is also true, with bond values increasing as interest rates decline. Companies with questionable credit must offer bonds with a higher rate of interest to attract investors called high-yield or "junk" bonds. Such bonds pose a substantial risk of default.

The length of time until maturity of the bond is an important factor. The longer the maturity, the greater the influence of changing interest rates on the value of the bond. Much like stock mutual funds (see below), bond mutual funds offer a diverse portfolio of bonds with varying interest rates and maturity dates. You must be aware, however, that a bond mutual fund does not have the same characteristics as an individual bond. Bond mutual funds do not offer a fixed interest rate and never mature.

Equity Investments

Equity means ownership. As the holder of an equity investment, you participate in the profit and loss of the underlying entity. There is no guaranteed return on equity investments. If the company is profitable, and is thought to be a good investment by other investors, the value of the stock goes up. If the company is not profitable or is not regarded as a good investment by the markets, your investment goes down. Although equities involve a certain amount of risk, over the last century, they have proven to be the best-performing long-term investment vehicle. Listed below are a few different types of equity investments.

Stocks

A share of a stock represents an ownership interest in the issuing company. Stockholders own a portion of the issuing company and participate in its profits and growth. Stocks are categorized by their "market capitalization." Market capitalization is the number of outstanding shares of a company multiplied by the share price. Companies with a capitalization under one billion dollars are generally considered "small cap" stocks. Companies with assets of between one and ten billion dollars are "Mid cap" stocks, and companies with a capitalization in excess of ten billion dollars are "large cap" stocks. Historically, large cap stocks have tended to be older, more stable companies. The most desirable "blue chip" stocks continue to be older large cap stocks with a consistent track record of profitability such as IBM, Wal-Mart, General Motors, etc.

Mutual Funds

Mutual funds offer you the opportunity to own a variety of stocks and bonds through a single investment. A professional money manager oversees the fund and makes investment decisions. Your choices are dizzying, with well over 12,000 mutual funds from which to choose. Interestingly, there are more mutual funds than there are individual publicly traded stocks!

Each mutual fund has its own investment philosophy, which must be clearly defined in the fund's prospectus. For example, a **growth fund** must invest primarily in stocks. A **capital preservation fund** must invest primarily in certificates of deposit. **Balanced funds** may invest in a variety of securities such as stocks, bonds, and international securities, while maintaining a cash reserve for flexibility. The key is to purchase quality funds that match your risk tolerance and investment objectives.

The first step in evaluating a fund is to compare it against the track record of similar funds over a designated period, usually the last 3 and 5 years. Although past performance is no guarantee of future results, it is the best available indicator (unless you have a crystal ball). You can find this information in the fund's prospectus. A much more accessible source of performance information is Morningstar, which ranks mutual funds in a number of categories using a one-to-five-star rating system. You can find these rankings in the reference section of your library. Morningstar's Web site, www.morningstar.com also has a wealth of data designed for novice as well as experienced investors.

Individual Stocks or Mutual Funds?

Other than the commission on purchase and sale, there is no cost in holding individual stocks. Gain on the sale of stocks held for more than one year are eligible for long-term capital gains tax treatment. In contrast to stocks, mutual funds charge an "internal" annual fee, and you have no control over whether the mutual fund manager sells issues during the year, exposing you to short or long term capital gains. Despite these apparent shortcomings, the diversification and ongoing management available in mutual funds makes them extremely attractive.

To properly diversify a stock portfolio, you would have to identify and research hundreds of companies and invest over $200,000. For example, to purchase 100 shares (extra costs and commissions are incurred if an "odd lot" of fewer than 100 shares is purchased) of stock in 40 different companies with an average share price of $55 you would have to invest $220,000, plus commissions. Once purchased, you would have to monitor each stock and make adjustments as necessary to account for changes in the market.

Apart from diversification, mutual funds offer ongoing affordable professional management. It is the fund manager's job to monitor the fund on a daily, if not hourly, basis. Fund managers are immune to the emotional attachments that individual investors often form with individual stocks. For these reasons, mutual funds (or managed accounts discussed below) should form the foundation of your investment portfolio, with individual stocks purchased only if you have substantial investment in the stock market.

Managed accounts are similar to mutual funds in that they use a professional investment manager who follows a particular investment strategy. The difference is that the securities in a managed account belong only to you, as opposed to a mutual fund that commingles all investor's money in a single fund with each investor owning a share. Because the investment manager works only on your account, managed accounts typically require a minimum investment of at least $100,000. The annual fee for managed accounts is usually between two and three percent of money under management. The fee covers all commissions and internal fees.

Load versus No Load

All mutual funds charge their costs of operation to the fund. Management fees are measured as a percentage of the value of the fund, and are known as the fund's "expense ratio" and "trading costs." Such expenses are said to be **"internal"** since they are not charged directly to the investor. The expense ratio and trading costs (combined) are typically between 2% and 3% of annual assets under management. You won't see these expenses on your statement. Instead, they will offset your annual return.

Load Funds

Some funds have a front-end commission, or "load," that is charged directly to investors. Such load funds can charge commissions up-front (called "Class A" shares), or at the time of sale ("Class B" shares). The "back-end load" on Class B shares is assessed against your account if you sell the investment within the "contingent deferred commission" period. For example if you invested $10,000 in Class B shares with a four year, 4% contingent deferred charge and liquidate the account after one year you would pay a $400 commission (4% times $10,000). There would be no sales charge at all for money left in the account for five years, or more.

No Load Funds

No-load funds do not pay commissions. In theory, all of your dollars are working for you rather than being eaten up in commission. In reality, no-load funds must be evaluated based on their historic rate of return and their internal expenses. Some no-loads are a bargain while others lag in the only category that matters: net investment return. Unfortunately, with no brokerage fees to be earned, you're typically on your own when it comes to evaluating no-loads.

Annuities

An annuity is a contract between the investor and the insurance company whereby the insurance company accepts a lump sum payment from the investor in exchange for a systematic stream of income payments to the investor usually beginning at retirement. Money invested in the annuity accumulates on a tax-deferred basis. Annuities can be used to supplement your Social Security and pension payments. Annuities are best when used during life for retirement or other monthly income needs since the unused portion does not receive a stepped-up basis at the owner's death. There are several different types of annuities that fall into two broad categories: deferred annuities and immediate annuities.

Deferred Annuities

The term "deferred" refers to the fact that monthly annuity payments will begin at some future date. Income earned during the deferral period is not taxed until paid. For an additional fee, paid to the issuing insurance company, the annuity will provide a death benefit to a beneficiary of your choosing. There are three different types of deferred annuities: variable annuities, fixed annuities and market indexed annuities.

Variable Annuities

Variable annuities are invested in professionally managed stock and bond portfolios, called *sub-accounts*. The value of a variable annuity changes with the value of the sub-accounts. Since dividends, interest and capital gains remain invested until you make withdrawals, you control when income taxes are paid. Remember that withdrawals of taxable amounts will be subject to income tax, and prior to age 59 ½, may be subject to a 10% penalty tax. Variable annuities are by far the most popular type of annuity sold today.

Fixed Annuities

In exchange for a lump-sum payment (or periodic payments) to an insurance company, a fixed annuity offers a competitive interest rate for a specified time period, usually 1, 3, or 5 years. Fixed annuities preserve principal and lock in a guaranteed rate of return.

Market Indexed Annuities

Market indexed annuities are tied to the performance of the market as a whole as typically measured by the "S & P 500." Indexed annuities offer a guaranteed return in the event the market performs below the guaranteed target rate. The guarantee allows investors to participate in the upside growth potential of the market without the downside risk.

Immediate Annuities

A lump-sum deposit establishes the immediate annuity, which provides payments, either at a fixed or a variable interest rate, typically on a monthly basis. With an immediate annuity, income stream payments begin right away. The first payment must be made within one year of purchase. Immediate annuity payments may be for a specified period, or for the greater of a specified period, or your lifetime.

Real Estate

Historically, real estate has been an excellent hedge against inflation, and is a good investment if you are able and willing to undertake or continue the responsibility of ownership. The federal tax code accords preferred tax status to your principal residence, allowing you to deduct mortgage interest and property taxes and also forgives the first $250,000 (single) or $500,000 (married) of gain on sale. Additionally, your principal residence is not counted for Medicaid eligibility purposes (see "Medicaid" in Chapter Twelve). The economic, tax and emotional advantages of owning your own home, condominium, or co-op are compelling. More than a mere investment, your home should be a permanent part of your investment portfolio.

Investment property such as apartments and commercial buildings can add diversification to your investment portfolio and provide protection against a down market. Investment real estate is often thought of as a "tax shelter" in that profits can be offset by the "depreciation deduction." However, despite the investment and tax benefits on investment real estate, you may simply be unable or unwilling to take on the management responsibilities associated with ownership. Investment real estate is not like a stock or other passive investment. If you own investment real estate, you must be actively involved with its day-to-day management.

You should consider selling investment real estate inherited from your spouse if you are not equipped to manage it yourself or if your new life plan doesn't include the active management that such properties requires. Your new stepped-up basis (see "Stepped Up Basis" in Chapter Two) will allow you to sell your investment real estate with little or no gain.

Tangible Investments

Tangible investments are those you can touch, such as gold, silver, coins, stamps and collectibles. Historically, these investments have been an excellent hedge against inflation. The reverse is also true: during periods of low inflation, tangible investments tend to perform poorly. Additional problems with tangible investments include lack of marketability, difficulty in determining value and inability to produce income.

A Word of Caution

Some investments are simply too risky for the vast majority of surviving spouses. You should not invest in limited partnerships, commodities and investments that are not publicly traded. You should respectfully decline any invitation to invest in any closely held (that is, not publicly traded) business. Such enterprises are not regulated and involve an inappropriate level of risk. If a family member or close friend is asking you to invest, you should defer to your attorney, accountant or financial planner, and let them decline on your behalf. Don't worry about being the bad guy. Worry more about being the poor guy.

Life Insurance and Retirement Distribution Options

As noted in Chapter Four ("Settlement Options"), you will be given the option to take your late spouse's life insurance benefit in a lump sum or a variety of monthly distribution options. You may have a similar option with respect to your late spouse's company retirement plan. Which option is right for you? The answer depends on your confidence in yourself and the confidence you have in the insurance company or your late spouse's employer. You may also have the same considerations with respect to company retirement plans.

The problem with the various non-lump-sum settlement options is that they are inflexible. Once you elect to take a monthly payment, you cannot adjust the amount or the timing of the distribution, and they are not adjusted for inflation. Non-lump-sum options also tend to end at your death, leaving no legacy for your children. Unless you have no children and/or no faith in your ability to manage money, you should elect to receive your spouse's life insurance death benefit in a lump sum. For these same reasons, and for the reasons discussed in the following chapter (Chapter Six: IRA and Retirement Distributions), you should also elect to take a lump sum distribution of your late spouse's IRAs and retirement accounts and roll them into your own Individual Retirement Account (IRA).

Naturally, the election to take lump sums makes you responsible for your own future. You must exercise immediate control of the distributions and integrate them into your financial plan and investment portfolio. Without the security of a monthly check for the rest of your life, your long-term financial well-being rests squarely on your shoulders. However, you and your heirs will benefit from these decisions if you properly manage the distributions.

If your spouse was eligible to receive a traditional pension from his or her employer, call the benefits department of the company and determine the value of the benefit. Pension distributions, like IRA and other retirement distributions, are taxable to you when received. Although taxable, IRA and retirement account savings are there to be used in your retirement. Don't be afraid to spend this money to make a better life for yourself while you can still enjoy it.

Choosing a Financial Advisor

Choosing a financial advisor is one of the most important decisions after your spouse's death. Choose someone with experience, someone with roots in your community, someone you trust and who will take the time to work with you. All financial advisors have to be compensated. Nonetheless, it is important that you understand how he or she is compensated so that you can judge whether their recommendations are motivated by their compensation.

Generally, financial advisors are compensated in one of three ways:

- On a **commission plan**, the advisor earns money from the purchase or sale of investments. A commissioned advisor should be expected to monitor, adjust and review your portfolio on a regular basis. The temptation of unscrupulous commissioned planners is to "churn" accounts (i.e., unnecessarily buying and selling investments) in order to generate commissions. Be aware of activity in your account. You should only grant your commission-based advisor the power to transact in your account without your permission if you have a long- standing relationship, and the planner has proven his or her trustworthiness.
- On a **fee plan**, you may be offered several options including a flat fee for the financial planning service, an hourly rate or a percentage of assets under management. The last option would motivate the planner to increase the value of your portfolio, which is also in your best interest.
- Under a **combination plan**, the advisor charges a fee to develop a financial plan, and also receives a commission to help manage the recommended investments.

There is no right or wrong way to compensate a financial advisor. Whom you choose should not be dictated so much by how they are compensated but on the basis of their experience, track record and the services to be provided. Retain an advisor who will take the time to develop a financial plan that takes into consideration your spending habits, risk tolerance, and your life plan. Work with someone who will monitor your plan and make specific recommendations based on changes in the market and in your short-term and long-term financial needs.

Experience counts. Ask about specific professional experience, length of time as financial advisor and with their current firm. Inquire whether the advisor has a college degree, and what licenses and designations they hold. For example, to obtain the "Certified Financial Planner" or "CFP" designation, the advisor must have passed a rigorous series of exams and must meet ongoing continuing education requirements. Although degrees and professional designations are no guarantee of an advisor's future performance, at least you will know that they have dedicated time and effort to their craft.

Most firms require that client accounts remain with the firm when an advisor leaves or changes firms. You should know in advance how the transfer of your account would be handled in the event your advisor leaves his or her firm.

Inquire about the number of support staff available to administer your account while your advisor is away from the office.

Ask about the procedures for discontinuing the association. How will your sensitive documents be returned and how quickly will you receive them? Are you entitled to a refund of fees if you are dissatisfied?

Conclusion

You financial security is key to your future. It is an area in which you literally cannot afford to procrastinate. Start by locating a competent financial advisor that you can trust. Work closely with him or her to develop a financial plan. Ask questions until you are satisfied that you fully understand your advisor's recommendations. Continue to develop your money skills. The fact that you have a financial advisor or advisors doesn't absolve you from the ultimate responsibility of controlling your own financial destiny. Knowing where you stand and having a plan will lead to a fuller happier life. Good luck.

Chapter Six

IRA and Retirement Distributions

P. Mark Accettura, Esq.

OVER THE LAST two decades, IRAs, 401ks, simplified employee pensions ("SEPs"), and other account-based retirement plans have gained widespread acceptance and popularity. For the most part, they have come to replace traditional employer-provided monthly pension benefit plans. Such account balance plans can easily be transferred from employer to employer (or to an IRA), and are therefore better suited to our mobile workforce. The move to account based plans has also shifted the responsibility for retirement savings from the employer to the employee.

The result of the last twenty years of employee-based retirement savings is that IRAs, 401k and other retirement accounts constitute a significant portion of the net worth of most Americans. If neither you nor your late spouse is eligible for a pension benefit from a previous employer, you might find that, other than social security, your retirement accounts are the sole source of your retirement income. Therefore, how you manage, invest, and take distribution from your retirement accounts will be critical to your personal financial security.

At death, your late spouse's retirement accounts pass to the named beneficiary on each account. Federal law requires that qualified pension and profit sharing plan participants (but not IRA, SEP, or 403b owners) name their surviving spouse as the primary beneficiary. A beneficiary other than the surviving spouse can be named in such plans only with the written consent of the spouse. Although IRAs, SEP plans, and 403(b) plans do not require that one's spouse be named as primary beneficiary, it is nonetheless likely that your late spouse named you as beneficiary. As beneficiary, several options are available to you. You may:

1. Take a distribution of the entire account and then roll it over into your own IRA.
2. Leave the money in your late spouse's account and access the account as needed.
3. Take a lump sum distribution of the account and elect "10-year averaging."
4. "Disclaim" the interest.

What is appropriate for you will depend on a number of factors including the size of your late spouse's retirement accounts, your late spouse's age at the time of his or her death, your age, and your need for income. The rules pertaining to retirement account distributions are extremely complex. Although the discussion that follows may be beyond the comprehension of many readers, it is too important to leave out of this book. You will need the advice of a competent tax attorney, financial advisor or CPA to assist you in the subject matter of this chapter. Please be patient, and learn what you can.

The "Stretch" Philosophy

Except in the case of Roth IRAs, distributions from retirement accounts are taxable to you as ordinary income. Generally, sound tax advice dictates that you accelerate your deductions and defer taxable income. As you develop your financial plan (Chapter Five), you should blend taxable and non-taxable sources of income to allow you to live the lifestyle to which you became accustomed when your spouse was living, while at the same time minimizing income tax. If you have significant alternate sources of income, you may not need to take immediate distributions from your retirement accounts. With a little planning, you can postpone retirement distributions until you are 70 ½ (see Required Minimum Distributions below). With artful planning, you can "stretch" retirement distributions over your life as well as your children's lives. Of the four options described above, the best potential for postponing distributions can be achieved by electing Option 1 and rolling your late spouse's retirement accounts over into your own IRA.

Rollover

A "roll over" is a distribution of your spouse's entire interest in the retirement account (IRA, etc.), that within sixty days is deposited into your own IRA. Rollovers are tax-free. Only a surviving spouse can roll over a deceased participant's interest. Once rolled, you become the owner of the rollover account and therefore are entitled to name a beneficiary of your own choosing. Of the options available, it is almost always best to roll your late spouse's IRA, 401k, or company retirement plan into your own IRA. Rolling over allows you the greatest investment and distribution flexibility. By rolling over, you are in complete control of the investment house, investment advisor, and investment mix of your new IRA. With your own IRA, you will have a greater ability to defer distributions both during your life, and to your beneficiaries after your death. The flexibility of your own IRA is in marked contrast to leaving your spouse's account in his or her former employer's retirement plan. Such plans often offer limited investment options, minimal financial planning advice and restrictive distribution options. *The only time you should not roll your spouse's account over is if you are younger than age 59 ½ and need immediate access to the funds.*

Required Minimum Distributions "RMDs"

Retirement distributions may not be deferred indefinitely. You must begin taking annual "required minimum distributions" ("RMDs") when you reach age 70 ½. You may take your **first** RMD by April 1st **following** the calendar year you attain the age of 70 ½ (the "required beginning date" or "RBD"). Future RMDs must be taken by December 31 of the year in question. Thus, if you wait to take your first distribution until the latest possible time (April 1 of the following year), you will be required to take a double distribution in the second year. To avoid a double RMD, it is advisable to take your first year RMD by December 31 of the year you reach age 70 ½ rather than waiting until April 1 of the following year.

Example: Mary attains 70 ½ during 2001 and takes her first RMD March 31, 2002. Mary must take her 2002 RMD by December 31, 2002, resulting in a double RMD distribution in 2002.

RMDs are determined by dividing your retirement plan account balance (as of the previous December 31) by the Applicable Devisor from the Uniform Table below that corresponds to your age. If you have more than one IRA, 403(b), 401(k) or qualified plan, all such plans must be aggregated for purposes of meeting the RMD requirement. Required Minimum Distributions are just that, minimums. You may always take more than the minimum. Roth IRAs are exempt from the RMD rules.

THE "UNIFORM TABLE"

TABLE FOR DETERMINING APPLICABLE DIVISOR

AGE	APPLICABLE DIVISOR	AGE	APPLICABLE	AGE	APPLICABLE DIVISOR
70	26.2	86	13.1	102	5.0
71	25.3	87	12.4	103	4.7
72	24.4	88	11.8	104	4.4
73	23.5	89	11.1	105	4.1
74	22.7	90	10.5	106	3.8
75	21.8	91	9.9	107	3.6
76	20.9	92	9.4	108	3.3
77	20.1	93	8.8	109	2.8
78	19.2	94	8.3	110	2.6
79	18.4	95	7.8	111	2.6
80	17.6	96	7.3	112	2.4
81	16.8	97	6.9	113	2.2
82	16.0	98	6.5	114	2.0
83	15.3	99	6.1	115+	1.8
84	14.5	100	5.7		

Example: On December 31, 2001, Mary has $703,285 in her IRA. She is 73 years old. Her RMD for 2002 is $703,285 ÷ 23.5 = $29,927.02

Rolling Over Versus Not Rolling Over

Distributions at death before Required Beginning Date

If your spouse died before attaining age 70 ½, and you are named as his or her beneficiary, you may elect to either roll your spouse's interest to your own IRA or leave the plan intact. If you choose the rollover option, your RMDs are based on **your** age. Thus, if your late spouse was older than you, rolling over his or her account will allow you to postpone RMDs until **your** 70 ½ year. If you decide not to roll over, you must begin taking distributions in the year your late spouse would have attained age 70 ½. RMDs must be taken under one of the following two methods:

1. Under the "5-year rule" (nothing required to be distributed in the first four years following death, but the entire account must be distributed by December 31st of the fifth year after death); or
2. Annual distributions over **your** life expectancy (which is **faster** than the Uniform Table which calculates minimum distributions on the basis of the joint lives of **two** individuals 10 years apart in age).

If you choose to roll over, you will begin taking RMDs based on the Uniform Table. At your death, your new beneficiaries (for example, your children) may take the balance of your interest over their life expectancies. By contrast, if you do not roll over, any benefits remaining in your late spouse's account at your death must be paid to the contingent beneficiaries named by your late spouse over your remaining life expectancy (which is likely to be substantially shorter than that of your beneficiaries).

Example: Jim, age 68 and Mary, age 62, are married with two children. Jim has an IRA worth $1,000,000. Jim dies. Mary can:

1. Rollover the entire account into her name. If she rolls over, she does not have to start RMDs until **she** reaches the age of 70 ½ and she can use the Uniform Table. After her death, the children can take the remaining balance over each of their life expectancies, not Mary's

2. Not rollover the account. If the account is not rolled over, Mary must take the RMD the year Jim would have turned 70 ½. She must either take the entire account within 5 years, or over her life expectancy. Her life expectancy is figured on a table with shorter lives than the Uniform Table. Any balance remaining after Mary's death must be paid out to the children over Mary's life expectancy, not the children's.

Not rolling over might be advantageous if you are substantially younger than 59 ½ and need immediate access to your late spouse's retirement accounts. *If you roll over, and take distributions from your IRA before you are 59 ½, the distributions would be subject to a 10% excise tax, in addition to the regular income tax. If you leave your spouse's account intact, withdrawals are considered to be paid on account of your spouse's death, an exception to the pre-59 ½ premature distribution 10% excise tax.* For example, if you are 52-years-old at your spouse's death and were to roll over your deceased spouse's retirement plan, you could not take a distribution from the rollover IRA without a 10% penalty until you attained 59 ½ (a 7 ½ year wait). By contrast, if you leave your spouse's account intact, withdrawals may be taken without penalty (they would, however, be subject to income tax), since the distributions are on account of the death of the participant (an exception to the 10% penalty on pre-59 ½ distributions).

If you are not the designated beneficiary, your spouse's entire account balance must be distributed to the named beneficiary in accordance with either the five-year rule described above, or over the life expectancy of the beneficiary. Under the life expectancy method, distributions must commence no later than the end of the calendar year following your spouse's death. If your spouse named multiple beneficiaries or a trust, life expectancy is determined based on the life expectancy of the oldest beneficiary or the oldest trust beneficiary. If a trust is named as beneficiary, it is extremely important that a copy of the trust (or a certification of trust that complies with IRS Regulations) be supplied to the Plan Administrator (IRA Custodian) prior to December 31 of the year following death.

Distribution on death after RMDs have begun

The rules for distributions after RMDs have begun (meaning that your spouse was at least 70 ½ at the time of his or her death) are very similar to those for pre-RMD death described above. First, you may roll your spouse's interest over into your own IRA. Once rolled, RMDs are based on **your** age, not your late spouse's. Consequently, if you are younger than 70½, RMDs will cease until **your** required beginning date (except that you must take your spouse's RMD for the year of his death). When RMDs do begin, you are eligible to use the Uniform Table. At your death, your beneficiaries will be able to take the balance of your account over their life expectancy. If you do not roll over, distributions during your life and after your death must be based on your life expectancy (rather than the longer Uniform Table during life and your children's life expectancy after your death). Thus, the case for rolling over is even more compelling where death occurs after RMDs have begun. In addition to the extended deferral available to you and your children, you may be able to discontinue RMDs altogether after your spouse's death if you are not yet 70 ½.

Post-Death Planning

Whether your spouse died before or after his required beginning date, the beneficiary of his or her retirement accounts is not officially determined until December 31 of the year following death. This delay allows for significant post mortem planning. In other words, there is time to "clean up" a messy beneficiary designation. For example, if your late spouse named multiple beneficiaries under his or her retirement account or named his or her trust as beneficiary, the age of the oldest named beneficiary (or trust beneficiary) must be used for purposes of calculating RMDs. *If one of the multiple beneficiaries is a charity, all beneficiaries must take their distribution in the year of death!*

With proper post mortem planning, however, the share of an older beneficiary or a charity can be distributed before December 31 following death (i.e., the "clean up" deadline). In so doing, only the life expectancy of the oldest **remaining** beneficiaries are counted, lowering RMDs for all remaining beneificiaries. *Also, an older beneficiary (such as you) can "disclaim" (essentially give) his or her interest to younger beneficiaries (your children) during the clean-up period, eliminating you, the older beneficiary, from the calculation.* Finally, separate accounts may be created for each beneficiary by the end of the year after death. With separate accounts, each beneficiary's RMD is calculated separately based on the age of each such beneficiary.

If a trust is named as beneficiary, a copy of the trust (or a certification of trust that complies with IRS Regulations) must be supplied to the Plan Administrator (IRA Custodian) prior to December 31 of the year following death.

Ten Year Averaging

If your spouse was age 50 by January 1, 1986 you should calculate "10-year averaging" on a lump sum distribution of your spouse's entire account. Although somewhat radical, this approach can sometimes produce surprising results. Note that 10 year averaging is available only for employer-sponsored retirement plans and not for IRA, SEP, or 403(b) distributions.

Conclusion and Course of Action

Your late spouse's retirement accounts are likely an integral part of your financial security. You should control all aspects of such accounts including investment matters and the timing of distributions. The fact that the accounts are fully taxable for income tax purposes (and estate tax for that matter) dictates that you plan to defer distributions as long into the future as legally possible. Unless you are substantially younger than 59 ½, you should roll your deceased spouse's accounts into your own IRA. You should name your revocable trust as beneficiary of all retirement accounts, or create separate accounts for your beneficiaries. Spreading RMDs over children's lifetimes not only provides maximum income tax deferral, but also provides financial safety for your children and perhaps your grandchildren.

Chapter Seven

Settling the Estate: Probate and Trust Administration

P. Mark Accettura, Esq. and Samuel A. Hurwitz, Esq.

CHAPTER TWO: "GETTING ORGANIZED" discusses how to get started, documents to locate, items to save, and whom to contact. Key among those duties is to identify all of the assets in which your late spouse had an ownership interest. The **Asset Inventory with Values Worksheet** discussed in Chapter Two (and reproduced in Appendix "A") is intended to help you catalog your late spouse's assets, identify how each is owned, and approximate their value. How your late spouse's assets were owned will determine how they pass at death. The methods of passage, and your responsibilities as surviving spouse and fiduciary, are the subject of this chapter.

There are essentially three ways that assets pass at death: 1) by operation of law, 2) through the probate process, and 3) pursuant to the terms of a trust. For purposes of this chapter, we will assume that you have been appointed as personal representative under your spouse's Will and, if applicable, trustee of his or her trust.

Assets that are held jointly, name a beneficiary, or are payable on death pass "by operation of law." As a matter of state law, the joint owner, designated beneficiary, or named payee **automatically** becomes the new owner at death. No further action is required to effectuate the transfer of this type of asset.

Assets owned in your late spouse's name alone that do not name a beneficiary must pass through probate. Probate is a court-supervised process by which orphan assets (assets in your spouse's sole name that do not name a beneficiary) pass to your spouse's rightful heirs. Probated assets pass according to the terms of your spouse's Will. If your late spouse had no Will, he or she is said to have died "intestate." In such case, the laws intestacy of the State of your late spouse's residence at the time of his or her death will determine his or her rightful heirs.

> **Intestate (Intestacy):** To die without leaving a valid Will. State laws of intestate succession determine the rightful heirs of a decedent's intestate property where the decedent died without a valid Will. The laws of most states provide that the intestate property of an individual leaving a spouse and children of the marriage would pass as follows: the first $100,000 and one-half of the balance to the surviving spouse, with the balance to be divided equally among the children.

> **Heir:** An heir is a person entitled to inherit under the laws of intestacy.

How do you know when probate is required? A banker, stock broker, or real estate agent will advise you that since a particular account, stock, or parcel of real estate is in your late spouse's name alone, they are going to need evidence of your authority to act in your late spouse's place and stead. They will not accept a copy of your late spouse's Will since, as they may tell you, only the probate court has the authority to interpret the terms of a Will. Instead, they will need "letters of authority" or other decree of the probate court appointing you as your spouse's "personal representative." The probate court will not contact you. Obtaining court authority requires that you submit to the court's jurisdiction by filing a petition with the court. For our purposes, the term "personal representative" is defined as follows:

> **Personal Representative:** A person, or committee of individuals, or sometimes a corporate fiduciary like a bank,

appointed by the probate court, to administer the probate estate of the decedent. Sometimes called an "executor" or "executrix." The person named in the decedent's Will has first priority to be appointed as personal representative. If the individual named in the Will is unable or unwilling to act as personal representative, or the decedent died without a Will, the surviving spouse has first priority.

Deserved or not, probate has gained the reputation of being time consuming and costly. In reality, each probate estate is different. Your experience will depend on the size of the estate, the quality of your legal representation, the cooperation of your family, and if different, your late spouse's family.

Assets owned in trust pass according to the terms of the trust document. No transfer of title takes place, since the trust continues to own property both before and after the death of the trust creator ("grantor"). The grantor's death makes the trust irrevocable since the grantor was the only person with the power to amend or revoke the trust. Most revocable trusts provide that the grantor shall act as initial trustee until his or her death. A successor trustee, appointed by the grantor in the trust instrument, takes over the management of trust assets after the grantor's death.

Fiduciary Responsibility

It is possible, in fact likely, that you will act as your late spouse's personal representative and successor trustee. When acting as personal representative or trustee, you are considered a "fiduciary" under state law. Being a fiduciary means that you have a legal obligation to exercise a high standard of care in the management and distribution of your late spouse's property. It is important that you fully understand and fulfill your fiduciary responsibilities. If you breach any such duty, you could be personally liable to the estate or trust, as well as heirs and beneficiaries for damages. The probate court could also remove you as fiduciary in favor of another family member, or officer of the court. While the risk of personal liability and removal are extremely low for traditional families, it could be quite high if your family has a history of hostility and conflict. You should be especially diligent in your duties if your late spouse had children not of the marriage, as these relationships can become strained after your spouse's death.

Although they vary from state to state, some version of the following fiduciary responsibilities apply in all fifty states. You must:

1. Exercise reasonable care in carrying out your duties,
2. Exercise loyalty (i.e., you must act in the best interest of the estate or trust and not for your own benefit),
3. Not commingle estate and trust property with your own property,
4. Act as a prudent investor concerning estate and trust assets,
5. Keep beneficiaries reasonably informed,
6. Provide beneficiaries with accurate and timely accounts of estate and trust assets and income.
7. Report and pay income and estate tax, and
8. Distribute estate and trust assets in strict compliance with state law or the terms of the trust document.

Categorizing Assets

The starting point in estate and trust administration is to determine into which of the three following categories each and every asset falls.

Assets Passing by Operation of Law

Joint Ownership and Survivorship Rights

Assets owned jointly in a form known as "joint tenancy with rights of survivorship," pass by operation of law to the surviving joint owner(s). An example is a brokerage account titled in the name of "Mary Barnes and John Barnes as JTWROS." If John dies, the account automatically belongs to Mary. Even though ownership transfers **automatically**, Mary would be well advised to remove John's name and social security number from the account at his death. This can be accomplished by presenting the brokerage house with a copy of John's death certificate. Real estate owned jointly with your spouse is a form of joint ownership called "tenancy by the entirety" in many states. At your spouse's death, ownership of the real estate, like your principal residence or vacation home, passes automatically to you without need of any court procedure.

"Tenancy in common" is a form of joint ownership that does not automatically pass the decedent's share at death. Instead, the share of the deceased owner must be "probated" (unless it is owned in trust) in order to transfer title to his or her heirs. For instance, if Mr. A, Mr. B and Mr. C own a piece of real estate together as "tenants in common," and Mr. A dies, his one-third ownership interest does not pass to Mr. B and Mr. C. Instead, the beneficiaries named in Mr. A's Will become the new owners. If Mr. A did not have a Will, his share will pass according to the laws of intestacy.

Even though jointly owned assets pass at death with relative ease, it would be incorrect to assume that such ownership constitutes sound estate planning. In reality, the automatic transfer at death and the lifetime rights accorded to joint owners make joint ownership a poor estate planning tool. See "Joint Ownership As a Trust Substitute" in Chapter Nine.

Assets Passing by Beneficiary Designation

Some assets allow the owner to name a beneficiary. Such assets pass at death to the individuals (or trust) named in the "beneficiary designation." This type of designation is usually found on insurance policies, retirement plans, IRAs, 401(k)s and annuities. Assets naming a beneficiary pass automatically without resort to a probate court proceeding.

Pay-on-death ("POD") and transfer on death ("TOD") accounts are another form of beneficiary designation. A number of states permit POD and TOD designations on individual securities, bank, and brokerage accounts. POD and TOD designations direct the financial institution to transfer the security or account to the named designee upon the death of the account owner.

Assets Passing Through Probate

Assets owned by your late spouse that were not held with a joint tenant, did not name a beneficiary, and were not owned in trust, will comprise your late spouse's probate estate. There are two major types of probate: formal and informal. With formal probate, the court supervises each step of the probate process. The judge must approve each step of the process including the sale and distribution of all estate assets. With informal probate, the court does not supervise the fiduciary. Instead, the court intervenes only if an interested party (i.e. beneficiary) complains about the fiduciary's actions.

Whether you choose formal or informal probate will depend on a number of factors including the number of creditors making claim to the estate and your relationship with the other heirs. Formal probate is more appropriate where you anticipate conflict. With the court approving each step of the process, there is little room for disgruntled creditors or heirs to claim you acted inappropriately. Formal probate can be significantly more expensive than informal probate, since numerous hearings must be held before the judge. Your attorney must attend each hearing. All heirs must receive notice of the time and date of each hearing, giving them an opportunity to object to your actions. Since most attorneys charge an hourly rate for their services, the more time your attorney spends in court, the more expensive the process.

Routine estates without expected challenges can be handled informally. Informal probate tends to be cheaper and faster, and all things being equal is preferred. If you choose informal probate and a conflict arises, you can elect to resolve a particular issue with a formal hearing. In fact, the preferred approach is to administer the estate informally, with final distributions approved by a formal hearing. Final court approval validates all of the fiduciary's actions, and prevents later challenges by disgruntled heirs.

Assets Owned in Trust

Assets owned in trust do not require a probate proceeding. Instead, upon the grantor's death, the successor trustee takes over the management of trust assets. As a fiduciary, the successor trustee has a legal obligation to prudently manage trust property and to strictly implement the terms of the trust. Depending on its terms, the trust may operate for only the time it takes to value, liquidate and distribute assets, or it may last for many years, with the successor trustee managing assets for minor or disabled beneficiaries.

Applicable Law

The laws of the **state** of which your late spouse died a resident govern the administration of his or her probate and trust estate. The probate court of the **county** of his or her residence has jurisdiction to handle estate and trust matters. For purposes of this chapter, we have assumed that your state has adopted the Uniform Probate Code ("UPC"). To date, approximately 18 states have adopted some variation of the UPC. Even if your state has not adopted the UPC, the concepts that follow nonetheless apply to you with minor modification.

Ongoing Administration

The balance of this chapter discusses the role of the fiduciary in administering each step of the probate estate or trust administration process. Generally, administration consists of five (5) separate steps. Each of the following steps compares your responsibility in formal probate, informal probate, and finally, trust administration:

1. Appointment of Fiduciary;
2. Admission of the Will;
3. Asset Inventory and Administration;
4. Dealing with Creditors;
5. Making Final Distributions.

To promote smooth administration, you should go above and beyond the strict legal requirements outlined below. The death of a loved one is extremely stressful on the entire family, often breathing new life into old conflicts and jealousies. This is especially true if there are beneficiaries who are not your biological children. They will undoubtedly wonder "What's she doing with dad's money?" One way to lessen these feelings is to be as open and honest as possible. Upon request, beneficiaries are entitled to a copy of your late spouse's Will and trust. Rather than make them ask, consider providing them with a copy of relevant documents as soon as possible. Another peacekeeping strategy is to speak through your attorney. Beneficiaries may feel more comfortable asking questions like "What do I get, and when?" to a third party. It may also be easier for them to hear bad news such as "You don't get anything until your step-mother's death" from someone other than you.

The term "estate" is often used loosely. It may refer to a probate estate, a trust estate, or a **taxable** estate. In general usage, the term "estate" means all that a person owns, whether tangible, intangible, personal, or real property. A "probate estate" consists of those assets that need to go through probate to transfer legal title from the decedent to the new owner. A "trust estate" refers to assets owned in trust. The phrase "taxable estate" means the assets that the IRS includes when computing the estate tax. When the term "estate" is used in this chapter without further explanation, you should infer its meaning from the context in which it is used.

Step One: Appointment of Fiduciary

Appointment of Personal Representative in Formal Probate

The first step in a formal probate proceeding is to file a petition, along with your spouse's Will (if any), requesting the appointment of one or more persons to serve as personal representative. The petitioning party, which can be any beneficiary or heir, asks the court to appoint the personal representative named in the petition. A copy of the petition and a notice of hearing must be sent to all "interested parties," which includes all heirs and beneficiaries named in the Will. In making its determination, the court gives priority to the person named in the Will. If the person named in the Will (if other than the surviving spouse) declines or is unable to serve, the next priority goes to the surviving spouse. Next in line will be children. This priority scheme will also apply if there is no Will.

A hearing will be held to determine whether the person nominated to be personal representative has priority and whether there are any objections to the appointment. Someone with higher priority can appear at the hearing and object to the appointment. Any interested party may object to the appointment, even if the nominated individual has priority, on a showing that the nominated person is not suitable to act as personal representative due to lack of expertise, conflict of interest, or some other valid reason.

Once the court has made its determination, it will issue "**letters of authority**" which you as personal representative must present as evidence of your authority. It is advisable to order five to ten original copies of the letters of authority since each financial institution will likely request an original copy.

The personal representative represents the estate in all matters including the preparation and filing of all income, gift, and estate tax returns. The personal representative is also charged with gathering and securing the estate's property, preparing all necessary court filings, paying proper estate expenses and distributing the estate's property to the named beneficiaries or heirs. As a personal representative and fiduciary you must use your best efforts; act in the best interest of the estate, and not for your own benefit; protect and preserve the estate's assets; productively invest the assets of the estate; account for all income and expenses; keep the interested parties informed of the progress of the estate's business; and ultimately distribute the estate to the beneficiaries named in the Will or to the heirs.

The court may require the estate to purchase a bond to protect the estate and its beneficiaries against any wrongdoing of the personal representative. If a bond is required, the annual premium is paid by the estate. A bond is usually not required where the surviving spouse is appointed as personal representative, especially where the estate will pass entirely to the surviving spouse.

Appointment of Personal Representative in Informal Probate

The procedure for appointing the personal representative in informal probate is the same as it is in formal probate except that there is no court hearing. Instead, the court clerk will simply issue letters of authority appointing the person named on the petition as long as he or she has priority under state law, or the written consent of everyone who has an equal or higher priority. The duties and standard of care of the personal representative are the same in both formal and informal probate.

Appointment of Trustee

In a typical revocable trust, the grantor acts as initial trustee. The trust document appoints a successor trustee to act upon the death of the grantor/initial trustee. For the successor trustee's appointment to become effective, he or she must sign an "Acceptance of Trust." In the Acceptance of Trust, the successor trustee accepts the appointment and agrees to faithfully execute the duties of trustee. No court filing is needed.

A trustee is a fiduciary, and must act in the best interests of all beneficiaries. State law typically requires the successor trustee to notify trust beneficiaries (usually within 28 days after signing the Acceptance of Trust) of the grantor's death and their right to review the trust provisions affecting their interest in the trust. No bond is required unless provided for in the trust document.

Step Two: Admission of Will

Admission of the Will in Formal Probate

The second step, which often occurs contemporaneously with the first, is a declaration by the probate court that the Will offered by the petitioner is the decedent's genuine last Will. Once a court rules that the Will is the decedent's last Will, it is "admitted to probate."

Prior to admitting the Will to probate, the court will entertain objections by any interested party who wishes to contest the Will. The Will may be disallowed if it can be shown that the testator (the person making the Will) lacked mental capacity, or that undue influence was exercised over the testator in making his Will. The law generally provides that anyone of sound mind can leave his or her property to whomever he or she desires (except if the effect is to disinherit a spouse as discussed below). However, if the court finds that the Will was fraudulently prepared or altered, that the testator was not competent, or was unduly influenced, it will invalidate the Will. If the Will is invalidated, the court will look to any previous Will prepared by the testator and consider it for admission. If there is no prior valid Will, the decedent's property will pass under the law of intestacy.

Shortly after your appointment as Personal Representative, you must send notice of your appointment, as well as notice of the admission of the Will, to all interested parties. The law also requires that you publish a notice to creditors (discussed in Step Four) at this time.

Admission of the Will in Informal Probate

The court clerk will examine the application, the associated papers and the Will. If the application lists everyone named in the Will as an interested party, the Will appears to be properly signed and witnessed, and all the associated papers are in order, the clerk will admit the Will to probate without a court hearing.

Admission of the Will in Trust Administration

Trusts need not be filed with the probate court since, absent an independent lawsuit to overturn the validity of a trust, there is no requirement that the court rule on the genuineness of a trust. If your spouse had a trust that was not fully "funded" (see "Trust Funding" in Chapter Nine), assets in his or her sole name must be probated. In that case, his Will would be admitted to probate and Steps One through Five pertaining to formal or informal probate would have to be followed. Your spouse's Will would likely be a "Pour Over" Will, naming his or her trust as the beneficiary of his or her probate assets. As such, probate assets will transfer, or "pour over" into his or her trust to be administered according to Steps One through Five as such steps pertain to trusts.

Step Three: Asset Inventory and Administration

Asset Inventory and Administration in Formal Probate

Within a few months of appointment, the personal representative must prepare a list of the estate's property called an "inventory." The inventory lists each item of property in the probate estate and its corresponding value. Personal items and household effects are often listed as a single entry with a single aggregate value. An "inventory fee," based on the aggregate value of the property listed on the inventory, is charged by the probate court. All beneficiaries and heirs are entitled to see the inventory, which must be filed with the probate court.

Each year the estate remains open, the personal representative must prepare, sign, and file federal and state income tax returns (see "Tax Reporting" in Chapter Eight). Annual accountings of estate income and expense must also be filed with the court, and made available to beneficiaries and heirs. Most formal estates run their course in nine to eighteen months, requiring only one or two income tax filings. If an estate can be completed in less than twelve months, it should elect a twelve-month non-calendar fiscal year. In doing so, the estate will only be required to make a single income tax filing (see Chapter Eight).

Asset Inventory and Administration in Informal Probate

Informal estates are subject to the same inventory and income tax return requirements that apply to formal estates, except that the inventory need not be filed with the court.

Asset Inventory and Trust Administration

There is no specific inventory requirement for trusts. However, depending on the terms of your spouse's trust and the law of your state, you may be required to furnish beneficiaries with trust asset information, as well as annual accountings. To avoid having to account to your children, your spouse's trust may exempt you from such disclosures. On the other hand, if it was a second marriage, your late spouse's trust may require asset and accounting disclosure to keep current beneficiaries (you) and contingent beneficiaries (his children) apprised of trust activity.

While probate estates continue only so long as necessary to appoint a fiduciary, pay creditors, and distribute assets to beneficiaries and heirs, trusts may last for years. Trusts avoid probate, minimize estate tax, and allow the grantor to provide structure and security for his or her surviving spouse and children. You could say that probate administration is accidental while trusts administration is by design. That is why the cost and delay of probate should be avoided. Trust administration, on the other hand, is a necessary byproduct of the grantor's wish to keep a guiding hand on his or her loved ones after death. Trusts that provide for immediate distribution require little or no ongoing administration. Trusts that operate for the surviving spouse's lifetime, or until the grantor's children reach a particular age, must be administered according to their terms for their duration.

As the surviving spouse, trust assets will likely be held for the balance of your life to allow you to maintain the lifestyle you enjoyed while your spouse was alive. Even if your late spouse's trust makes liberal provision for you, you nonetheless have a duty to contingent beneficiaries even if they are your natural children. You must prudently invest trust assets, file Federal and state income tax returns, and preserve trust assets for contingent beneficiaries. Your duties as trustee end at your death, or when the trust's last dollar is distributed, if earlier.

Family/Marital Trust Division

If your spouse's trust holds assets in excess of the Applicable Exclusion Amount ($1,000,000 in 2002) it will divide into two separate trusts: a "family trust" (sometimes called a "bypass" or "credit shelter" trust) and a "marital trust." Trust assets equal to the Applicable Exclusion Amount are first allocated to the family trust. Assets in excess of $1,000,000 (if any) are allocated to the marital trust. The division of trust assets between the family and marital trust allows for the full utilization of your spouse's unified credit, and avoids estate tax at his or her death (unless you are not a U.S. citizen). The family trust is not subject to estate tax since it is within the Applicable Exclusion Amount. No estate tax is imposed on the marital trust since transfers to the marital trust qualify for the unlimited marital deduction.

Some marital trusts permit you to designate the beneficiary of the balance of the trust at the time of **your** death (a "**general power of appointment**" or "POA"), and some do not (a "qualified terminal interest property" or "**QTIP**" Trust). In either case, the balance of the assets remaining in the marital trust at your death will be included in your taxable estate. With a QTIP marital trust, amounts remaining in the marital trust at the time of your death are paid to the family trust to be held or distributed for the benefit of the contingent beneficiaries **named by your late spouse**. QTIP trusts are especially useful in second marriages. Trust assets are used for the support of the second spouse for the balance of her life with the balance distributed to the grantor's natural children at the second spouse's death. If the marital trust is the POA variety, amounts remaining in the marital trust at the time of your death are paid to the family trust only if you fail to designate different contingent beneficiaries at the time of your death.

By definition, you may not designate contingent beneficiaries of your spouse's family trust, since such a power would cause the family trust to be included in your taxable estate, defeating the purpose of creating the family trust; that is, to bypass your estate and fully utilize the Applicable Exclusion Amount of your late spouse.

Income and principal from both the family and marital trusts are available to you to allow you to enjoy the lifestyle to which you became accustomed while your spouse was alive. How and when you take income and principal is important to minimize income and estate tax. Obtaining the best income and estate tax result is no simple task. Often, the best estate tax result comes at a high income tax cost, and vise versa. However, minimizing both taxes can be done with a little planning.

Best Income Tax Result. The family and marital trusts are separate taxable entities, subject to the highest marginal income tax rate. Fortunately, trusts are entitled to a deduction (to the extent of trust income) for distributions made to beneficiaries. The effect of the "distribution deduction" is to shift income tax liability from the trust to its beneficiaries. Since trust beneficiaries are likely to be in a much lower tax bracket than the trust, shifting the tax burden to beneficiaries is good for all of the parties involved. Unfortunately, making distributions from the family trust may not make good estate tax sense.

Best Estate Tax Result. Assets of the family trust have already passed under your spouse's Applicable Exclusion Amount, and are not includible in your taxable estate at your death. Thus, assets of the family trust will never be (estate) taxed again, no matter how much they appreciate after your spouse's death. So, "let it grow, let it grow, let it grow." To achieve the greatest growth, the family trust should be invested for long-term growth, and you should take distributions from the family trust only to the extent needed to maintain your lifestyle. If you need income, you should take it from the marital trust. You should spend down the marital trust since it is included in your taxable estate. In short: spend marital, don't spend family. This advice is tempered by the fact that income left in the family trust will be taxed at the highest marginal income tax rate.

The Problem. The problem, simply stated, is that for income tax purposes, family trust income should be distributed annually. For estate tax purposes, little or no distributions should ever be made from the family trust.

Solution. To avoid unfavorable income tax results, the family trust should be invested in growth, low-income, or non-income producing investments. By investing for growth and not for income there is no income tax reason for making distributions from the family trust. With the income tax problem solved, family trust assets can be allowed to grow estate tax free. The following diagram illustrates the division of a single trust into a family and marital trust as described above:

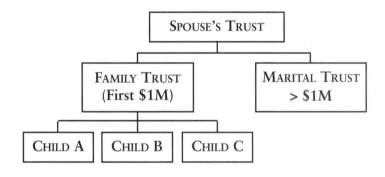

Step Four: Dealing with creditors

Dealing with creditors in formal probate

Although there may be room for compromise, your late spouse's debts are not automatically extinguished at death. How and when creditors are paid depends on a number of factors including whether they are "secured" or "unsecured," known or unknown, and whether your spouse was the sole obligor of a debt. The probate code contains notice procedures that must be strictly followed to guarantee that creditor's claims are completely extinguished. As with most things in life, when paying creditors timing is everything. You shouldn't pay creditors or beneficiaries too quickly. You need to be sure that each creditor has an enforceable claim and that the estate has sufficient assets to pay all creditors in full. Beneficiaries should be paid only when all creditor claims are **finally** determined. The risks are high. You, as the personal representative, can be personally liable to either creditors or beneficiaries if you fail to properly assess their relative entitlements. By following the instructions in this Step Four and Step Five, you can protect yourself from liability.

First, you remain personally responsible to repay home loans and other debts for which you co-signed. Additionally, "**secured**" creditors, such as mortgage companies and other lenders, have a mortgage, "lien," or other security interest securing their loan. If a secured creditor is not paid, they can pursue the secured assets directly. For example, a mortgage company will bring a foreclosure action on real estate for which they hold a mortgage. A car loan or leasing company will simply come and take the car. Your spouse's "**unsecured**" creditors can make a claim against your spouse's probate estate or his or her trust during the publication period described below.

You may wonder: "How do creditors know when someone dies?" The short answer is: "You tell them." As personal representative, you must make a reasonable attempt to locate creditors. Most creditors can be located from a simple review of your spouse's incoming mail or his checkbook. You might also consider contacting a credit agency to run a credit report. Known creditors must be sent a **Notice to Known Creditors**. In most states, known creditors have four months from their receipt of the **Notice to Known Creditors** (or four months from the date of the published Notice to Creditors (described below), whichever is longer), to file their claim against the estate, or be forever barred.

You must also publish a **Notice to Creditors** in a legal newspaper in the county of your spouse's residence to inform unknown creditors of his or her death. In most states, unknown creditors have four months from the date of the published notice (the "publication period") to file a claim against the estate, or be forever barred. Merely publishing the claims notice in the newspaper will not bar the claim of a known creditor or a creditor you should have known about. Such creditors may have up to six years to pursue their claims. Therefore, if in doubt, send a notice. Sending notice reduces the claim period for both known and unknown creditors from the normal six year "statute of limitations" (the period a creditor has to bring a lawsuit to collect its debt) to four months. Although the notice requirements may seem like an added burden, in reality they provide closure and certainty. You can rest assured knowing that no creditor will come out of the woodwork after the publication period has passed and you have disbursed the estate.

As personal representative, you may allow or disallow claims. Allowed claims are simply paid. Disallowed claimants must receive written notice of the disallowance. Failure to disallow a claim is a deemed acceptance (state laws vary as to how much time must pass before a deemed allowance occurs). A disallowed creditor must file a lawsuit to further pursue its claim.

Compromising Claims

If the estate contains only illiquid, or not readily available, assets such as real estate, you should contact creditors and ask them to wait until funds become available. Many creditors will be willing to either wait for full payment, or negotiate a quick settlement of the debt. Credit card companies, for example, are often willing to accept a lesser sum, say 80%-85% of the debt in exchange for immediate payment.

If the estate's assets are insufficient to pay all creditors, state law determines which creditors get paid first. *Except as provided below, neither you (acting in your fiduciary capacity) nor any beneficiary is personally obligated for your late spouse's personal debts.* If the estate does not contain sufficient assets to pay all creditors in full, the probate code dictates the following priority of claims:

1. Funeral and burial expenses, and administrative expenses such as the personal representative's fees, attorney fees, and accountant fees. Since funeral and burial expenses are given such high priority, it is usually safe to pay them as soon as possible.

2. Statutory allowances such as the homestead exemption and the family allowance (see Step Five, below) that provide immediate living expenses to the surviving spouse and children of the decedent.
3. State and federal taxes. You will be **personally liable** if you distribute the estate's assets before tax obligations have been paid in full.
4. Medical/hospital bills related to you spouse's last illness.
5. All other claims on a pro rata basis.

Property passing by operation of law is not subject to the claims of your late spouse's individual creditors. For example, life insurance proceeds are not part of your spouse's probate estate and therefore are not subject to creditors' claims (unless the proceeds pass to his or her estate or his or her revocable trust). Similarly, joint property with full rights of survivorship passes directly to the joint owner, outside of the decedent's estate and is generally not subject to creditors' claims (except secured creditors with a lien or other security interest in the joint property). However, property in your spouse's revocable trust is subject to such claims.

Liability of the Personal Representative

Generally, as personal representative you are not liable for your late spouse's individual debts, or for debts incurred in the administration of the estate (such as funeral, attorney, accounting, and appraisal fees). However, you may become personally liable if you breach one of the fiduciary responsibilities described earlier in the chapter, or if you distribute estate assets to yourself or other heirs at the expense of valid creditor claims. Beneficiaries can be quite anxious to receive their inheritance, exerting subtle and not so subtle pressure on you to "hurry things up." If bold, they may even outright ask, "When do I get my money?" *You must resist the temptation to appease such heirs, so as to avoid personal liability.* Rather than have to ask heirs to return improperly paid distributions, it is cheaper and easier to postpone distributions until all estate liabilities are identified and quantified. You may decide to make **interim distributions** to heirs at any time, but you should postpone final distributions until the publication period ends, and all tax returns are filed and accepted by the taxing authorities.

Creditors and Informal Probate

With the exception of the closing procedure for informal estates (see Step Five, below), creditors are treated the same in formal and informal probate.

Dealing with Creditors in Trust Administration

In most states, revocable trusts may elect, but are not required, to utilize the creditor notification procedure. If a trustee chooses not to utilize the notification process, creditors have up to six years to present their claims, rather than only four months. The procedural requirements for notifying potential creditors are virtually the same for trusts as for probate estates. The same rationale for time limiting claims also applies.

Step Five: Making Final Distributions

Distribution of Property in Formal Probate

The fifth and final step is to distribute what's left of the estate after payment of your spouse's debts, taxes, and estate administration expenses. If the probate estate is small, the probate code gives priority to the surviving spouse and children of the decedent. The allowances, which are modest, take priority over the claims of all the other beneficiaries and most creditors.

Disinherited Spouse

In addition to a family allowance, the surviving spouse, if disinherited, may elect "against the Will," and take a portion of what he or she would have received under the laws of intestacy. Each state defines the surviving spouse's entitlement differently. Some states base the surviving spouse's elective share on the "augmented" estate. That is, the probate estate plus assets owned in trust as well as life insurance proceeds. Other states do not augment the estate, measuring the spouse's elective share as only a percentage of the probate estate. Interestingly, in states that do not augment the estate, a spouse could put all his or her property into a trust for his or her children, or others and purchase life insurance to benefit his or her children, or others, and legally disinherit his or her surviving spouse.

Division of Assets

When allocating assets among beneficiaries, the value and character of each asset must be considered. To assure equitable division, assets that will subject the beneficiary to income tax such as IRAs, 401ks, and bonds (and other "income in respect of a decedent," or "IRD"), must be allocated so as to proportionately distribute the income tax burden. Illiquid assets like real estate should be sold prior to distribution. Personal property, such as furniture, jewelry, and tools can be divided among beneficiaries in a lottery system, with numbers drawn from a hat to determine the order of choice.

There are two general categories of gifts in a Will: specific bequests and residuary bequests. A **specific bequest** is the gift of an identifiable item to a particular person, such as: "I give my 1982 Buick to my nephew, David Smith"; or, "I give my tangible personal property such as furniture, clothes, books and jewelry to my children, equally." **Residuary bequests** consist of everything not given in a specific bequest: "I give the rest, remainder and residue of my estate to my children, equally."

The significance of whether a gift is a specific or residuary bequest arises where there are insufficient assets to satisfy all gifts. In such a situation, the specific bequests are dispersed before the residuary ones. If a Will gives a diamond necklace to Mabel, $10,000 to David and the whatever is left (the "residuary") to Fred, and the estate has only the necklace and $10,000, Fred will get nothing. If the estate has only the $10,000 and no necklace, Mabel and Fred get nothing and David gets the $10,000.

Minors as Beneficiaries

Assets of the estate cannot be distributed to a minor. A fiduciary, known as a "conservator," must be appointed to receive, hold, and manage distributions on behalf of minor beneficiaries. Once appointed, the conservator must account to the court annually until the minor reaches the age of majority (age 18 in most states). At such time, the remaining funds are given to the child outright. A major advantage of revocable trusts is that they may hold the share of a minor beneficiary in trust, with no requirement that the trustee annually account to the court. Often, trusts manage the share of young beneficiaries such as children and grandchildren until they are out of college. Even then, distributions may be made in increments (say equal shares at age, 25, 30, and 35), to allow young beneficiaries time to mature. There is no such flexibility allowed in probate. At age 18, newly emancipated minors are free to spend their inheritances as they please. A scary thought.

Procedure for Distribution

Prior to final distribution, a final accounting and an itemized list of proposed distributions must be prepared and sent to all interested parties and unpaid creditors. A hearing is held to approve the final accounting and proposed distributions. A party wishing to object to the fiduciary's performance, or to the final distributions can do so at the hearing. Failure to object forever bars future complaints. Once approved by the court, final distributions can be made. It is advisable to obtain a receipt from each recipient showing that the distribution has been made and that the recipient waives further claim.

Distribution of Property in Informal Probate

Informal distributions are handled much the same as in formal probate, except that no hearing is required. A final account is sent to interested parties and creditors, and receipts received at the time of distribution. Without a final hearing to cut off claims, creditors and disgruntled beneficiaries can bring an action at any time in the future. *For that reason, it is advisable to formally close an informal probate estate.*

Distribution of Property in Trust Administration

No formal procedure is necessary to make final distribution of trust assets. Nonetheless, it is advisable that as trustee you prepare a final accounting and obtain receipts from all beneficiaries.

Small Probate Estate Procedures

Most states provide for an abbreviated probate procedure for small estates. Depending on your state, the simplified procedure is available for estates of up to $25,000 (not counting funeral expenses and some spousal and family allowances). The dollar limit is based only on probatable assets, and therefore does not include assets held in trust or assets that pass by operation of law. The abbreviated procedure typically involves the filing of a single document, and does not require public notice to creditors. Small estate procedures usually require a single visit to the county probate court.

Compensation of Fiduciaries

You are entitled to compensation for services rendered as a personal representative or trustee. Compensation is based on a number of factors, the most important of which tends to be the actual time spent in furtherance of your duties. Accordingly, it is important that you keep track of the time you spend on estate business, as well as your out-of-pocket expenditures.

Conclusion

The law of estate and trust administration is extremely complex and the liability is too great to learn on the job. You cannot rely on the probate court staff to walk you through the probate process. Probate courts do not render legal advice and are not staffed to educate the general public on probate procedure. Fulfilling your fiduciary responsibilities requires that you hire professionals. The Uniform Probate Code states: "The fundamental duties of a trustee include the use of the skill and prudence which an ordinary capable and careful person will use in the conduct of his own affairs." You are not held to the standard of what you happen to know, but what you should know to completely and competently discharge your duties. Ignorance is no excuse when it comes to fiduciary responsibility. If you don't have accounting, investment, or legal experience you will need professional help. To fully discharge your duties and avoid liability, you need to engage the services of an accountant

(Chapter Eight), an investment advisor (Chapter Five) and an attorney. How to locate and choose professionals in these areas is discussed in the respective chapters and in the Directory of Resources.

Finding a Lawyer

It is important to retain a lawyer who specializes in estate administration and estate planning to assist you in administering your late spouse's estate or trust.   Since trust and estate administration involves complicated tax issues, you should choose a lawyer with experience and advanced training in taxation. A lawyer with a post-law degree in taxation ("LL.M") is preferred. The trust department of your bank or brokerage house often has names of attorneys they have worked with and can give you a referral. You can also use the Directory of Resources section of this book to obtain names of attorneys in your area, along with their qualifications. You may also have friends, acquaintances or co-workers who have used a lawyer, in circumstances similar to your own, who can either recommend or steer you away from a particular attorney.

Finally, what you learned by administering your late spouse's estate should be helpful as you plan your own estate. Chapter Nine will help you avoid the pitfalls discussed in this chapter.

Comparison of Formal Probate, Informal Probate, and Trust Administration

	Formal Probate	Informal Probate	Trust Administration
Appointment of Fiduciary **Step 1**	1. File petition with court; 2. Schedule court hearing and notify legally defined interested parties ("I.Ps.") 3. Attend court hearing;	1. File application with court 2. Clerk reviews papers and issues order; 3. Send court approved papers to I.Ps.;	1. Sign acceptance of trust 2. No court filing;
Admission of Will **Step 2**	Requires court hearing as described above	Requires court filing, as described above	Not Applicable
Inventory **Step 3**	Prepare and send to Interested Parties;	Prepare and send to Interested Parties	Depends on Terms Trust
Notice to Creditors **Step 4**	Publish in newspaper; Send to known creditors	Publish in newspaper; Send to known creditors	Publish in newspaper; Send to known creditors
Accountings	1. Prepare and send to Interested Parties; 2. Court hearings to approve or not	1. Prepare and send to Interested Parties; 2. No Court hearing	Depends on terms Trust
Tax Returns, Income and Estate	Required	Required	Required
Estate Tax Savings Opportunties	No	No	Yes
Final Distribution **Step 5**	1. Have court hearing; 2. Distribute per court order	1. Distribute per Will or law of Intestacy; 2. No court hearing or order	1. Distribute per terms of Trust; 2. No court hearing

If line 39 (taxable income) is—		And you are—				If line 39 (taxable income) is—		And you are—			
At least	But less than	Single	Married filing jointly	Married filing separately	Head of a household	At least	But less than	Single	Married filing jointly	Married filing separately	Head of a household
		Your tax is—						Your tax is—			
95,000						**96,000**					
95,000	95,050	24,320	21,102	26,023	22,413	96,000	96,050	25,250	21,942	27,103	23,34
95,050	95,100	24,336	21,116	26,041	22,429	96,050	96,100	25,266	21,956	27,121	23,35
95,100	95,150	24,351	21,130	26,059	22,444	96,100	96,150	25,281	21,970	27,139	23,37
95,150	95,200	24,367	21,144	26,077	22,460	96,150	96,200	25,297	21,984	27,157	23,39
95,200	95,250	24,382	21,158	26,095	22,475	96,200	96,250	25,312	21,998	27,175	23,42
95,250	95,300	24,398	21,172	26,131	22,491	96,250	96,300	25,328	22,012	27,183	23,42
95,300	95,350	24,413	21,186	26,131	22,506	96,300	96,350	25,343	22,026	27,211	23,43
95,350	95,400	24,429	21,200	26,149	22,522	96,350	96,400	25,359	22,040	27,229	23,46
95,400	95,450	24,444	21,214	26,167	22,537	96,400	96,450	25,374	22,054	27,247	23,46
95,450	95,500	24,460	21,228	26,185	22,553	96,450	96,500	25,390	22,068	27,265	23,49
95,500	95,550	24,475	21,242	26,203	22,568	96,500	96,550	25,405	22,082	27,283	23,49
95,550	95,600	24,491	21,256	26,221	22,584	96,550	96,600	25,421	27,301		23,51
95,600	95,650	24,506	21,270	26,239	22,599	96,600	96,650				
95,650	95,700	24,522	21,284	26,257	22,615						
95,700	95,750	24,537	21,298								

Schedule A—Itemized Deductions

(Schedule B is on back)

SCHEDULES A&B
(Form 1040)

Department of the Treasury
Internal Revenue Service (F)

► Attach to Form 1040. ► See Instructions for Schedules A and B (Form 1040)

Name(s) shown on Form 1040

Medical and Dental Expenses

Caution: Do not include expenses reimbursed or paid by others.

1 Medical and dental expenses (see page A-1)
2 Enter amount from Form 1040, line 34
3 Multiply line 2 above by 7.5% (.075)
4 Subtract line 3 from line 1. If line 3 is more than line 1, enter -0-

Taxes You Paid
(See page A-2.)

5 State and local income taxes
6 Real estate taxes (see page A-2)
7 Personal property taxes
8 Other taxes. List type and amount ►

9 Add lines 5 through 8

Interest You Paid
(See page A-3.)

10 Home mortgage interest and points reported to you on Form
11 Home mortgage interest not reported to you on Form
to the person from whom you bought the ho
and show that person's name, identifyin

Note: Personal interest is not deductible.

12 Points not reporte
for special rules
13 Investment interest
page A-3.)
14 Add lines 10 through 1

Gifts to Charity

If you made a gift and got a benefit for it, see page A-4.

15 Gifts by cash or check. If
more, see page A-4
16 Other than by cash or check
see page A-4. You MUST attac
17 Carryover from prior year
18 Add lines 15 through 17

Casualty and Theft Losses

19 Casualty or theft loss(es). Attach For

Job Expenses and Most Other Miscellaneous Deductions
(See page A-6 for expenses to deduct here.)

20 Unreimbursed employee expenses—
dues, job education, etc. You MUST atta
or 2106-EZ if required. (See page A-5.)

21 Tax preparation fees
22 Other expenses—investment, safe deposit box, e
type and amount ►

23 Add lines 20 through 22
24 Enter amount from Form 1040, line 34
Multiply line 24 above by 2% (.02)
Subtract line 25 from line 23. If line 25 is more than line

1040 U.S. Individual Income Tax Return

Department of the Treasury—Internal Revenue Service
For the year Jan. 1–Dec. 31, 1998, or other

Your first name and initial

If a joint return, spouse's first name and initial

Home address (number and street). If you

City, town or post office, state, and ZIP

Label
(See page 18)
Use the IRS label. Otherwise, please print or type.

Presidential Election Campaign
(See page 18.)

Do you want $3 to go to this
If a joint return, does your spo

Filing Status
Check only one box.

1 ☐ Single
2 ☐ Married filing joint
3 ☐ Married filing separ
4 ☐ Head of househol
enter this child
5 ☐ Qualifying wi

Exemptions

6a ☐ Yourself. If your
b ☐ Spouse
c Dependents
(1) First name

Form 4868
Department of the Treasury
Internal Revenue Service

Application
To File U

General Instructions

Purpose of Form

Use Form 4868 to apply for 4 mo
1040EZ, Form 1040A, or Form
to get the extra time you
information available to
• Properly estimate your
• Enter your tax liabilit
• File Form 4868 b
You are not req
estimate as du
Payment Pe
with your ap
payment of
You d
ente

Chapter Eight

Tax Reporting

P. Mark Accettura, Esq.

IT SEEMS THAT in most marriages, one spouse gets the dirty duty of acting as the family accountant. If your late spouse was in charge of tax returns, you may not have much experience in such matters. They may even scare the hell out of you. Even as you read now, you may have just remembered that your dog needs more water in his dish, or that you need to check your supply of furnace filters. Though you may be tempted, try not to "check out." It is not expected that you will learn to prepare tax returns by reading this chapter, only that you understand what returns are due and their function. Certainly, tax returns cannot be ignored.

Unless you have a strong accounting background, you will need the assistance of a Certified Public Accountant ("CPA"). You are best advised to contact a CPA as soon as possible to begin to gather the information you will need to timely file the tax returns described in this chapter. Even if you intend to hire a CPA, reading this chapter will make you a better teammate in a "taxing" undertaking. If you already use the services of a CPA, it is best to continue with someone who knows you and understands your situation.

Naturally, you continue to be responsible to file a personal income tax return (Form 1040), but the rules change somewhat as a result of your spouse's death. If you are the personal representative of your late spouse's estate, or the trustee of his or her trust, you must also file income tax returns for the estate or trust. If your late spouse's taxable estate exceeds the Applicable Exclusion Amount ($1,000,000 in 2002), you may be required to file a federal estate tax return. If you or your late spouse made taxable gifts, you may be required to file gift tax returns (Form 709). The following returns are discussed in great detail in this chapter:

Personal Income Tax: *U.S. Individual Income Tax Return (Form 1040)*

Income taxation of trusts and estates: *U.S. Income Tax Return for Estates and Trust (Form 1041)*

Estate and Gift Tax:
U.S. Estate (and Generation-Skipping Transfer) Tax Return (Form 706)

U.S. Gift (and Generation-Skipping Transfer) Tax Return (Form 709).

Form 1040

Despite your spouse's death, for a limited time you may still take your late spouse's exemptions and file a joint tax return. You are eligible to elect "married filing jointly" status in the year of your spouse's death, which in most cases produces the best tax result. However, you may choose to file separately ("married filing separately") if your late spouse was in trouble with the IRS, or you believe he or she may have committed tax fraud in the year of death. If you were to file jointly, you would expose yourself to his or her tax debts or even his or her fraud. In some cases, married filing separately may even generate more Schedule A deductions. That would be the case if there were large medical expenses incurred in the year of death. Your accountant should prepare Form 1040 using each status to determine which filing status nets you the best result. If you file jointly, you must sign both personally and as your spouse's personal representative.

You may file jointly for two tax years **following** the year of your spouse's death as a "qualifying widow or widower with dependent child," if **all** of the following conditions are met: (1) You were entitled to file a joint return in the year of death, whether or not you actually did; (2) You have not remarried; (3) You have a child, stepchild or foster child that qualifies as your dependent; and (4) you provide more than one-half the cost of maintaining your home, which is the principal residence of the child. If the above conditions are **not** met, you must file as a "single" taxpayer, and will likely pay a significantly higher tax.

> **Example:** Mr. Brown's wife died in 2001. As of 2002, Mr. Brown had not remarried and continued throughout 2002 to maintain a household for himself and their child. In 2001 Mr. Brown was entitled to file as married filing jointly with his deceased wife. For year 2002 he again qualifies for the more advantageous joint tax tables. He will be eligible to file a joint return for 2003 if he continues to meet the requirements described above.

When filing Form 1040 in the year of death (or short Form 1040A for taxpayers with minimal deductions and taxable income of less than $50,000), several disclosures must be made. In the name and address section on the top of Form 1040, you must indicate that your spouse is "deceased" and enter the date of death. Additionally, in the signature block on page 2 you must also indicate, "deceased." Your signature should be followed by the words "filing as surviving spouse."

The following is an example of the relevant portions of pages one and two of Form 1040:

Form **1040**	Department of the Treasury - Internal Revenue Service **U.S. Individual Income Tax Return**	2000	(99)	IRS Use Only - Do not write or staple in this space.

For the year Jan. 1-Dec. 31, 2000, or other tax year beginning _____ , 2000, ending _____ , 20 ____ OMB No. 1545-0074

Label (See instructions on page 19.)

L A B E L

Your first name and initial **Wendy**   Last name **Barnes**   Your social security number

If a joint return, spouse's first name and initial **Harry ("Deceased")**   Last name **Barnes, DOD: 1/10/01**   Spouse's social security number

Use the IRS label. Otherwise, please print or type.

H E R E

Home address (number and street). If you have a P.O. box, see page 19.   Apt. no.

▲ **Important!** ▲ You **must** enter your SSN(s) **above.**

City, town or post office, state, and ZIP code. If you have a foreign address, see page 19.

You   Spouse

Presidential Election Campaign (See page 19.)   Note. Checking "Yes" will not change your tax or reduce your refund. Do you, or your spouse if filing a joint return, want $3 to go to this fund? . . . . ▶   Yes ☐ No ☐   Yes ☐ No ☐

Filing Status

Check only one box

1 ☐ Single
2 ☐ Married filing joint return (even if only one had income)
3 ☐ Married filing separate return. Enter spouse's social security no. above and full name here. ▶
4 ☐ Head of household (with qualifying person). (See page 19.) If the qualifying person is a child but not your dependent, enter this child's name here. ▶
5 ☐ Qualifying widow(er) with dependent child (year spouse died ▶ ____). (See page 19.)

Sign Here

Joint return? See page 19.

Keep a copy for your records.

Under penalties of perjury, I declare that I have examined this return and accompanying schedules and statements, and to the best of my knowledge and belief, they are true, correct, and complete. Declaration of preparer (other than taxpayer) is based on all information of which preparer has any knowledge.

Your signature **Wendy Barnes**   Date   Your occupation   Daytime phone number

Spouse's signature. If a joint return, **both** must sign. **Wendy Barnes, Filing As Surviving Spouse**   Date   Spouse's occupation **Deceased**

May the IRS discuss this return with the preparer shown below (see page 52)? Yes ☐ No ☐

Paid Preparer's Use Only

Preparer's signature ▶   Date   Check if self-employed ☒   Preparer's SSN or PTIN **111111111**

Firm's name (or yours if self-employed), address, and ZIP code ▶   EIN **111111111**   Phone no. **(555)-555-555**

.1220 1 000   Form **1040** (2000)

Unless you moved in the year of your spouse's death, Form 1040 is filed with the same IRS center that you filed with the previous year. If you are not your spouse's personal representative, Form 1040 is filed with the IRS center determined by the residence of the personal representative.

If you did not remarry, your joint return for the year of death will include your late spouse's income and deductions **up to the date of death**. It will also include your income and deductions for the entire year. Income from your spouse's employment, retirement plans, or other income paid to you in the year of death is included on the joint return. Income from your spouse's employment, retirement plans, or investments paid to your late spouse's **estate** or **trust** must be reflected on Form 1041 discussed below.

1040 Estimated Tax Payments

The passing of your spouse may affect both your level of income and tax withholding. If your spouse was working, income tax was withheld from his or her paycheck. Naturally, once the paychecks stop so does the withholding. After your spouse's death, you may begin to live off of other sources of income such as retirement distributions, or proceeds from the sale of investment assets. If tax is not withheld from these new sources of income, you could be subject to withholding penalties. Federal and state law requires that either 100% of the prior year's tax liability (or approximately 110% percent for individuals with more that $150,000 of adjusted gross income) or at least 90% of current annual tax liability either be withheld from payroll or paid to the government in what are called "quarterly estimated payments." Failure to properly withhold can result in substantial penalties. Unfortunately, the death of your spouse does not exempt you from the withholding rules. Estimated taxes are paid four (4) times during the year: April 15th, June 15th, September 15th, and the following January 15th. *Considering the substantial income fluctuations that naturally occur in the year of death, it is likely that estimated payments will be necessary.*

Replace Social Security Number with New Tax Identification Number

To ensure proper income tax reporting, you should promptly notify the appropriate financial institutions of your spouse's death. Your spouse's name should be removed from your joint accounts, with your social security number added on each account. Trust and probate assets should be changed to reflect the new tax identification numbers issued by the IRS from information you submit on Form SS4. Financial institutions are required to file information returns (Form 1099) with the IRS. The IRS uses this information to determine whether taxpayers have accurately reported their dividend, interest and other income. Failure to promptly change tax identification numbers, especially on estate or trust assets, will result in misreporting of 1099 income. Post-death income would be improperly reported to the IRS as income of your late spouse rather than income of the estate or trust. If, in fact, you receive 1099s that do not reflect the responsible taxpayer, you must first report the income on the return of the taxpayer listed on the 1099. You then deduct the erroneous income from the return in what is called a "nominee distribution," identifying the correct taxpayer. The responsible taxpayer must then report the income.

The following is an example of page one of Form SS-4:

Form **SS-4** (Rev. April 2000) Department of the Treasury Internal Revenue Service	**Application for Employer Identification Number** (For use by employers, corporations, partnerships, trusts, estates, churches, government agencies, certain individuals, and others. See instructions.) ▶ Keep a copy for your records.		EIN OMB No. 1545-0003
Please type or print clearly.	1 Name of applicant (legal name) (see instructions)		
	2 Trade name of business (if different from name on line 1)	3 Executor, trustee, "care of" name	
	4a Mailing address (street address) (room, apt., or suite no.)	5a Business address (if different from address on lines 4a and 4b)	
	4b City, state, and ZIP code	5b City, state, and ZIP code	
	6 County and state where principal business is located		
	7 Name of principal officer, general partner, grantor, owner, or trustor - SSN or ITIN may be required (see instructions) ▶		

Medical Expenses

Substantial un-reimbursed medical expenses are often incurred in the year of death. Such expenses are generally not paid until after death. The general rule is that medical expenses are deductible when paid. However, an election can be made that will allow you to deduct medical expenses in the year **incurred** (rather than when later paid) as long as they are paid within one year of the date of death. The election is made on Form 1040 (see example on page 143). Alternatively, you may elect to deduct medical expenses on the estate tax return (Form 706) in lieu of an income tax deduction. However, since there is rarely any estate tax due at the death of the first spouse, it will almost always be preferable to elect to take medical expenses as an income tax deduction. Medical expenses may not be deducted from trust or estate income (Form 1041).

Income Tax Deduction for Estate Tax Paid

Income in respect of a decedent, or "IRD," is income earned during the life of the decedent that is paid out after death. Typical items of IRD include pension, IRA, and 401k distributions, bond interest, annuity payments, as well as the decedent's last paycheck. Since IRD is subject to both income and estate tax, it is subject to **double** tax.

Fortunately, recipients of IRD are entitled to an **income** tax deduction that somewhat offsets the effect of the double tax. The amount of the deduction is determined by computing the federal estate tax with the IRD included and then re-computing the tax with the IRD excluded. The income tax deduction is the difference between the two results.

ELECTION TO ACCRUE MEDICAL EXPENSES ON FINAL INCOME TAX RETURN ATTACHMENT TO FORM 1040

The undersigned executor of the above-named taxpayer hereby elects to deduct the taxpayer's following medical expenses paid within one year of death on the taxpayer's final income tax return. In accordance with IRS Sec. 213(c) and Reg. 1.213-1(d)(2), such medical expenses have not been claimed under IRC Sec. 2053 on Form 706 and further, taxpayer hereby waives the right to deduct such expenses in the future for estate tax purposes under IRC Sec. 2053.

Form 1041

Estates and irrevocable trusts (including revocable trusts that become irrevocable upon the death of the grantor) must file and report income tax on an annual basis. The first taxable year of a probate estate or a revocable trust begins the day of the decedent's death. As noted above, it is important that all assets owned by the estate or trust carry the proper tax identification number. Tax preparation will be a lot easier for you and your accountant if 1099s properly match income with the responsible taxpayer.

Form 1041 must be filed annually for so long as the estate or trust has income that exceeds $600. Since probate estates can usually be wrapped up in a calendar year or two, only one or two 1041s will be required. Trusts, depending on their terms, may last for many years. For example, a trust for the benefit of the surviving spouse for the balance of his or her lifetime, or for children until their "35th birthday," may continue for decades after the decedent's death.

The following is an example of page one of Form 1041:

Form **1041**	Department of the Treasury - Internal Revenue Service **U.S. Income Tax Return for Estates and Trusts**	**2000**	

For calendar year 2000 or fiscal year beginning _____ , 2000, and ending _____ | OMB No. 1545-0092

A Type of entity:	Name of estate or trust (If a grantor type trust, see page 10 of the instructions.)	C **Employer identification number**
☐ Decedent's estate		
☐ Simple trust		D Date entity created
☐ Complex trust	Name and title of fiduciary	
☐ Grantor type trust		E Nonexempt charitable and split-interest trusts, check applicable boxes (see page 10 of the instructions):
☐ Bankruptcy estate - Ch. 7		
☐ Bankruptcy estate - Ch. 11	Number, street, and room or suite no. (If a P.O. box, see page 10 of the instructions.)	
☐ Pooled income fund		☐ Described in section 4947(a)(1)
B Number of Schedules K-1 attached (see instructions) ▶	City or town, state, and ZIP code	☐ Not a private foundation ☐ Described in section 4947(a)(2)
F Check applicable boxes:	☐ Initial return ☐ Final return ☐ Amended return	G Pooled mortgage account (see page 11 of the instructions):
	☐ Change in fiduciary's name ☐ Change in fiduciary's address	☐ Bought ☐ Sold Date:

The decedent's personal representative is responsible for filing Form 1041 on behalf of the estate, as is the trustee on behalf of the trust. As noted in Chapter Seven, personal representatives and trustees are "fiduciaries," and as such, must prepare and sign all returns. If your late spouse had several trusts, each must be assigned its own tax identification number and must file Form 1041 annually. For example, your late spouse may have had an Irrevocable Life Insurance Trust (See Chapter Ten, "Irrevocable Trusts"), as well as sub-trusts contained within his or her revocable trust known as family and marital trusts (See Chapter Seven).

Probate estates may elect a non-calendar **fiscal year.** The filing of the first return constitutes the irrevocable election of a tax year. The first taxable year of an estate begins on the date of the decedent's death and ends on the last day of any month that is not more than twelve months from the date of death. For example, if your spouse died June 15, 2001, you may elect a fiscal year ending as late as May 31, 2002. A non-calendar year fiscal year allows you more time to get organized after the death of a spouse, as well as limited income tax deferral. In the example above, year 2001 income would be reported on the May 31, 2002 tax return, allowing you to report 2001 trust or estate income on your 2002 personal income tax return.

Except in the limited circumstance of **trusts** that elect to be taxed as estates, trusts must report income on a **calendar year** basis. If as personal representative and trustee, you so elect, the trust will be treated and taxed as part of the estate and not as a separate trust. The election allows the filing of a single Form 1041 and the election of a single non-calendar fiscal year. Combined reporting may continue for up to six months after the IRS issues its final determination of estate tax liability. If no estate tax return (Form 706) is required to be filed, combined income tax reporting may continue for up to two years after the date of your late spouse's death. The election is made on the first Form 1041 filed for the estate and is irrevocable. The election is most useful for estates and trusts that by their terms will be fully disbursed within a year or two following death, and is of little use for trusts that will continue for many years after the death of your spouse.

> *For Example:* Harry is married to Wendy. He has a revocable trust and dies on June 22, 2001. Wendy discovers a sizable bank account in Harry's name alone (she wonders why he didn't tell her about it!), and must therefore open a probate estate. Both the trust and estate earn enough income to require the filing of income tax returns. Wendy receives distributions from the trust between June 23 and December 31, 2001. Wendy is required to pay income tax on those distributions reporting them on Form 1040. If the trust uses the calendar year as its tax year, which is the usual requirement, Wendy will have to report the distributions as part of her 2001 income. However, if the trust elects to be taxed as an estate, it does not have to use the calendar year and can chose any tax year (as long as the first year is not longer than 12 months). Let's say that Mary as Harry's personal representative chooses May 31, 2002 as the estate's fiscal year. If Mary also elects to have the trust taxed as an estate, the trust distributions Wendy received in 2001 will not be counted as income to her in 2001. Instead, trust income will be added to estate income and reported on the estate's first tax return for the year ended May 31, 2002. Accordingly, Mary will report first year trust and estate income as part of her 2002 income, allowing her to defer trust income an entire year. In addition, Mary only need file one Form 1041 covering **both** the estate and trust.

The due date for filing Form 1041 is the 15th day of 4th month following close of the tax year (April 15th for calendar fiscal years). **Trusts** are granted an automatic extension of time to file (not an extension to pay) for 90 days by filing form 8736. An additional 90 days extension (beyond the first 90 day extension) may be granted by filing Form 8800, if "reasonable cause' can be established.

By contrast, **estates** are not automatically granted an extension of time to file Form 1041. An estate must show "reasonable cause" as to why the return cannot be filed on time. The maximum extension allowed is 6 months from the original due date. As with all extensions, an extension of time to file is not an extension of time to pay the tax. Accordingly, a tax payment ("tentative tax") must be made on or before the original due date. If the tentative tax paid with the request for an extension is insufficient, penalties and interest on the shortfall may be imposed. Form 2758 is used to apply for an extension to file Form 1041.

Avoiding the Tax Trap

Trust and estate income is taxed at an extremely high marginal rate. Income not distributed during the year is taxed to the trust or estate. Distributions to trust beneficiaries during the year or within 65 days after the end of the year generate a distribution deduction to the trust or estate. Such distributions are included in the income of the recipient beneficiary at his or her marginal tax rate. The effect of the distribution deduction is to shift income tax liability from the trust or estate to the recipient beneficiaries. Since trusts and estates are in a much higher tax bracket, distribution of income to beneficiaries is desirable. The trustee or the personal representative must be ever vigilant against accumulating income in the estate or trust and thereby paying unnecessary income tax.

The following chart compares the tax rate of married couples filing jointly to that of trusts and estates:

TAXABLE INCOME	MARRIED COUPLES	TAXABLE INCOME	ESTATE TRUST
$0 - $45,200	15%	$0 - $1,800	15%
$45,200 - $109,250	28%	$1,800 - $4,250	28%
$109,250 - $166,500	31%	$4,250-$6,500	31%
$166,500 - $297,350	36%	$6,500 – $8,900	36%
$297,350 -	39.6%	$8,900 -	39.6%

As you can see, the tax rate is substantially higher for 1041 income. An estate or trust reaches the maximum tax rate of 39.6% with only $8900 of taxable income, while a married couple filing jointly doesn't reach the maximum tax rate until they have $297,350 of taxable income.

As noted, trusts and estates are permitted a distribution deduction for distributions to beneficiaries during the tax year or within **65 days of the end of the year.** The 65-day rule allows the trustee or personal representative time to assess trust or estate income tax liability for the year and to make distributions to shift income tax liability to the beneficiaries. For calendar year trusts and estates, the 65-day period coincides with the deadline for issuance of 1099s. Taxpayers, including trusts and estates, must receive forms 1099 by January 31st. The 65-day rule allows trustees and personal representatives time between January 31 (when they receive trust and estate 1099s) and March 5th (the deadline for making distributions) to assess their tax liability and to make trust or estate distributions that will achieve the optimal application of the marginal tax rates between the entity and the beneficiary. Distributions within the 65-day period relate back to the previous tax year. The trust or estate is allowed to deduct distributions in the 65 day period as if made during the previous tax year. Likewise, beneficiaries must report the distribution as if received on the last day of the trust or estate's immediately preceding tax year.

Distributions generate a deduction only to the extent of the trust or estate's distributable net income ("DNI"). Basically, DNI is the trust or estate's taxable income for the year. Distributions in excess of DNI are not deductible to the trust or estate and are not taxable to beneficiaries. Distributions are first considered distributions of DNI and qualify for a distribution deduction. Specific bequests such as "$10,000 to my cousin Vinny" are not considered taxable distributions. The tax Code recognizes that the decedent probably did not want cousin Vinny to pay income tax on the remembrance left to him by the decedent.

Form K-1 is an attachment to Form 1041. A separate K-1 is prepared for each beneficiary to reflect his or her share of trust or estate income and loss. Beneficiaries must wait to prepare their 1040 until they have received their K-1. The K-1 will not only indicate the amount of income and loss to be included on their personal return, but also the character (i.e., capital versus ordinary, long term versus short term).

The following is an example of page one of Form K-1:

SCHEDULE K-1 (Form 1041)	Beneficiary's Share of Income, Deductions, Credits, etc.	OMB No. 1545-0092
Department of the Treasury Internal Revenue Service	for the calendar year 2000, or fiscal year beginning _____ ending _____ ▶ Complete a separate Schedule K-1 for each beneficiary.	2000

Name of trust or decedent's estate

☐ Amended K-1
☐ Final K-1

Beneficiary's identifying number ▶	Estate's or trust's EIN ▶
Beneficiary's name, address, and ZIP code	Fiduciary's name, address, and ZIP code

	(a) Allocable share item		(b) Amount	(c) Calendar year 2000 Form 1040 filers enter the amounts in column (b) on:
1	Interest	1		Schedule B, Part I, line 1
2	Ordinary dividends	2		Schedule B, Part II, line 5
3	Net short-term capital gain	3		Schedule D, line 5
4 a	Net long-term capital gain: a 28% rate gain	4a		Schedule D, line 12, column (g)
b	Unrecaptured section 1250 gain	4b		Line 11 of the worksheet for Schedule D, line 25
c	Total for year	4c		Schedule D, line 12, column (f)
5 a	Annuities, royalties, and other nonpassive income before directly apportioned deductions	5a		Schedule E, Part III, column (f)
b	Depreciation	5b		
c	Depletion	5c		Include on the applicable line of the appropriate tax form
d	Amortization	5d		
6 a	Trade or business, rental real estate, and other rental income before directly apportioned deductions (see instructions)	6a		Schedule E, Part III
b	Depreciation	6b		
c	Depletion	6c		Include on the applicable line of the appropriate tax form
d	Amortization	6d		
7	Income for minimum tax purposes	7		
8	Income for regular tax purposes (add lines 1, 2, 3, 4c, 5a, and 6a)	8		
9	Adjustment for minimum tax purposes (subtract line 8 from line 7)	9		Form 6251, line 12
10	Estate tax deduction (including certain generation-skipping transfer taxes)	10		Schedule A, line 27
11	Foreign taxes	11		Form 1116 or Schedule A (Form 1040), line 8
12	Adjustments and tax preference items (itemize):			
a	Accelerated depreciation	12a		
b	Depletion	12b		Include on the applicable line of Form 6251
c	Amortization	12c		
d	Exclusion items	12d		2001 Form 8801
13	Deductions in the final year of trust or decedent's estate:			
a	Excess deductions on termination (see instructions)	13a		Schedule A, line 22
b	Short-term capital loss carryover	13b		Schedule D, line 5
c	Long-term capital loss carryover	13c		Schedule D, line 12, column (f) and (g)
d	Net operating loss (NOL) carryover for regular tax purposes	13d		Form 1040, line 21
e	NOL carryover for minimum tax purposes	13e		See the instructions for Form 6251, line 20
f		13f		Include on the applicable line
g		13g		of the appropriate tax form
14	Other (itemize):			
a	Payments of estimated taxes credited to you	14a		Form 1040, line 59
b	Tax-exempt interest	14b		Form 1040, line 8b
c		14c		
d		14d		Include on the applicable line of appropriate tax form
e		14e		

For Paperwork Reduction Act Notice, see the Instructions for Form 1041.　　　　Schedule K-1 (Form 1041) 2000

JSA
0F1610 2.000

1041 Estimated Tax Payments

If an estate or trust owes more than $1,000 in tax for the current year, it must make estimated tax payments. The rules of estate and trust estimated payments are the same as those for individuals; that is, either 100% of the prior year's tax (110% percent for trusts and estates with adjustable gross income of more than $150,000) or 90% of the current year tax due. Like individuals, estimated tax payments for trusts and estates must be made in four quarterly installments. Unlike individuals, estates and revocable trusts that become irrevocable at death, are not required to make estimated tax payments until the first tax year ending 2 years after the decedent's death.

For example, if your spouse dies March 15, 2000 and you adopt a January 31, 2001 fiscal year, the first tax year that estimated tax payments are required is the year ended January 31, 2003 (i.e. the first tax year ending two years after March 15, 2000). If the estate closes prior to February 1, 2002, no estimated tax payment is ever due.

Costs of Administration

Estates and trusts may deduct expenses incurred for the collection of assets, the payment of debts, and the distribution of the property to beneficiaries and heirs. Administration expenses include executor's commissions, real estate commissions, attorney's fees, court costs, appraiser's fees, interest, accounting fees, and brokerage fees. Administration expenses are deductible either against income on Form 1041 or as an expense of the estate on Form 706. *Since it is unlikely that estate tax is due at your spouse's death, you should deduct administrative expenses on Form 1041.*

You and Your CPA

You should meet with your CPA no later than two or three months after your spouse's death. If you don't have a CPA, or your CPA is not qualified to assist you in the matters discussed in this chapter, see "Choosing a CPA" at the end of this chapter. The initial meeting with your CPA is needed to plan a strategy for the most appropriate fiscal year for your late spouse's estate and trust(s).

Once you have agreed on a tax year, you should agree to meet again sometime within the 65-day period discussed above. At the second meeting, you and your CPA can review income and expenses of the estate and trust(s) and determine what distributions should be made from the estate or trusts to achieve the optimal income tax result.

To better track income and expenses, you should maintain a checking account for the estate and each trust (using the appropriate tax identification numbers). All disbursements should be made from each appropriate checking account. Each check register will provide a clear record of administrative expenses and evidence of distributions made to beneficiaries.

With these things in mind, and having already met with your CPA at least twice after your spouse's death, you should bring the following information to your CPA at tax time:

1. Your last three federal and state personal income tax returns;
2. All current year 1099s (1099-DIV, 1099-INT, 1099-MISC, 1099-R);
3. All current K-ls and W2s;
4. Evidence of deductible expenses;
5. Evidence of distributions to beneficiaries;
6. The tax identification numbers of the estate and any trusts (bring copies of filed SS4s);
7. The name, address, and social security number of all estate and trust heirs and beneficiaries.

Form 706

For the most part, the unlimited marital deduction eliminates the possibility of any estate tax at the death of the first spouse. Only where the surviving spouse is a non-U.S. citizen, or where the surviving spouse is not the beneficiary of a substantial portion of the decedent's estate, will an estate tax be due at the death of a married individual. You should immediately consult an estate tax attorney if you are not a U.S. citizen.

Even though it is unlikely that estate tax is due as a result of your spouse's death, Form 706 must nonetheless be filed if your late spouse's gross estate, plus his or her lifetime taxable gifts, exceeds the "Applicable Exclusion Amount". The Applicable Credit Amount for 2002 is $1,000,000 and is scheduled to increase to $3,500,000 by 2009 before the estate tax is scheduled to be repealed in 2010:

YEAR	APPLICABLE CREDIT AMOUNT
2001	$675,000
2002 - 2003	$1,000,000
2004 - 2005	$1,500,000
2006 - 2007	$2,000,000
2009	$3,500,000
2010 and after	$0 *

*The repeal of the federal estate tax in 2010 will occur only if Congress votes to ratify the repeal at a future date.

The following is an example of page one of Form 706:

Form 706 is extremely difficult to prepare, and should be prepared by an estate tax attorney, or by CPA familiar with estate and gift taxation. Form 706 is due nine months after death. Although nine months may seem like a long time, the detailed information that must be compiled makes Form 706 a challenge to complete in the allotted time. As your late spouse's personal representative, you must sign form 706. If you can demonstrate sufficient cause, a six-month extension of time to file may be granted by filing Form 4768. *The six-month extension is only an extension of time to file and not an extension to pay.* An estimated tax payment, if applicable, must accompany Form 4768.

To coin a phrase, Form 706 is "where the rubber meets the road" in estate planning. Form 706 is where you tell the IRS your late spouse's life story. In addition to current asset and liability information, a detailed history of all taxable gifts must be disclosed. Copies of your late spouse's Will and trust must be submitted along with Form 706. Although no tax may be due, important elections such as the election to treat the marital trust as a QTIP trust, the election to value assets six months after the date of death (Alternate Valuation Date), the election to qualify the family business as a Qualified Family Owned Business Interest ("QFOBI"), among others, must be made on Form 706.

The starting point in completing Form 706 is to determine your late spouse's gross estate. *Basically, the gross estate consists of all assets in which your late spouse had an interest during life including life insurance, IRAs, 401ks, real estate, cash, stocks, annuities, promissory notes receivable, bonds, jewelry, and personal property, as well as interests in closely held businesses, whether held in individual name or in his or her revocable trust (See Chapter Nine, "Planning to Avoid Estate Tax").*

All assets that make up your late spouse's "gross estate" must be valued as of the date of death (See Chapter Two for the specific information that needs to be gathered). Various deductions, including debts, are deducted from the gross estate to arrive at the "adjusted gross estate."

Difficult to value assets such as real estate and interests in closely held businesses must be appraised by a licensed appraiser. The single most audited and litigated issue is the value of assets listed on Form 706. Having a professional appraiser value difficult to value assets will minimize your chances of audit and enhance your peace of mind. Although appraisals are expensive (other than those for residential real estate), potentially running in the thousands of dollars, they greatly increase the chances of having your 706 accepted "as filed." All appraisals should be in writing and attached to Form 706 when submitted to the IRS.

If the estate declines in value after death, you may elect to report the value as of the date that is six months after death (i.e. the **"Alternate Valuation Date"**). Assets sold or distributed during the six-month period are valued as of the date of sale or transfer.

You can expect to receive an initial response from the IRS within six months of filing Form 706. At such time, the IRS may simply issue a closing letter accepting the return as filed, or it may request further information, or audit the return. Returns filed at the death of the first spouse have a low audit profile and are typically accepted as filed.

Disclaimer

You may elect to "disclaim" property left to you by your late spouse. Assets disclaimed by you pass to those who would have received your late spouse's assets had you predeceased him or her. At first blush, disclaiming assets may sound insane. However, disclaiming assets may make excellent tax sense if your spouse left everything to you and consequently failed to use his or her unified credit. By disclaiming assets you can fully use your late spouse's unified credit, effectively doubling the amount you can leave to children free of estate tax (See Chapter Nine, "Planning to Avoid Estate Tax"). To be qualified, the disclaimer must be irrevocable, in writing, and made within 9 months of death. You may not accept possession of disclaimed assets (for example, cashing the proceeds of a life insurance policy would make the policy ineligible for disclaimer), and the disclaimed assets must pass to someone other than you.

State Inheritance Tax

All 50 states have some form of inheritance tax return. Each state has different forms and rules, but all tend to evolve from federal law. You should obtain a copy of your state's forms and instructions. Thirty-three states have adopted a form of "pick-up" tax, where the state collects a portion of the federal estate tax that would have been due the federal government if not for the **state death tax credit** available on the federal return. The remaining states have a separate tax not limited to the federal state tax credit.

Gifts and Form 709

Taxable gifts made during life reduce the amount the decedent may leave tax-free at death. Taxable gifts are gifts in excess of the $10,000 gift tax exclusion (See Chapter Nine "Gifting"). Form 709 must be filed for any year a taxable gift is made. Taxable gifts for which no Form 709 was filed should be documented after death. As personal representative, you must prepare and sign Form 709. Significant tax savings may be available where you and your late spouse made lifetime gifts but failed to file Form 709. You may "split" the gift on Form 709, and essentially double your gift tax exclusion.

Form 709 is due on April 15th following the year in which the gift is made. A six-month extension is permitted. Post mortem gift tax returns must be filed by April 15th of the year following the year of death or the due date of Form 706 whichever is earlier. The minimum penalty for failing to file a 709 is $100, even if no tax is due.

Generally, gift tax returns should be filed on a timely basis in order to start the running of the statute of limitations. The IRS has only three years from the date of filing Form 709 to audit the return. By contrast, there is no limit on the time the IRS can audit gifts where no Form 709 was filed. Carefully documenting gifts limits the IRS's ability to scrutinize gifts years later, even after the death of the donor.

The following is an example of page one of Form 709:

Form **709**	United States Gift (and Generation-Skipping Transfer) Tax Return		OMB No. 1545-0020
Department of the Treasury Internal Revenue Service	(Section 6019 of the Internal Revenue Code) (For gifts made during calendar year 2000) ▶ **See separate instructions.**		**2000**

1	Donor's first name and middle initial		2 Donor's last name		3 Donor's social security number	
4	Address (number, street, and apartment number)				5 Legal residence (domicile) (county and state)	
6	City, state, and ZIP code				7 Citizenship	

Part 1 - General Information

		Yes	No
8	If the donor died during the year, check here ▶ ☐ and enter date of death		
9	If you received an extension of time to file this Form 709, check here ▶ ☐ and attach the Form 4868, 2688, 2350, or extension letter		
10	Enter the total number of separate donees listed on Schedule A - count each person only once. ▶		
11a	Have you (the donor) previously filed a Form 709 (or 709-A) for any other year? If the answer is "No," do not complete line 11b		
11b	If the answer to line 11a is "Yes," has your address changed since you last filed Form 709 (or 709-A)?		
12	Gifts by husband or wife to third parties. - Do you consent to have the gifts (including generation-skipping transfers) made by you and your spouse to third parties during the calendar year considered as made one-half by each of you? (See instructions.) (If the answer is "Yes," the following information must be furnished and your spouse must sign the consent shown below. If the answer is "No," skip lines 13-18 and go to Schedule A.)		
13	Name of consenting spouse	14 SSN		
15	Were you married to one another during the entire calendar year? (see instructions)		
16	If the answer to 15 is "No," check whether ☐ married ☐ divorced or ☐ widowed, and give date (see instructions) ▶		
17	Will a gift tax return for this calendar year be filed by your spouse?		
18	**Consent of Spouse -** I consent to have the gifts (and generation-skipping transfers) made by me and by my spouse to third parties during the calendar year considered as made one-half by each of us. We are both aware of the joint and several liability for tax created by the execution of this consent.		

Consenting spouse's signature ▶   Date ▶

Other Returns

If you or your late spouse were involved in a business enterprise, you will need to continue payroll and tax filings for such enterprise. Corporations must file Form 1120, S corporations file Form 1120S, and partnerships and LLCs file Form 1065. Sole proprietorships file Form 1040 (Schedule C) and Form 1040 (Schedule E) must be filed for real estate investments. If you find any of these tax returns in your late spouse's files, you need to follow up with your CPA, or the CPA who prepared the return, to make sure that you do not have a continuing obligation with respect to the listed entity.

Word to the Wise

All federal and state tax returns are filed under penalty of perjury. If you are signing returns, make sure they are accurate to the best of your knowledge. Ask questions. Don't be persuaded to omit income or assets from any return. You're the one that is on the hook and the one that will suffer the consequences of any misadventure. You may be thinking: "How does the IRS know I have this?" The answer is: "Don't risk it." The value of a good night's sleep in your own home is too great to put at risk.

Record Retention

You are required to maintain records that would allow the IRS to confirm income, expenses, or tax liability. The IRS says that records should be held until the expiration of the statute of limitations for the return to which they relate. The statute of limitations ordinarily expires three (3) years after the return is due. The three (3) year period does not apply in cases of fraud or failure to file. Since you have the burden of showing that returns have been filed, it is advisable to permanently retain filed tax returns. You should also **permanently** retain the following items:

1. Cancelled checks for all tax payments;

2. All estate tax returns (Form 706) as well as all gift tax returns (709s);

3. Closing letters received from the IRS and state agencies stating that your estate and inheritance tax returns have been accepted and your case is closed.

Although voluminous, you should save cancelled checks for at least six years. Cancelled checks can verify tax payments, satisfaction of a debt, or the making of a loan.

Choosing a CPA

If you already have a CPA, ask whether he or she is familiar with the topics discussed in this chapter. Not all CPAs have experience in the income taxation of trusts and estates. Even fewer have experience with estate (Form 706) and gift (Form 709) tax returns. So don't accept a fast answer that he or she "does this stuff all the time." You might ask how many of each return mentioned in this chapter the CPA prepares each year. You might even engage him or her in a discussion about some of the things you have learned from this chapter and judge for yourself whether the answers jibe with what you have read. You should also ask about fees and how many years he or she has been practicing.

If you do not already have a CPA, ask your estate planning attorney to recommend one. If for some reason your attorney cannot help you, every state has an affiliate of the American Institute of Certified Public Accountants (AICPA) that licenses, supports and promotes local CPAs. The state association will be able to provide you with a list of CPAs in your area. You should call at least three CPAs from the list, and interview at least two. Most CPAs will be happy to meet with you for a free consultation. If you have access to the Internet, you should visit each accountant's website. Be patient if you are trying to contact a CPA during tax season (February through April).

Chapter Nine

Basic Estate Planning

P. Mark Accettura, Esq.

WHEN WE ARE MARRIED, our spouse is our logical and default care-taker. Forged in the wedding vows, and perhaps never ratified thereafter, it is agreed that each will watch over the other in sickness and in health. The law, in fact, recognizes the presumed authority of a competent spouse to speak for an incompetent one, and a surviving spouse to speak for the estate of a deceased spouse.

Now that you are single, you have no logical or presumed care-taker. You must provide for your own sickness and death. You must decide who will make your medical and financial decisions in the event you become incapacitated, and who will manage your estate at death. Other important questions must also be answered. If you have minor children, who will care for them, shepherding them through their youth, teens, twenties, and perhaps beyond? Who will care for your handicapped children, children in bad marriages, children who are substance abusers? The answers to these questions are found in the process of estate planning, the subject of this chapter.

Estate planning is the process of assessing one's lifetime and testamentary goals. Lifetime goals typically include providing for your own care in the event of incapacity. Testamentary goals include when, how, and to whom to distribute your assets at death, as well as planning to avoid probate and to minimize estate tax.

A typical estate plan, to the extent there is such a thing, begins with a Will, a durable power of attorney and a revocable trust. Each of these documents allows for the appointment of trusted individuals, or institutions, known as "fiduciaries," to carry out your wishes at the time of your incapacity or death. The scope and complexity of your estate plan is individual to you, and increases with the size of your estate and the degree to which your family deviates from the traditional nuclear family.

This Chapter discusses the following important estate planning topics:

- Estate planning building blocks: Wills, durable powers of attorney and revocable trusts.
- How to get started.
- Why joint ownership and beneficiary designations should not be used as substitutes for estate planning.
- The importance of "funding" your revocable trust.
- Sizing up your estate and avoiding estate tax.
- Gifting to avoid estate tax.
- Planning for children of all ages with special needs.

Estate Planning Building Blocks

Last Will and Testament ("Will")

A personal representative (also known as "executor" or "executrix") is appointed to make funeral arrangements, disburse personal property, and if necessary, to represent your estate in probate court. Your Will is the proper document to appoint the Guardian of minor children. When used in conjunction with a revocable trust, the Will is known as a "pour over Will," and serves to transfer un-funded assets (see "Funding Your Revocable Trust" below) into trust at death. A pour over Will acts as a safety net to catch any asset not transferred to trust during life and "pour" them over to your trust. Unfortunately, assets transferred into trust via the pour over Will must pass through probate.

Durable Powers of Attorney

Durable powers of attorney permit you to name trusted individuals to act on your behalf in the event you become incapacitated. Durable powers of attorney fall into two broad categories: powers pertaining to general personal matters (general powers), and powers pertaining to health care (health care powers).

General powers permit you to appoint an "agent" to handle all of your personal affairs such as banking, preparation of tax returns, sale of an automobile, and application for employee or government benefits as if you yourself were present.

Health care powers allow you to appoint someone (sometimes called a "patient advocate" or "health care surrogate") to make your medical decisions including "pulling the plug" in the event of terminal illness.

The Patient Self Determination Act requires all federally funded healthcare facilities to inform patients of their right to appoint a health care surrogate. All fifty states now allow for the appointment of a substituted decision maker with life cessation powers. Each state has its own terminology and rules. Your state may recognize "Durable Powers of Attorney," "Living Wills," "Health Care Proxies," or "Advance Directives." *You should be aware that health care powers executed in one state are not necessarily effective in other states.* Accordingly, separate health care powers should be drafted if you are splitting time between or among states.

Most powers of attorney come into effect at the time of your incompetence (some non-medical powers come into effect at their creation), and in all cases, end at your death. The term "durable" signifies that the power being granted continues to be effective despite your disability. A general non-medical power of attorney grants your agent the power to handle all of your **personal** affairs. The power of the agent does **not** extend to assets owned by your revocable trust, since assets owned in trust are not considered to be personally owned by you. Your revocable trust addresses the issue of your disability by appointing a successor trustee to manage trust assets in such event.

Since the likelihood of becoming incompetent dramatically increases with age, it is important that you have powers of attorney. Absent proper planning, your affairs would come within the jurisdiction of the probate court. If you become incompetent without durable powers of attorney in effect, a public hearing must be held to determine your incompetency before appointing a family member, friend, or a court appointee to act as your Guardian and Conservator. Powers of attorney avoid such costly and intrusive probate proceedings.

Revocable Trusts

Today, most estate plans employ revocable trusts. Their versatility and ease of administration make them indispensable for small and large estates alike. Revocable trusts may be used to avoid probate, provide for children of current or prior marriages, and to minimize federal estate tax. Revocable trusts are effective upon execution, and continue for so long as mandated by their terms. Assets passing at your death avoid probate since your death does not affect the continued existence of the trust.

For income tax purposes, your revocable trust is not a separate taxable entity while you are alive. It operates under your social security number, is not taxed, and is not required to file a separate income tax return. Income of the trust is taxed to you at your individual tax rate. Thus, while you are alive the trust is ignored for federal and state income tax purposes.

How to Get Started

Choose Fiduciaries

Start by identifying the people you wish to act on your behalf in the event of your incapacity or death. Your appointees should be competent to act, understand your wishes, and be likely to carry them out. The three most important jobs tend to be the guardian of minor children, your patient advocate charged with making medical decisions, and your successor trustee appointed to manage trust assets after your disability or death. It is advisable to choose both primary and contingent fiduciaries for all appointments in the event your first choice is unable or unwilling to act.

Name Beneficiaries

Who is to inherit your estate? If you have children, treat them equally, except in extremely rare circumstances. Unequal shares will surely leave a legacy of hurt feelings and estrangement among your children. If your late spouse has children from a previous marriage, you must decide how to remember them. If your late spouse has a trust, stepchildren may already be remembered. How you treat stepchildren will depend on a number of factors including what your conscience tells you, and whether your late spouse remembered them in his or her trust. Ideally, you and your late spouse executed trusts balancing the needs and expectations of your children and the surviving spouse. If so, those trusts must be strictly administered according to their terms. The relationship between step-children and a step-parent is often strained. Latent hurt and resentment matures to outright anger and mistrust over what will happen to "dad's money." If your late spouse made no provision for his or her children, you should consider making a gift of money or personal property as an olive branch to encourage continued involvement with them.

Control From the Grave

Young beneficiaries shouldn't inherit too early. If you have small children, you are now the last line of defense between them and the outside world. Having their inheritance held in trust will facilitate their secure future. A trustee of your choosing should manage your assets in the event of your premature disability or death. Trusts permit you to postpone your children's inheritance and encourage college attendance. Certainly, eighteen year olds (the age of majority in most states) cannot be permitted unfettered control of their inheritance; neither can beneficiaries with emotional or substance abuse problems or beneficiaries who are either unable or unwilling to work, or who have a predilection for gambling, or otherwise wasting money. It is your duty to protect your children in the event you aren't around to parent them. You have the opportunity to speak to them through the words of your trust.

Joint Ownership as a Trust Substitute

Assets that pass by operation of law, such as jointly owned assets and assets that name a beneficiary, are not governed by the terms of your Will or trust. Instead, they pass automatically at your death, and as a result can have unintended results. For example, if your Will and trust reflect your wish that your entire estate be distributed to your three children equally, your assets will nonetheless pass to a single child added as co-owner on a bank or brokerage account, merely as a matter of convenience.

A great many married couples own some or all of their assets jointly. At death, the couple's assets automatically pass to the surviving spouse. Although the automatic transfer may have seemed smooth and painless at the time, couples with a net worth in excess of the Applicable Exclusion Amount ($1,000,000 in 2002) have permanently lost a significant tax planning opportunity. Had both spouses prepared revocable trusts and transferred one-half of their assets to each trust, the couple could have doubled the amount they can leave to their children free from federal estate tax.

A couple whose combined net worth is likely to remain below the Applicable Exclusion Amount, should consider adopting a "joint trust." A joint trust combines the benefits of joint ownership with those of a trust. Both spouses are the grantors and trustee of the joint trust. On the death of the first spouse, the surviving spouse is in complete control of the trust and even retains the power to amend the trust. Since the trust does not become irrevocable on the first spouse's death, none of the trust administration discussed in Chapter Seven is required at the first spouse's death. Probate is avoided on the death of both spouses. Unlike joint ownership, joint trusts (like other revocable trusts) can hold assets for the benefit of children beyond the age of 18.

If your late spouse did not have a trust, and you are now the sole owner of your marital assets, you should avoid the temptation of adding your children's names to your accounts. Although jointly held assets pass to the surviving tenants by operation of law, and therefore avoid probate, there are a number of reasons not to use joint ownership as a form of estate planning. First, joint ownership accords significant lifetime rights to the new joint tenants, and exposes your assets to the claims of their creditors. For example, if you add your children as joint tenants on your home, you cannot sell or mortgage your home without their consent. Even if the children consent to the mortgage or sale of the home, they would technically be entitled to their share of the proceeds from the sale, a result you certainly did not intend. Your children's creditors will lick their chops when they learn that your children have an ownership interest in your assets. In the event one of your children divorces, a son-in-law or daughter-in-law may claim a spousal interest in your home.

You cannot provide for contingent beneficiaries through joint ownership. For example, parents often wish to leave their assets to their children equally, with the share of a deceased child passing to his or her children (i.e. grandchildren). This objective cannot be achieved by titling assets jointly. Under joint ownership, only the surviving named beneficiaries inherit, leaving the children of deceased children out in the cold. The share of a child who prede-ceases you will be allocated only to your surviving children.

In short, don't gamble on joint ownership and other operation of law transfers. The best way to minimize estate tax, retain control of assets, insulate assets from children's creditors, and ensure that assets pass to the intended beneficiaries, is to re-title assets into the name of your revocable trust.

Funding Your Revocable Trust

The preparation of revocable trust documents is only the first step in eliminating probate and minimizing estate tax. Once drafted, you must "fund" your trust. The process of funding assets into trust can be somewhat laborious, but is essential to achieving the full benefit of revocable trusts. Funding is the process of transferring ownership (or a beneficial interest) in assets into trust during life. Assets owned in trust during life avoid probate at death.

The procedure for funding depends on the type of the asset being funded. Real estate, brokerage accounts, business interests, and bank accounts are funded by making the trust the **owner** of the asset. The trust name must contain the name of the Grantor, the Trustee(s), and the date the trust was created. A typical trust name would be "Wendy Barnes as Trustee for the Wendy Barnes Trust dated September 1, 2001." However, in light of the space limitations on typical ownership and beneficiary forms, it may be necessary to abbreviate the trust name down to its most important elements. The following name can be used in place of the full trust name described above: "Wendy Barnes Trust dated 9/1/01."

Real Estate

A "Warranty Deed" or "Quit Claim Deed" is used to transfer ownership of real estate into trust. Some advisors favor "recording" funding deeds, (i.e. filing the deed with the county register of deeds), while others prefer to record deeds only upon the death of the grantor. The fact that property is subject to a mortgage does not prevent you from transferring it to trust. Ownership of your principal residence in trust does not affect your eligibility for the $250,000.00/$500,000.00 forgiveness of gain on sale available under federal Law. However, for Medicaid eligibility purposes, a principal residence owned by a revocable trust is not eligible for the homestead exemption (see "Medicaid" in Chapter Twelve).

Qualified Plans and IRAs

Ownership of qualified retirement plans and IRAs cannot be changed without causing the entire account to become immediately taxable. Artfully drafted beneficiary designation forms are necessary to properly fund such retirement accounts into trust. As a general rule, married participants should name their spouse as **primary** beneficiary, with the revocable trust of the participant named as the **contingent** beneficiary. A two-part beneficiary designation allows the greatest flexibility in negotiating the complex and perilous income and estate tax rules that apply to retirement plan assets. Unmarried participants should either name their revocable trust as primary beneficiary or their children directly. Retirement plan and IRA distributions are discussed in greater detail in Chapter Six.

Personal property

Other than automobiles and other vehicles whose titles are regulated by state motor vehicle law, no action is required to fund personal property into trust. Since personal property (e.g., furniture, jewelry, art work and other household items) cannot be re-titled (i.e., there's no title for a table or chair!), such property cannot be transferred into trust. Instead, the disposition of personal property is governed by your Will. Rather than addressing items of personal property directly in the document, most Wills permit the use of a "separate writing," disposing of items of personal property. Automobiles and other items capable of being re-titled should not be transferred into trust. For liability purposes, automobiles, recreation vehicles, and other motor vehicles should be owned by the user of the vehicle (See "Planes, Trains, and Automobiles" in Chapter Four).

Often missed items

Savings bonds, stock certificates and undeveloped real estate lots tend to be overlooked during the funding process. Overlooked assets require a probate proceeding to transfer title. For this reason, it is important to be diligent in identifying all of your assets and then make sure that they are all transferred to trust.

Planning to Avoid Estate Tax

Don't be lulled into a false sense of security by the fact that no estate or inheritance tax was due at your spouse's death. As a general rule, no estate tax is imposed on the death of the first spouse, irrespective of the couple's net worth. *Federal estate tax is built on the belief that the surviving spouse shouldn't be burdened by estate tax. Instead, the estate tax is imposed at the death of the surviving spouse, that is, **your** death.*

Since a good number of estates exceed $1,000,000, it is important that spouses plan together in order to fully utilize their respective

Applicable Exclusion Amount. *A properly planned estate for a married couple allows the couple to leave up to $2 million to the next generation free of Federal estate tax.* To accomplish this result, and gain the full benefit of each spouse's Applicable Exclusion Amount, each spouse must prepare a revocable trust during his or her lifetime. Each trust is drafted to allow the surviving spouse nearly full access to the trust assets during the surviving spouse's lifetime, without having the trust assets included in the surviving spouse's estate.

As the Applicable Exclusion Amount goes up over the next several years due to recent legislation, you may not need to each have a trust. A joint trust may suffice. However, you should be aware that future changes in the estate tax law could also reduce the Applicable Exclusion Amount, or halt its increase. For those in second marriages who want to lock in their children's inheritance, a two trust arrangement may be necessary.

If you didn't do any estate planning while your spouse was alive and your spouse left you more than the Applicable Exclusion Amount, you will have to play catch-up. With your spouse gone, more sophisticated estate planning strategies will be required to reduce your estate tax liability. They include outright gifts to your children and grandchildren, use of irrevocable trusts, family limited liability companies, as well as a number of charitable options described below. These more sophisticated estate planning techniques are discussed in Chapter Ten: "Advanced Estate Planning."

The following chart illustrates the scheduled increases in the Applicable Exclusion Amount between the years 2001 and 2010. If your estate exceeds these figures, or if your late spouse has a trust and your combined estate exceeds two times the figure shown for the year of your spouse's death, estate tax will be owed at your death unless you take action.

For decedents dying and gifts made during the year:	Applicable Exclusion Amount
2001	675,000
2002 and 2003	1,000,000
2004 and 2005	1,500,000
2006 and 2008	2,000,000
2009	3, 500,000
2010 and after	0

The starting point in determining whether you exceed the taxable limit is to determine your "gross estate." Items included in your gross estate include all property in which you have a beneficial interest at the time of death. The most obvious examples are cash, stocks, bonds, real estate, business interests, artwork and other personal tangible property. The following is a more complete list of property included in your gross estate:

Tangible
- Cash (dividends, etc.)
- Cars and other vehicles (including boats and recreation vehicles)
- Precious metals, jewelry and furs
- Antiques, collectiblest and works of art
- Household goods, clothing

Real Estate

- All homes, condominiums, time shares, business and investment properties, as well as undeveloped and agricultural land.

Intangible
- Stocks and bonds
- Savings and Checking Accounts
- Money Market and Certificates of Deposit
- Mutual Funds
- Vested interest in profit sharing and other miscellaneous plan, stock options, 401(k) and personal property, IRA Plans, etc.
- Life insurance
- Trademarks and royalties/ partnerships/sole proprietorships/corporations
- Miscellaneous receivables (mortgages, promissory mortgages, promissory notes, promissory notes, rents due)

The full **face** value of life insurance is included in your estate if you maintained any "incidents of ownership" over the policy, such as the right to change the beneficiary or borrow from the policy. To avoid estate tax, it may be advisable to own life insurance in an irrevocable trust (see "Irrevocable Trusts" in Chapter Ten). An irrevocable trust separates you from any incidents of ownership in the policy, thereby excluding the proceeds from your estate.

The full value of your IRA, 401(k) and other retirement plan is included in your estate. Distributions from these plans are **also** subject to income tax. The possibility of double taxation on retirement type assets requires special planning described in Chapter Six.

Debts and certain expenses are subtracted from your gross estate to arrive at your "adjusted gross estate." Further deductions reduce the adjusted gross estate to arrive at the taxable estate. The tentative tax is computed using tables provided by the IRS. The tentative tax is then reduced by your unified credit. *The practical effect of all of these calculations and manipulations is that the first $1,000,000 (2002) of your taxable estate can be left to your beneficiaries tax-free.* The estate tax begins to apply only to the extent your taxable estate exceeds $1,000,000 (in 2002). The following diagram illustrates the circuitous journey from the gross estate to the estate tax due.

Gross Estate
(Funeral and Administrative)
(indebtedness and taxes)
(losses)
Adjusted Gross Estate
(Marital Deduction)
(Charitable deductions)
Taxable Estate
x (times) Tax rate %
Tentative Tax
(Unified Credit)
(State death tax credit)
Estate tax due

Gifting

You may make gifts of up to ten thousand ($10,000) dollars per calendar year per beneficiary gift tax free. The right to make annual tax-free gifts is known as the "annual exclusion." The tax code does not limit the number of beneficiaries to whom gifts can be made nor does it require that the recipient ("donee") be related to the person making the gift ("donor"). Gifts may be made in cash or other property. Non-cash gifts are valued at their fair market value on the date gifted.

There is an **unlimited** exclusion (in addition to the $10,000 annual gift tax exclusion) for direct payment of a donee's medical expenses or tuition. Both the medical and educational exclusions are allowed without regard to the relationship between donor and donee, meaning the recipient need not be related to you. However, the payment must be made directly to the school, doctor or hospital that provides the service. The "unlimited marital deduction" allows unlimited gifts between spouses, as long as the donee spouse is a U.S. citizen. Unlimited gifts may be made to charities, even though there is a limit on their deductibility for income tax purposes.

If annual gifts to a single donor (other than a spouse or charity) exceed $10,000, the gift tax exclusion covers the first $10,000 and the excess is "taxable." However, rather than having to pay tax on the excess, taxable gifts reduce your Applicable Exclusion Amount dollar for dollar.

The following example shows the effect of taxable gifts on the Applicable Exclusion Amount:

> Mary gifts her son, Sam, $40,000 in calendar year 2001. The portion of the gift that exceeds $10,000 ($30,000) is a taxable gift. Accordingly, Mary's Applicable Exclusion Amount is reduced by the amount of the taxable gift, to $970,000 ($1,000,000 - $30,000). Thus, Mary may leave $970,000 free of estate tax at the time of her death.

To qualify for the annual $10,000 exclusion, a gift must be of a "present interest." A present interest is defined as the current right of a donee to the unrestricted enjoyment of the gifted asset. For example, Mary's $10,000 outright gift to her son Sam, described above, would qualify for the gift tax exclusion. However, a transfer of $10,000 in trust for Sam to be distributed to Sam at a future date, would not qualify as a gift of a present interest, since Sam would have no present right to the gift. Sam would have only a future interest in the property. Sam's gift could have been converted to a present interest had Mary's trust contained a "Crummey" provision (see "Irrevocable Trusts," in Chapter Ten).

The Economic Growth and Tax Reconciliation Act of 2001 increased the amount of lifetime taxable gifts you may make to $1,000,000. Unlike changes in the estate tax that would increase the amount one may leave at death to $1,500,000, then $2,000,000 then $3,500,000 followed by repeal of the estate tax, the limit on taxable gifts is not scheduled to increase beyond $1,000,000.

Special Needs Trusts

Disabled Children

Parents with disabled children face special estate planning challenges. The cost of supporting disabled children, especially ones with severe disabilities, is typically well beyond the financial means of most parents. They must rely on government programs to at least supplement the care they themselves are able to provide.

All but the wealthiest families must rely on government support to care for their disabled children. Supplemental Security Income (SSI), Medicaid, Medicare, and Social Security Disability Insurance (SSDI), though minimal, provide core support to disabled children. Eligibility for these programs is conditioned on both the child's incompetency as well as financial need.

It is not advisable to leave an outright inheritance to a disabled child or grandchild since it would disqualify the child from government benefits. The child's inheritance would have to be exhausted (to no more than $2,000 in most cases) before the child would again be eligible for government support. The disabled child, having lost his or her inheritance, would be worse off than when his or her parents were alive, since the safety net provided by the disabled child's parents would be gone. Only poverty level government benefits would remain.

The planning device that best addresses the needs of disabled children is known as a "special needs trust" (SNT) or "amenities trust." These trusts make inherited assets available to a disabled child without disqualifying the child from government benefits. Basically, a SNT directs the trustee to hold and administer trust assets to supplement, rather than replace, government benefits available to a disabled child. As a result, assets held in a properly drafted SNT are not considered part of the child's resources for SSI purposes.

To avoid disqualification, a SNT must provide that 1) expenditures from the trust are wholly within the discretion of the trustee and the beneficiary does not have the right to demand either income or principal; and 2) the trust cannot be used to provide for basic needs such as food, clothing or shelter.

Elderly Parents

Special needs trusts may also be used to provide for elderly parents. Monies left outright to aging parents will quickly disqualify them from Medicaid benefits. If you wish to provide for your parents in your estate plan, you should do so through a special needs trust. If you predecease them, your bequest will be used to supplement rather than disqualify them, from government benefits.

Jim, a fifty-five year old husband and father of two pre-teen children died leaving two parents in a nursing home. He had named his parents as beneficiary on life insurance policies totaling several hundred thousand dollars, thinking that as an only child it was his responsibility to care for his parents. Unfortunately, Jim's wife was not aware that Jim had left his life insurance to his parents. She stood by helplessly as money she could have used to raise her children was instead used to disqualify her in-laws from government benefits. Only after the life insurance proceeds were totally exhausted did the in-laws begin to receive Medicaid benefits. Had Jim used a SNT, Medicaid would have paid for his parent's basic care (with the money in trust used for specialized medical and dental care, clothing, and other non-government provided benefits). At the death of her in-laws, Jim's wife could have used the balance remaining in the SNT to raise her children.

Chapter Ten

Advanced Estate Planning

P. Mark Accettura, Esq.

THE TOPICS DISCUSSED in Chapter Nine apply to anyone considering an estate plan. The topics discussed in this Chapter Ten apply predominantly to individuals with a gross estate in excess of the Applicable Exclusion Amount (see "Planning to Avoid Estate Tax" in Chapter Nine). Even with the changes brought by the Economic Growth and Tax Reconciliation Act of 2001, the techniques discussed in this chapter are still useful. The changes in the estate tax law have a sunset provision. They will expire on December 31, 2010, unless reenacted by Congress and signed by the President before that date. Who knows what the politics will be in the future, especially if economic conditions worsen. There are also non-tax reasons for using these techniques such as transferring control of assets or family businesses to the next generation in an orderly manner, or tying up assets to prevent frivolous spending.

As noted in Chapter Nine, the **face amount** of life insurance is included in your estate. Irrevocable life insurance trusts are used to exclude the value of life insurance assets from the estate of the insured. If simply removing the life insurance from your estate will lower the value of your estate to be below the Applicable Exclusion Amount no further estate planning may be necessary. If, after excluding life insurance, you still have a taxable estate, consider implementing a family limited liability company to make structured gifts to family members and loved ones. Finally, irrespective of the size of your estate, consider making charitable transfers to fulfill your social contract.

Irrevocable Trusts

Life insurance provides liquidity to larger estates. At death, life insurance proceeds are available to satisfy the immediate needs of your family, as well as any estate tax (due within nine months of the decedent's death) that may be due. Unfortunately, the face value of life insurance is included in your gross estate, exposing the proceeds to estate tax. The solution is to create an irrevocable trust to be both the owner and beneficiary of the policy.

Irrevocable trusts are a valuable estate planning tool for larger estates. They are used to remove assets like life insurance from estates that would otherwise be taxable. Unlike revocable trusts, which may be amended or revoked at any time during the grantor's lifetime, irrevocable trusts may not be amended or revoked. Also, unlike revocable trusts, the grantor of an irrevocable trust may never act as trustee. Thus, once established, the grantor of an irrevocable trust relinquishes complete benefit and control of the trust.

As noted in Chapter Nine, your taxable estate consists of assets over which you exercise control at the time of your death. By relinquishing all such control in an irrevocable trust, you are able to exclude handpicked assets from federal estate tax. To avoid having the irrevocable trust assets leech back into your estate, you must also permanently forego the benefit or use of irrevocable trust assets. *Accordingly, when selecting assets to contribute to an irrevocable trust, you must select assets over which you are willing to permanently relinquish all control or enjoyment.* Life insurance makes an attractive irrevocable trust asset, since the true value of life insurance is not realized until your death. Consequently, the fact that the policy is outside your control has little economic impact on you during your life.

To avoid adverse gift tax consequences, strict procedures must be followed when making life insurance premium payments. Since the irrevocable trust is the owner of the policy, premium payments are no longer your responsibility. They become the responsibility of the trustee. Gifts of cash must be made to the irrevocable trust to allow the trustee to make premium payments. Transfers to the irrevocable trust are considered gifts to others since by definition you cannot be a beneficiary.

As noted in Chapter Nine, you may make gifts of $10,000 per beneficiary per year without incurring gift tax. However, in order to qualify for the gift tax exclusion, gifts must be of a "present interest." For a gift to be of a present interest, the beneficiary must be able to enjoy the gift currently. A transfer of life insurance premium payments to an Irrevocable Life Insurance Trust ("ILIT") is not by itself a gift of a present interest, since the beneficiaries of a typical ILIT don't receive a right to trust assets until the death of the grantor. However, gifts in trust are converted from future to present interest transfers by a device known as a "Crummey Notice."

A Crummey Notice is given to all ILIT beneficiaries contemporaneously with each contribution to the ILIT. The Crummey Notice notifies each beneficiary of his or her right to withdraw his or her prorata share of the contribution. Under the terms of the ILIT and the Crummey Notice, if such right of withdrawal is not exercised within thirty days, it lapses. Despite numerous attacks by the IRS, the courts have consistently upheld the Crummey Notice as a valid means of qualifying gifts to an irrevocable trust as present interest gifts. The following is a sample Crummey Notice:

CRUMMEY NOTICE

Please be advised that a contribution in the amount of $_____ Dollars has been paid over to the _____ Irrevocable Trust dated _____, 2001. You have the right within thirty (30) days of your receipt of this letter to contact _____, the Grantor of the Irrevocable Trust and request that your prorata share of the contribution to the Irrevocable Trust be paid to you. At the expiration of the thirty (30) day period, you will no longer be entitled to make such demand. Should you have any questions, please contact the undersigned.

_____
"Grantor"

Dated:

WAIVER OF WITHDRAWAL

I acknowledge receipt of this Crummey Notice. I waive my right to demand withdrawal of this gift from the trust. I do not waive my right to subsequent gifts made to the trust.

Dated: _____

It is the responsibility of the ILIT trustee to make annual life insurance premium payments. The insured/grantor should **not** make premium payments directly to the insurance company (bypassing the ILIT), as this could cause inclusion of the proceeds of the policy in the insured/grantor's estate at death. Instead, once the 30 day Crummey Notice period has lapsed (presumably no beneficiary has elected to withdraw his or her share of the annual contribution), the ILIT trustee may then make the annual premium payment to the insurance company. Note that it is inadvisable to name either the grantor or the grantor's spouse as trustee of the ILIT. As trustees, the grantor or grantor's spouse would have powers considered to be "incidents of ownership," causing the life insurance proceeds to be included in their estates. Accordingly, it is common practice to appoint other ILIT beneficiaries (such as grantor's children) as Trustee.

The complex operation of an ILIT, and the flow of premium payments is summarized by the following illustration:

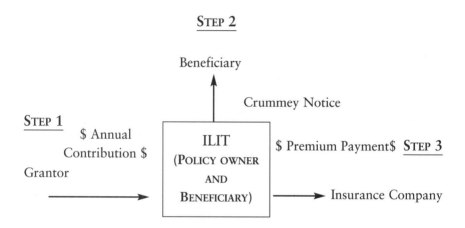

Family Limited Liability Companies

Whether through outright gift, transfers in trust, or charitable transfers, reducing estate tax liability involves some sort of gifting. The $10,000 dollar, per beneficiary, annual gift tax exclusion allows for substantial annual gifts. Assuming you begin a systematic gifting program early enough in life, significant estate tax reduction can be achieved over time. Not only are the gifted assets removed from your estate, but the future appreciation of the gifted assets is removed as well.

Having lost a spouse and experiencing your economic future as somewhat uncertain, you may be hesitant to make large gifts. You may not want to part with cash you believe you may need for a rainy day. You may be concerned that outright gifts to your children or other beneficiaries will negatively affect their work ethic. Or, you may simply not have sufficient **liquid** assets to make substantial cash gifts each year.

Most, if not all, of your gifting concerns can be addressed by using a Limited Liability Company ("LLC") as a gifting vehicle. Limited Liability Companies are relatively new. They offer the liability protection of a corporation but are taxed as a partnership. LLC owners are called "members," and their ownership is expressed as a percentage. Like shareholders in a corporation, members' liability is limited **to the extent of their investment in the LLC.** Members share in LLC profits and loss in direct proportion to their ownership.

Limited liability companies created for gifting purposes are often called "family" LLCs. Most family LLCs provide for the appointment of a manager who controls the day-to-day operation of the LLC. Naturally, you would appoint yourself as the manager to allow you to control investment of LLC assets as well as disbursement of LLC income and principal. Exclusive management authority allows you to make gifts without relinquishing control of the gifted assets.

To create an LLC, Articles of Organization must be filed with your state's Corporations and Securities Bureau. The initial LLC members then execute an Operating Agreement that sets forth the names and ownership interests of all members, appoints a manager, and establishes the rules of operation for the LLC. Once these steps have been completed, you can begin to transfer selected assets to the LLC. During your life, you act as manager, retaining full control of company stock, real estate, or other assets transferred to the LLC. After death, the successor manager appointed by you in the Operating Agreement implements the terms of the LLC to provide structure among the competing interests of your beneficiaries. Tension, and even outright conflict often manifest after the death of the family patriarch or matriarch. Such family disputes can be minimized by clearly defining ownership and authority succession in your LLC.

LLCs are the preferred vehicle for gifting business, investment and real estate assets. It is difficult if not impossible to divide a shopping mall, family farm, or apartment building into precise fractional shares. However, if such hard to divide assets are first transferred to an LLC, precise membership interests can be calculated and easily gifted. Once transferred, the LLC provides for the orderly management of the property by its appointed manager (you). As an added bonus, substantial gift tax "discounts" (discussed below) are available when LLC interests are gifted.

LLC interests, once gifted, are insulated from the claims of outside creditors. Unlike outright gifts, LLC gifts are relatively secure from the claims of your children's spouses and creditors. The LLC Operating Agreement prohibits members from making voluntary transfers and severely limits involuntary transfers due to the bankruptcy, divorce or insolvency of a member. Such events trigger an automatic "buy back" under the Agreement for a nominal price. Buyback may not even be necessary. The inherent lack of marketability of LLC interests make them unattractive to outside creditors. Even if a creditor were able to acquire a member's share, the creditor would only be an assignee, and as such would not be eligible to participate in LLC activity or management.

As a "pass through" entity, LLCs pay no tax. Instead, items of income and loss pass through to the members in proportion to their ownership interest, and are taxed at the member's marginal tax rate. As a separate entity, the LLC must file annual income tax returns (IRS Form 1065). Each member's share of income and loss is calculated on Schedule K1 of Form 1065, which must be given to members by January 31 of the following year. As a practical matter, members cannot file their personal income tax returns until they have received a copy of their K1.

LLCs are the preferred gifting vehicle for all gifts except gifts of life insurance (which should be made to an ILIT). While the manager of an LLC may both manage and enjoy LLC assets, the grantor of an irrevocable trust may neither retain an interest in the trust nor act as Trustee. While an irrevocable trust cannot be amended, modified or revoked, an LLC may be amended as circumstances change.

Valuation is a critical issue in gift and estate tax. In fact, the majority of gift and estate tax audits involve valuation issues. To avoid IRS problems, all gifts must be valued. For gifts of cash and publicly traded securities, the value of the gift can easily be determined. However, gifts of real estate and business interests require that you obtain a written appraisal from a licensed appraiser. If the gift is an interest in an LLC, determining value is a two-part analysis. First, the LLC's assets must be valued, and then the membership interests must be valued. Interestingly, the member's pro rata share of LLC assets is only the starting point in determining the value of the member's interest. A discount must then be applied to account for the member's lack of participation in management ("minority discount"), and the restrictions on transferability imposed by the operating agreement ("marketability discount"). The courts have reasoned that an outside purchaser would pay less to acquire the membership interest than to acquire the underlying LLC assets directly.

Valuation discounts allow you to make larger annual gifts. For example, a thirty five percent (35%) discount allows you to make a 35% larger gift within the annual gift tax exclusion. In the long run, the ability to make larger annual gifts can dramatically reduce your estate tax liability. The earlier gifts are made the better, since future appreciation of LLC assets will be owned by your beneficiaries instead of by you. The following example illustrates the operation of LLCs and the benefit of valuation discounts:

> Mary wishes to give her four children an interest in her water-front vacation home worth $1,000,000. Mary creates a limited liability company to which she transfers the vacation home. Mary appoints herself as manager. Without a valuation discount, Mary could transfer a 1% LLC interest to each of her children, representing a gift of $10,000 (1% x $1,000,000), all of which is sheltered from tax by Mary's annual gift tax exclusion. Since Mary's children are acquiring minority interests, and are subject to the transfer restrictions imposed by Mary in the LLC Operating Agreement, Mary is eligible for a valuation discount on the gifted interests.
>
> A 35% valuation discount (readily acceptable by the IRS in such circumstances) allows Mary to gift $15,385 ($10,000 gift exclusion ÷ (1 -.35)) annually to each child. Accordingly, Mary could make larger tax-free gifts of 1.538% to each child, retaining a 93.8 % interest in the LLC after the gift. Using the LLC, Mary is able to gift precise fractional interests in the vacation home annually. She also retains full con-

trol of the vacation home after the transfer, which would not have been the case if Mary had simply added her children to the deed as joint owners.

Mary would be advised to annually gift LLC membership interests until she gave away all but one (1%) percent of her interest in the LLC. Since in our example it would take Mary 16 years to gift 99% of her interest, she should consider gifts to grandchildren and other family members as well as making taxable gifts.

Charitable Transfers

Charitable transfers generate an income tax deduction if made during life (inter vivos gifts), and are deductible for estate tax purposes when made at death (testamentary transfers). The advantage of inter vivos gifts over testamentary transfers is that they are tax deductible for income tax purposes, and also remove the gifted asset from your estate. Lifetime gifts can substantially reduce the tax bite of high-income taxpayers with large estates. Apart from the obvious tax benefits associated with charitable giving, charitable transfers also fulfill your "social contract" by subsidizing programs, scholarships and other charitable endeavors that advance the charitable causes you support.

There are as many reasons for making charitable gifts, as there are charitable givers. Whether you want to give to charity in order to give something back to your community, for religious reasons, to better society, to repay an institution or cause that made a difference in your life, or just because you were brought up that way, why not give in a way that allows both the charity **and** you to benefit?

There are a myriad of options and gifting vehicles available to anyone with a charitable bent. Naturally, gifts can be made in cash. You may also gift personal property, appreciated stock, and real estate. The federal tax code also permits, and even promotes, a wide variety of gifting vehicles discussed below.

A charitable deduction is available for contributions to "501(c)(3)" organizations; which include churches, educational institutions, foundations and other organizations promoting charitable works. The philosophy behind the deduction is that taxpayers should be encouraged to support organizations engaged in charitable works that the government would otherwise be forced to provide.

To promote gifting, a number of "split interest" trust options are available. All split interests involve the division of the gifted assets into two component parts: income and principal. The most common split interest gifts allow you to retain the income from the gifted asset for a period of years or your lifetime with the charity receiving the remaining principal at your death. "Charitable remainder trusts," "pooled income funds" and "charitable gift annuities" fall into this category. "Charitable lead trusts," by contrast, reverse the sharing of income and principal, allowing the **charity** to enjoy the income from the gifted asset for **your** life, with your family owning the gifted asset outright at your death. You will need the assistance of an estate planning attorney to help choose the appropriate gifting vehicle for you. Most established charities have a planned giving professional on staff who can also provide valuable information.

Split interest gifts allow you a current income tax charitable deduction without requiring you to forfeit the entire enjoyment of the gifted asset. You give the charity future ownership and retain the income for a period of years (not exceeding 20) or life. Your charitable deduction is less than the fair market value of the gift since the charity cannot immediately enjoy the gift. A somewhat complicated calculation of the present value of the gift must be made to determine your income tax deduction (see below).

Charitable Remainder Trusts

Charitable remainder trusts ("CRT") are the most common gift splitting vehicle. Highly appreciated assets that have been transferred to a CRT can be sold tax-free, solving the problem faced by older taxpayers who are often saddled with highly appreciated assets that cannot be sold without substantial capital gains. Without a CRT, the standard of living of such individuals can suffer if the highly appreciated assets are not income generating. Despite their high net worth, people in this predicament have no spendable income.

The CRT itself is exempt from income tax, and therefore can sell highly appreciated property tax-free. After the transfer to the CRT, and the subsequent sale, the entire proceeds of the sale (undiminished by income tax) are available to pay an annual income.

You are entitled to a percentage (which must be at least 5%) of the value of the trust assets as valued on the first day of the year. Since the value of trust assets fluctuate, your income interest will change from year to year. CRT distributions are taxable to you to the extent that the CRT has income. The character of the income is the same as in the hands of the CRT. Distributions are first considered ordinary income, then capital gains, then tax-exempt income, and finally tax-free return of principal. The following example illustrates the use and operation of a CRT:

Assume that Mary (70 years old) has a substantial estate. She owns highly appreciated non-income producing stock worth $100,000 for which she only paid $5,000. If Mary were to sell the stock she would have a $95,000 capital gain. Hearing of the benefits of CRTs, Mary contributes the stock to a CRT. She elects to retain an 8% annual income interest for the balance of her lifetime. Based on tables provided by the IRS, Mary is entitled to a whopping $39,845 charitable income tax deduction (see chart) in the year the CRT is created.

In the first year, Mary will receive a distribution of approximately $8,000 (8% of $100,000) prorated to the extent the first year is not a full twelve-months. Mary, as Trustee of the CRT, will sell portions of the CRT stock as needed to pay herself her annual 8% amount. The sale of the appreciated stock by the CRT is not taxable to the CRT since it is tax exempt. The $8,000 received by Mary will be taxable to her as a capital gain since the trust had only capital gains. Note that if the CRT had ordinary income, the distribution to Mary would first be treated as ordinary income to the extent of the CRT's ordinary income, with the excess treated as capital gains.

The actual dollar figure distributed to Mary will change from year to year depending on the fair market value of the CRT on January 1 of each year.

The table below illustrates the income tax deduction available to an individual creating a CRT. The calculation assumes a $100K contribution. The deduction depends on the age of the donor and the income interest retained.

AGE

		50	60	70	80
	10%	11,405	20,262	33,042	49,860
RETAINED	9%	13,381	22,938	36,213	53,002
INCOME INTEREST	8%	15,890	26,159	39,845	56,441
	7%	19,107	30,062	44,020	60,210

Pooled Income fund

Pooled income funds are another type of split-interest gift. Unlike CRT's that are established by the donor, pooled income funds are created and operated by charities. Gifts to a pooled income fund are merged with the gifts of other donors, and, in that respect, closely resemble a mutual fund. As with CRTs, you are entitled to a deduction in the year of contribution. The charitable deduction is based on your age and the funds highest rate of earnings in the previous three years. You give money or property to the fund in exchange for fund units, which entitle you to a pro rata share of the fund's actual income each year for the remainder of your life. At your death, your share of the fund passes outright to the charity.

Gift Annuity

In a charitable gift annuity, you make a gift to charity in exchange for a guaranteed income for life. A charitable gift annuity is very much like buying an annuity in the commercial marketplace, except that you get an immediate charitable deduction equal to the excess of the contribution over what the annuity is worth, based on IRS tables.

Unlike the pooled income fund or CRT, income from the charitable gift annuity is an obligation of the charity that does not depend on investment results. The rate of return on the gift annuity is not variable, as in a pooled income fund, or negotiable, as in a CRT. As with any annuity, a portion of each year's annuity payment is tax-free allowing you to recover your "investment in the contract" over your life expectancy. The simplicity of charitable gift annuities allows for much lower contribution limits, typically in increments of five thousand ($5,000) dollars (depending on the charity). You may realize capital gain if appreciated assets are transferred to the charity to purchase the annuity.

Charitable Lead Trusts

A charitable lead trust is a CRT in reverse: the charitable beneficiary is entitled to the current *income* with the non-charitable beneficiary entitled to the remainder. The general rules of CRT's apply to charitable lead trusts with the exception that there is no requirement that the payout rate be a minimum of 5%. Charitable lead trusts are primarily used to save estate and gift taxes, and do not provide the same income tax saving opportunities as CRT's. To accomplish this result, you must postpone the receipt of the trust assets by your family until the charitable lead interest of the charity has expired.

Wealth Replacement Trust

If you fear that making substantial gifts will deprive your children of their inheritance, you should consider a "wealth replacement trust." Notwithstanding the bumper sticker credo, "I'm spending my children's inheritance," most parents want their children to be properly remembered. Fortunately, the needs of the family can be accomplished by creating a "wealth replacement trust" concurrently with the split interest trust.

A wealth replacement trust allows you to leave a substantially larger **tax free** inheritance to children. Here's how it works: basically, a portion of the income distributed to you from your CRT is used to purchase a life insurance policy inside a wealth replacement trust (which is simply an irrevocable trust). At your death, the charity receives the assets remaining in the CRT, and your family receives the life insurance proceeds from the wealth replacement trust. The net effect of this arrangement is as follows: 1. You get a substantial income tax deduction in the year you create the CRT. 2. Your taxable estate is reduced by the gift. 3. The charities of your choosing receive bequests at your death. 4. Your children receive tax-free life insurance proceeds. The following diagram illustrates the use of a CRT in combination with a wealth replacement trust:

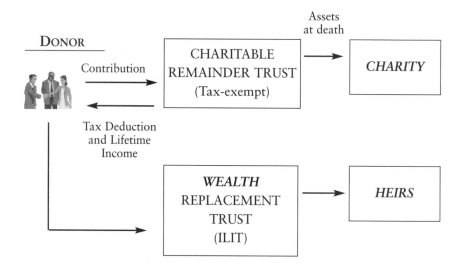

Chapter Eleven

Prenuptial Agreements

P. Mark Accettura, Esq.

IT IS ONLY natural to miss the intimacy and companionship of a good marriage. The growing number of mature singles, combined with our changing attitudes about marriage, contributes to a growing marriage rate among the mature. If you are considering marriage, congratulations! However, before you send out wedding invitations or purchase the Hawaiian honeymoon package, you need to consider what would happen if the marriage doesn't work out, or you die.

The fact that nearly half of all marriages in this country end in divorce is well publicized. Interestingly, the divorce rate in second marriages is substantially higher at nearly 60%. Essentially, the stresses that contribute to divorce among the mature are no different than those of the general population. Added concerns for mature couples include determining who is responsible for the cost of an extended illness or long-term nursing home care. Further, in the event of your death, you must be careful to balance the needs of your spouse with those of your children or other loved ones.

From a moral or philosophical standpoint, your children are not "owed" anything at your death. However, if you love your children you need to keep their interests in mind as you enter your new marriage. Stories of children who have lost a parent and are left to wonder whether their stepparent will leave them anything are legion. Such children are left with a legacy of pain, hurt, and mistrust. At the same time, the needs of a surviving spouse should not be ignored. He or she should be treated with respect and dignity. With proper planning, you can accommodate the needs and allay the fears of all parties. By clearly establishing the entitlements of your spouse and children, you will create an environment where all parties can get along.

Certainly, the stakes are higher in a second marriage. Your net worth is likely to be significantly higher than it was when you first married. You also have far fewer years to rebound from a financial setback such as divorce. Fortunately, you can protect yourself and your family with a little advance planning. What is required is an open and frank discussion about financial matters prior to marriage. Although such discussions may be somewhat awkward, it is important to identify sensitive issues before they ripen into full-blown conflict after marriage. It has been said that money is the last thing that people talk about before marriage and the first thing they fight about after the wedding. In fact, approximately 70% of all divorced couples cite disagreement over financial matters as the reason for the demise of their marriage. Rather than leaving your financial future to chance, you should commit your financial understanding to writing in a "prenuptial agreement," and your revocable trust should be consistent with the terms set out in your prenuptial agreement. The combination of these documents will ensure that your lifetime and post mortem wishes are realized.

All fifty states now recognize the validity of prenuptial agreements that meet the following general conditions: (1) the agreement must be in writing; (2) each party must make full disclosure of his and her personal financial information, including assets and income; (3) each party must be represented by separate independent legal counsel; (4) the agreement must be voluntarily entered into without fraud, mistake or duress (to prevent the appearance of duress, the prenuptial agreement should be executed before wedding invitations are sent out); and (5) the agreement must be fair when entered into.

Prenuptial agreements override state law with respect to the division of property both in divorce and at death. This is important considering that state laws grant significant rights to spouses. In divorce and at death, your spouse could be entitled to up to one-half of your estate. Worse, depending on how your assets are titled and beneficiaries designated, your spouse could be entitled to your **entire** estate at death.

In your prenuptial agreement, you can agree as to who is responsible for ordinary day-to-day living expenses as well as extraordinary expenses such as long-term care. Through full disclosure, you can clearly identify the owner of all assets and the responsible party on all indebtedness. At death, you can agree to divide your estate as you wish. For example, you might agree to leave all of your assets to your respective children at death, and little, if any, to your spouse. This might be the case where you each brought substantial assets to the marriage. Absent a prenuptial agreement, state law would grant your spouse the right to take his or her "marital share" of your estate (see Chapter Seven), at the expense of your children. Alternatively, you might agree to leave some of your assets, like your principal residence, outright to your spouse, with the balance to be held in trust for your surviving spouse's lifetime use. Under this scenario, the remaining trust assets would pass to your children at your spouse's subsequent death.

You might provide your surviving spouse with access to some or all of your assets after death to allow him or her to maintain the lifestyle you enjoyed together. If that is the case, the shared assets should be held in trust and an appropriate successor trustee appointed to oversee investment and disbursement of trust assets. A trust allows for the use of your assets after death without granting the survivor an ownership interest in trust assets. As noted in Chapter Seven, the trustee you appoint has a fiduciary obligation to strictly apply the terms of the trust. Typically, the trustee has wide discretion in making distributions of income and principal.

It may be appropriate for the surviving spouse to act as successor trustee. That would be the case in long-term second marriages, or second marriages where the spouse has a parent-like relationship with children not of the marriage. On the other hand, a new spouse may not be a suitable successor trustee considering the broad discretion granted under the terms of the trust. It could prove quite costly to rein in a spouse/trustee who is mismanaging trust assets. To avoid trust mismanagement and potential conflict between family members and the spouse, a neutral third party, like a bank or brokerage house trust department, should be considered as trustee. If you do not favor corporate trustees, you might make your spouse a co-trustee with another family member. Since you will both be bound by the same prenuptial agreement and will likely each have your own revocable trust, you will have to agree on a solution suitable to both of you, since "what's good for the goose, is good for the gander."

The trust you create should be qualified as a Qualified Terminal Interest Property ("QTIP") trust. QTIP trusts, discussed in detail in Chapter Seven, were created during the Reagan administration specifically to address second marriage situations. A QTIP trust allows the surviving spouse to enjoy the income and principal of the marital trust (a sub-trust for larger estates discussed in Chapter Seven in detail) during his or her lifetime, with no power to appoint the balance remaining in the marital trust at his or her later death. The result is that the you may provide for your surviving spouse, and at the same time be assured that the balance of the marital trust assets remaining at the surviving spouse's death will pass to your children. As an added bonus, QTIP trusts also save estate tax.

Special planning is required for retirement plan (such as company sponsored pension, profit sharing and 401(k) plans, and IRAs) assets. As noted in Chapter Six, retirement plan accumulations are subject to **both** income and estate tax. To achieve the best income and estate tax result, it is usually advisable to name your surviving spouse as the primary beneficiary of retirement benefits. Although naming your surviving spouse produces the best income tax result, naming your spouse as primary beneficiary in a second marriage situation may defeat the interests of your children. As primary beneficiary, your spouse could simply roll the retirement plan assets over into his or her own IRA and name a new beneficiary of his or her choice. Choosing a retirement plan beneficiary necessarily involves a tradeoff between the best possible income tax result, and assurance that your children will inherit the retirement plan proceeds. In light of the complex legal and tax issues involved, you should consult with an estate planning attorney before naming your beneficiary.

Special language **must** be included in the prenuptial agreement to waive an interest in a company retirement plan. Federal law grants spouses special rights that can only be waived after marriage. Since, by definition, prenuptial agreements are executed prior to marriage, a waiver of company retirement benefits in the prenuptial agreement is not effective. To make the waiver effective, the spouses must agree in the prenuptial agreement to affirmatively waive such rights after marriage.

Even if you marry without a prenuptial agreement, you may be able to accomplish your objectives with a "postnuptial" agreement. In most states, the same rules that apply to prenuptial agreements also apply to postnuptial agreements.

Chapter Twelve

Losing Independence
P. Mark Accettura, Esq.

As YOU MOVE forward, you should plan for the possibility that at some point you may not be able to live independently. Advances in medical science have greatly increased the likelihood that we will live beyond the point that we are able to care for ourselves. You may not be able to rely on your children, whose own personal obligations may make them unable or unwilling to provide for your care. As the old saying goes, "One parent can take care of ten children, but ten children cannot care for one parent." The statistics on aging and long term care are compelling. One in five Americans older than 65, and nearly half of those older than 85, will need assistance with everyday activities. Fifty percent of women and 30% of men over age 65 will require long-term care during their lives. Despite these statistics, nearly 60% of Americans have given "very little thought" or "no thought at all" as to whether and when they will need long term care.

The greatest concern for older Americans is that their entire wealth accumulation will be dissipated if they experience an extended stay in a skilled nursing care facility. According to a recent report, the average cost of a year in a nursing home is approximately

$45,000 a year, roughly equating to $125 per day. Since 1990, the cost of long-term care has increased at an annual average rate of 3% above the overall rate of inflation. Further, according to the New England Journal of Medicine, more than 50% of those who require 24-hour care will need such care for more than 2 ½ years.

Long-term care for the elderly has evolved to include various forms of home care and long term nursing home care, all of which are very expensive. Long-term care (LTC) ranges from help with day-to-day activities in the home (such as bathing, dressing, preparing meals, etc.) to more sophisticated services such as skilled nursing care. While typical health care services are cure oriented, long-term care involves treatment of chronic conditions and thus is said to be care oriented. Long term care can be provided in one's own home, an adult day care setting, in an assisted living/residential care facility, or a skilled nursing care facility.

The high cost of skilled nursing care is of special concern to "community spouses," that is, the non-institutionalized spouse of a skilled nursing care patient. Community spouses need assurance that their dependent spouse's care won't wipe them out financially. Whether or not you are married, the balance of this chapter will help you establish a plan to pay for long-term care without leaving you or your heirs penniless.

The primary sources of funding for the payment of LTC are: 1) Medicare; 2) private pay (including long term care insurance); and finally 3) Medicaid.

Medicare

Medicare covers LTC only under limited circumstances, and only for a limited period of time. Medicare will reimburse the cost of a stay in an approved skilled nursing facility which immediately follows a three-day or more hospital stay. Further, to be eligible, you must enter the skilled nursing facility within 30 days of your discharge from the hospital, and the skilled nursing facility stay must be for the same reason as the hospitalization.

Medicare only covers the first 100 days of the skilled nursing care stay, covering 100% percent of the cost of the first 20 days, and only the cost of the remaining 80 days to the extent that the cost **exceeds** $99.00. Slightly augmented coverage may be provided under private "medigap" coverage during the 100 day period, but medigap coverage does not otherwise cover LTC (see "Medigap" discussion in Chapter Three and Chapter Four).

The cost of LTC, after Medicare benefits are exhausted (if eligible at all), falls to the patient. The likelihood that you will have to pay privately is high, considering that Medicare paid only 10.6% of skilled nursing home cost in 1994. The patient will continue to be required to pay the cost of his or her own LTC until his or her assets are sufficiently exhausted to be eligible for **Medicaid**. Individuals with adequate means and who enjoy reasonably good health may insure against this potentiality by purchasing long term care insurance (see "Long Term Care" in Chapter Four).

SUMMARY OF MEDICARE SKILLED NURSING FACILITY COVERAGE

BENEFIT	MEDICARE PAYS	YOU PAY
First 20 days of Care	100% of Approved Amount	None of approved amount, but all of non-approved amount
Next 80 days of care	Only above $99.00 a day	Up to $99.00 a day
Beyond 100 days	Nothing	All Costs

Private Pay

Ultimately, you are responsible for the cost of your own long-term care. Medicare will cover a portion of the first 100 days after you leave the hospital, and Medicaid will cover the cost after you have depleted your personal assets. You are liable for the interim period. Depending on your assets, you entire net worth could be lost in the process. Do you have sufficient assets to cover the cost of your long-term care? You shouldn't rely on the government, since it only pays for subsistence level care through Medicaid. Nor should you rely on your children. If you are worried that you do not have sufficient assets, you should consider long-term care insurance discussed in Chapter Four. Even if you have sufficient assets for your care, you might nonetheless consider long term care insurance if you wish to preserve an estate for your children. Certain non-economic factors may also be at play. Were your parents or grandparents in a nursing home? Does Alzheimer's, dementia, or extreme longevity run in your family? These are questions you need to answer with the aid of your professional team.

Medicaid

Medicaid is a federally funded, state-administered welfare program restricted to the financially indigent. To qualify for Medicaid you must have exhausted substantially all of your non-exempt assets.

You are eligible for long-term care coverage under Medicaid if you are at least age 65, demonstrate financial need, and follow the Medicaid application procedures. With respect to financial need, you may have assets of no more than $2,000 and limited income. The following assets (sometimes referred to as "excluded assets") are not considered for purposes of the $2,000 limit:

1. Your automobile;
2. Your principal residence ("homestead");
3. Household goods, furniture and personal effects, including clothing and jewelry;
4. Up to $2,000 in a prepaid irrevocable funeral contract;
5. Cemetery plot;
6. Cash value of life insurance up to $1,500;
7. Income producing real property where the income derived from rents is at least 6% of the person's equity in the rented property;
8. An actuarially sound annuity (see Planning Techniques and Strategies, below); and
9. Miscellaneous other exemptions not relevant here.

With respect to **income**, there are two basic approaches depending on the state of your residence. In some states, if medical expenses exceed income, then the income test is met. Other states have strict income caps. In such states, if your income exceeds the limit set by the state, irrespective of your medical expenses, you are ineligible. Income is defined as both earned and unearned income and thus includes interest, dividends, rents, social security benefits and retirement benefits.

Clients often ask "How does the state know what we have?" The simple answer to this question is that you must file an Asset Declaration Form with the state and provide independent verification of the ownership and value of each asset and source of income.

Two of the most misunderstood and complicated aspects of Medicaid eligibility are the Divestment Rules and Spousal Impoverishment Rules.

Divestment

Gifting assets in order to qualify for Medicaid is called "divestment," and can be perilous. Recent legislation imposes sanctions on individuals (and their advisors) who divest assets in order to qualify for Medicaid. If you divest, you will be ineligible for Medicaid for a period of time illustrated in the example below. You may also make yourself unattractive to the very nursing homes to which you hope to gain entry. The more desirable facilities are either entirely private-pay, or allow a limited number of Medicaid patients. The Medicaid patients that are admitted typically start out as private-pay patients who have lived in the facility and have run out of money. In light of the national shortage of skilled nursing care facilities and beds, patients attempting entry as Medicaid patients from day one may only gain entry at the most undesirable facilities.

Divestment is the transfer of countable (i.e., non-excluded) assets for less than fair market value within (36) months of applying for Medicaid nursing home benefits. For transfers to or from a trust, a sixty (60) month look-back applies. It is important to understand that divestment does not occur if countable assets are converted to exempt assets of equal value. For example, paying off the mortgage on your home, buying a new car or purchasing an irrevocable funeral arrangement does not constitute divestment. The period of disqualification on account of divestment is measured by dividing the "uncompensated value" of the transferred assets by the average monthly private paid nursing home costs of the particular nursing home facility applied for.

> For example, if on the eve of entering a nursing home and applying for Medicaid, you give your son $120,000, you will be ineligible for Medicaid for thirty-two months ($120,000 divided by the average monthly cost of long-term care in your state ($3,750 is the national average in 2000)). There is no limit on the length of disqualification resulting from divestment.

Finally, a rule that appears to have no logical basis is that the transfer of one's **homestead** within the look-back period (unless the transfer is to a spouse or a disabled child) is considered a divestment. Transfer of exempted assets other than a homestead within the thirty-six (36) month period is not considered to be a divestment. Transfer of one's homestead to a revocable Trust is also considered a divestment.

Spousal Protection

In order to prevent the economic devastation of the community spouse, the Medicare Catastrophic Coverage Act enacted in 1988 treats the assets and income of a husband and wife as part of a common pot with the community spouse entitled to a guaranteed share. With respect to income, the community spouse's income may be supplemented from income of the resident spouse up to a minimum of $1,452 and a maximum of $2,175 per month in 2001. The community spouse is also entitled to one-half (1/2) of the countable assets (in addition to the excluded assets) not to exceed $87,000 but with a guaranteed minimum of $17,400. These values are indexed for inflation.

After the death of the patient, states are required to seek reimbursement for their outlay of long term care (Medicaid) benefits from the estate of the deceased Medicaid recipient. Some states define "estate" to include only the decedent's probate estate. Other states interpret the term estate more broadly to include jointly held property or even assets owned by the decedent's revocable trust. As of the date of this writing, only Michigan and Texas do not attempt to recover long-term Medicaid benefits from the estates of deceased recipients.

Planning Techniques and Strategies

There are several steps you can take to preserve your estate in the event you need long term nursing home care:

1. Purchase long term care insurance.
2. Hold on to your exempt assets, especially your home.
3. Convert counted assets into excluded assets. Examples include paying down the mortgage on your home, improving your home or acquiring a more expensive home.
4. Since the 6% income rule does not apply to homesteads, if you go into an nursing home, your home could be rented to family members for a very modest amount. Your family could in turn re-rent the property at the current fair market value rent. This arrangement would prevent all of the rental income from being treated as income eligible for nursing home care payment.
5. Investment real estate could be acquired (even a common tenancy in a family member's residence would qualify) as long as the 6% income to equity ratio is met.
6. Outright gifts and gifts to an Irrevocable or Testamentary Trust provide the greatest planning opportunity. Outright transfers more than thirty-six (36) months from the month in which application for Medicaid is made, or trusts more than sixty (60) months prior to such date are not counted for purposes of Medicaid eligibility. Use of trusts avoids an outright transfer of assets to family members who may dispose of the assets in a fashion unacceptable to you.
7. Consider monthly gifts in what has come to be known as "serial divestment." This technique involves monthly gifts in an amount that is less than the average monthly nursing home cost, as determined by state authorities. For example, if the average monthly nursing home cost is $3,750 (the current national average), a gift of $3,749 results in no disqualification. A gift of $3,750 would result in one month of disqualification.

Since each month is a new time period for computing gifts, $3,749 could be gifted **each** month with no disqualification. Serial divestment depends on two quirks in the law: first, that each month must be treated as a new gifting period, and second, that there be no partial period disqualification for gifts of less than the average monthly nursing home cost. You should consult with an attorney knowledgeable in such matters to determine if serial divestment is available in your state.

8. Purchase an actuarially sound annuity ("ASA"). An ASA is a commercially available or private annuity that does not have a guarantee period longer than the life expectancy of the applicant.

The Medicaid rules change frequently and vary from state to state. Therefore, any planning strategy must be reviewed in light of current and future law changes. Your strategy will depend on the nature and extent of your assets and your family situation.

Chapter Thirteen

Making Funeral Arrangements
P. Mark Accettura, Esq.

FUNERALS PROVIDE AN opportunity to grieve, to be with friends and family and honor the person who has passed. Like weddings, funerals are an important social occasion, balancing budget, custom, religious convention and personal preference.

Funerals are for the living; they do not benefit the dead. What you choose to do in your spouse's (or your) final arrangements is a personal matter. As you plan the funeral or memorial there are many things to consider. You may find it helpful to give some thought to the following questions before meeting with a funeral director:

- What funeral home or mortuary will handle arrangements?
- Will your spouse be buried or cremated?
- Will your spouse be embalmed?
- What type of casket or container will be chosen for the remains?
- Will the body be present at any after-death ceremony?
- Open or closed casket?
- Will there be a period of visitation by family and friends?
- What are the details of any ceremony you would like to have

before cremation or burial? Music? Readings? Will the service be at the funeral home or a church? Who will officiate?
- What will your spouse wear for cremation or burial?
- Will there be pallbearers? Who?
- What will be the final disposition of the remains? Where will they be buried, stored or scattered?
- How will the body be transported to the cemetery or gravesite?
- Will there be a ceremony to accompany the interment, burial or scattering? What are the details of that ceremony?
- Will there be a marker to show where the remains are buried or interred?
- Will there be a wake?

Choosing a Funeral Home

The job of the funeral director is to care for and safeguard the body until its final disposition. Funeral directors coordinate every aspect of the funeral, serve as dealers for caskets and containers, arrange for final disposition of the body, provide the funeral facility and complete the necessary paperwork.

You may choose a funeral home based on location, reputation or personal experience. Ask family, friends or co-workers for their recommendations. Clergy may be able to offer some helpful guidance. Naturally, you will want a funeral director with whom you feel comfortable.

In your initial investigation, get a price list. Under federal law (The Funeral Rule), funeral directors are required to provide you with a General Price List when you first talk, whether in person or by telephone. The General Price List establishes the price or range of prices for all of the services and merchandise regularly offered by the funeral home. The list is yours to keep whether or not you complete arrangements with a particular establishment.

If your spouse died out-of-state or in any distant location, you should contact the funeral home **in the city where the funeral services will take place** to make arrangements. They will make arrangements to pick up the body and have it transported. If you contact a funeral home in the city where the death took place, you will end up paying a basic arrangements fee to both providers at an extra cost of $1,000-$1,500 or more.

Another option for selecting a funeral home is to seek out a local memorial or funeral society. These non-profit, non-sectarian groups began in the early part of the 1900's to cut funeral costs through cooperative buying power. Memorial societies survey the price lists of funeral homes in their area and negotiate discounts for their members at cooperating funeral homes. Lifetime membership in a memorial or funeral society typically runs about $40.

In addition to providing a wide range of funeral planning services, memorial societies also serve as consumer "watchdogs" over the funeral industry. It was their efforts that resulted in the Federal Trade Commission's enactment of The Funeral Rule in 1982 protecting funeral consumer rights.

Funeral Costs

Funerals can be expensive. The average cost (nationally) of a funeral today is around $4800. However, funeral costs can vary widely depending on the funeral home, where you live and the types of goods and services you choose to purchase.

Generally, the costs of a funeral can be divided into two categories:

1. Services and facilities provided by the funeral home, funeral director and his staff; and
2. Merchandise, such as caskets and urns.

The Arrangement Conference

The meeting with the funeral director during which funeral goods and services are discussed and purchased is called the "arrangement conference." At this meeting, the funeral director will provide you with a **General Price List** (if he has not done so already) in compliance with Federal Trade Commission rules. The General Price List outlines the price of all of the goods and services regularly offered by the funeral home.

General funeral services include:

- The services of the funeral director, including the arrangement conference, the filing of necessary paperwork and the use of the funeral home for the custodial care of the body until final disposition. These services comprise the **Basic Arrangements Fee** and may not be declined.
- Funeral goods and merchandise including caskets, urns and buried containers such as graves liners and vaults.
- Transportation of the body from the place of death and to the place of final disposition.
- Care of the body, including embalming (or refrigeration) and preparation for viewing.
- Use of the funeral home facilities for visitation or viewing and the funeral ceremony, if held at the funeral home.
- Miscellaneous items, such as register books; music, burial clothing, flowers, acknowledgment cards and the preparation of an obituary or death notice.

In addition to the items covered by the funeral home's price list(s), funeral arrangements will include cash advance items that the funeral home pays to outside service providers such as the cemetery or crematory, clergy and fees for certified copies of the death certificate. You may pay these fees directly or through the funeral home. The funeral home may not add a service or handling fee on advanced outside service fees.

Itemized Statement

Once you have made your selections you will be given an **Itemized Statement of Services and Merchandise**. This document will include a detailed outline of the specific merchandise and services you have selected, the price of each, a total cost and an estimate of cash advance items for which you will be responsible. In most cases, the Itemized Statement will also include contractual language that legally obligates you to pay for the cost of the funeral and outlines the terms of payment. Payment arrangements vary widely. Some funeral homes require full payment of the entire funeral before a single service is rendered, while others will advance the entire cost of the funeral allowing the family up to thirty days to pay.

The Funeral Rule

Past abuses and unethical practices by some funeral care providers resulted in the 1982 enactment of the Funeral Rule by the Federal Trade Commission. In general, the Funeral Rule requires full price disclosure and outlines both required and prohibited activities for the death services industry.

Some activities prohibited under the Funeral Rule include:

- Pressuring the customer to select particular merchandise or services or suggesting that any products provided are inadequate or unsatisfactory.
- Charging a handling fee for paying third parties on your behalf.
- Charging a handling fee for using a casket obtained from some other source.
- Charging for goods or services not selected by the customer.
- Charging an extra fee for filing the death certificate.
- Misrepresenting laws and rules regarding funeral directing and required services.
- Charging interest on unpaid balances unless these fees have been explicitly disclosed in the Itemized Statement.

If you believe that a funeral director is pressuring you or that you have been the victim of a prohibited activity, you may report him/her to the agency regulating their activities in your state or to the Federal Trade Commission (see the Directory of Resources at page 253).

Cremation

Although earth burial continues to be the most common disposition of human remains, cremation is becoming more common. During cremation the body is placed in a casket or container which is then placed in a cremation chamber. After a period of approximately three hours at a temperature between 1500 and 2000 degrees, all organic materials are consumed by either heat or evaporation. At completion only a residue of ash and bone fragments remains. This residue is processed into fine particles and placed either in a container provided by the crematorium or an urn purchased by the family.

Because cremations obliterate any evidence of the cause of death, some states impose a minimum waiting period following death before a cremation may take place. During this "waiting period" the body must be preserved by embalming or refrigeration.

Cremation services may be purchased directly from a crematorium (which may or may not have additional facilities on site to conduct a funeral or memorial service) or may be arranged through a funeral home or mortuary.

Following cremation there are several options for disposal of the cremains, including burial, placement in a columbarium, retention by a family member or scattering of the cremains in a place of significance (subject to state and local law restrictions). Earth burial of a box or urn in a cemetery is another option. Many cemeteries will allow burial of an urn above a casketed spouse or parent in a single grave as a way of preserving space.

Caskets, Urns, Vaults, and Grave liners

A casket is the single most costly item in a traditional funeral and accounts for a large percentage of funeral costs. Prior to the passage of rules protecting consumers funeral homes used to wrap the costs of a funeral around the price of a casket marking them up several hundred percent to cover other costs. Since 1982, all aspects of the funeral must be priced separately.

Caskets are available in a wide variety of materials (wood, metal, plastic, fiberglass, even cardboard) and styles. The one you choose depends on your budget and the importance you place on such things. Caskets are widely available from cemeteries, independent dealers and on the Internet. Although not required, as a matter of convenience, most families purchase the casket from the funeral home provider.

Like caskets, urns (used to hold cremains) come in a wide variety of prices and styles. Prices vary from about $50 for a simple plastic box to $7000 or more. The more expensive urns are priced according to the materials used and the artistry involved in their creation. Urns may be made from wood, metal, glass or pottery. In general, if the cremains are to be buried you will be required to have at least a sheet metal or copper box.

Burial vaults and grave liners are outside containers into which a casket is placed when it is buried, ostensibly to protect the casket. A grave liner is similar to a vault, but of lighter construction. Like caskets, they can be made from a variety of materials including concrete, steel, copper and fiberglass. The difference in materials is reflected in the price.

Though most areas of the country have no laws requiring the use of vaults or grave liners, most cemeteries require their use in order to keep the ground from sinking or collapsing over the grave.

Obituaries and Death Notices

An obituary is a published notice of death written by newspaper staff and controlled by the newspaper's editorial policy. You may provide as much, or as little information as you wish, however there is no guarantee that it will be used. Make an effort to write a thoughtful paragraph or two about your spouse and submit it to your news-hungry local newspaper. It is much more likely to run locally (as opposed to the big city newspaper) and be seen by the people in your community.

Death notices are paid advertisements that must be published. Take the time and make the investment to properly memorialize your spouse with an appropriate death notice. List your spouse's family members and his or her accomplishments. Although it costs more, run the death notice for at least two days to be sure that it is seen by as many people who knew your late spouse as possible.

Rites and Rituals: The Funeral Service

The funeral service has three primary rites: the visitation, the service and the interment. Each rite is distinct and serves a particular purpose. You may choose all or none of them. Together they form a strong and for some a necessary form of emotional and spiritual expression.

Visitation

The visitation is a time when family and friends come together to share their experiences and memories about the deceased and to comfort one another. Depending on whether the body is present and whether there is an open casket, it is also a time when family and friends can view the deceased and see the reality of death. The visitation typically takes place at a funeral home, but it is also acceptable for the family to receive friends at their home.

It is increasingly common to have a memory board or memory table at the funeral home during the visitation. Personal items that were meaningful to the deceased and collections of family photographs can be displayed so that visitors can recall the full dimension of the life being celebrated.

The Service

There are no legal requirements as to the form of the funeral ceremony itself. Most people choose some form of religious ceremony that follows their own cultural traditions. The service is a time for an affirmation of life, a memorialization of and tribute to the deceased through thought, prayer or eulogy. Services may be held at the funeral home, mortuary or at a place of worship. Most services last from twenty minutes to half an hour, but can last longer particularly if they involve prescribed religious rites. The funeral service should include aspects that are meaningful and comforting to the mourners.

Interment

The final rite of the funeral service is the committal or interment. The committal service whether it be at graveside for a burial or the scattering of cremains is the symbolic demonstration that a life has ended. It is the time when we say our final goodbye. Committal services may or may not include a brief ceremony. You are permitted to witness the cremation and witness (or even participate in) the filling of grave with dirt. Far from being macabre, following the committal or interment to its final conclusion is regarded by some, like Thomas Lynch in "Tract" below, as a an integral part of the process.

Cemeteries

Cemeteries link us to our history. Great heroes, poets, scientists and soldiers lie beside our friends, neighbors and family. Whether a body is casketed or cremated, most people opt for final disposition of the remains in a cemetery. There are two primary "styles" of cemetery – the traditional cemetery and the memorial park or garden.

Traditional cemeteries are distinguished by gravesites marked by upright gravestones and monuments. They may also contain decorative sculptures, fountains, tombs and mausoleums or columbaria. Because traditional cemeteries tend to be older, many of them have extensive landscaping with an abundance of mature trees.

Memorial parks or gardens are a more recent development. They are characterized by broad expanses of lawn and gardens with flat bronze or stone markers. They too, may include many decorative elements. In recent years both types of cemeteries have frequently incorporated scattering gardens for the broadcasting of cremains.

A standard cemetery plot (approximately four feet by ten feet) generally costs several hundred dollars. Plots are available in pairs, side-by-side, for spouses. Urban areas command higher prices. And like any other real estate, location is a major determinant of price. Plots located in more "desirable" sections of the cemetery tend to be more costly. Prices also escalate for plots with a view.

Due to the scarcity of ground in older cemeteries, additional options have been developed to create additional space. One method is two-deep burials, where one casket is buried at eight feet and a second later layered on top. Mausoleum buildings with floor to ceiling vaults to house caskets are also common.

In making cemetery arrangements, there are a number of factors to consider in addition to price:

- Does the cemetery require the use of a burial vault?
- Are there restrictions on the type of monument or marker that can be used?
- Does the price include perpetual care and maintenance?
- What are the approximate opening and closing fees?
- Are there provisions for the disposition of cremains as well as casketed remains?
- Are there plots available in the same area (to provide for the burial of an entire family)?

Because they are not regulated in the same way as funeral homes (the Funeral Rule does not apply), cemeteries can charge whatever the market will bear. Generally, some portion of the purchase price of a plot goes to an endowment to provide for maintenance of the cemetery in perpetuity.

Although you will receive a "deed" to the cemetery plot you purchase, it assures you only of the right to bury whomever you please in the plot. Actual ownership of the land remains with the cemetery owners. Typically there are restrictions on the resale of a plot if you decide not to use it.

Opening and closing fees for a gravesite usually run several hundred dollars. These fees cover not only the digging and filling of the grave, but also boundary marking, the filing of all necessary paperwork, use of the lowering device and re-grading and re-sodding of the plot.

Alternative Plans

Immediate burial or direct cremation is an option for those who choose not to have a traditional ceremony or where cost is paramount. Immediate burial is the disposition of the human remains without a visitation, viewing, or ceremony other than a graveside service. The body does not require embalming for immediate burial and the cost of a graveside service is included in the package price, though generally, the price of a casket is not. Similarly, direct cremation is the disposition of remains by cremation without formal ceremony. Both immediate burial and direct cremation will appear as separate items on the funeral homes price list.

Pre-planning

Pre-planning your funeral relieves your survivors of this responsibility and allows for your personal expression. Pre-planning, which may include pre-paying, also has some financial advantages. Not only do pre-planned funerals tend to be less expensive; pre-paid funerals are not counted for Medicaid eligibility purposes. (see "Medicaid" in Chapter Twelve).

There are two parts to pre-planning: pre-arranging and pre-funding. Pre-arranging involves recording your wishes as to choice of funeral home, whether you wish to be buried or cremated, the name and location of the cemetery and the details of the ceremony. *Do **not** document your wishes in your Will, as it will likely to be read long after your funeral or memorial service.* Pre-funding is an agreement with a funeral provider as to the goods and services to be provided at a future date at an agreed price. Pre-funding is regulated by state law. Before executing a pre-funded contract you should determine:

- Is there a price guarantee? For which items or services?
- What happens to interest earned on pre-paid funds?
- Is there a pre-payment penalty (on installment plans)?
- Can you make changes to the contract?
- What about substitutions if your choices are not available?
- Are there geographic restrictions? What happens if you move?

In "Tract," noted poet, author and undertaker, Thomas Lynch of Milford, Michigan muses on directing his own funeral, the usefulness of graveside rituals, the weather, dirt and the love of his family.

TRACT
Thomas Lynch

I'd rather it be February. Not that it will matter much to me. Not that I'm a stickler for details. But since you're asking – February. The month I first became a father, the month my father died. Yes. Better even than November.

I want it cold. I want the gray to inhabit the air like wood does trees: as an essence not a coincidence. And the hope for springtime, gardens, romance, dulled to a stump by the winter in Michigan.

Yes, February. With the cold behind and the cold before you and the darkness stubborn at the edges of the day. And a wind to make the cold more bitter. So that ever after it might be said, "It was a sad old day we did it after all."

And a good frosthold on the ground so that, for nights before it is dug, the sexton will have had to go up and put a fire down, under the hood that fits the space, to soften the topsoil for the backhoe's toothy bucket.

Wake me. Let those who want to come and look. They have their reasons. You'll have yours. And if someone says, "Doesn't he look natural!" take no offense. They've got it right. For this was always in my nature. It's in yours.

And have the clergy take their part in it. Let them take their best shot. If they're ever going to make sense to you, now's the time. They're looking, same as the rest of us. The questions are more instructive than the answers. Be wary of anyone who knows what to say.

As for music, suit yourselves. I'll be out of earshot, stone deaf. A lot can be said for pipers and tinwhistlers. But consider the difference between a funeral with a few tunes and a concert with a corpse down front. Avoid, for your own sakes, anything you've heard in the dentist's office or the roller rink.

Poems might be said. I've had friends who were poets. Mind you, they tend to go on a bit. Especially around horizontal bodies. Sex and death are their principal studies. It is here where the services of an experienced undertaker are most appreciated. Accustomed to being personae non grata, they'll act the worthy editor and tell the bards when it's time to put a sock in it.

On the subject of money: you get what you pay for. Deal with someone whose instincts you trust. If anyone tells you you haven't spent enough, tell them to go piss up a rope. Tell the same thing to anyone who says you spent too much. Tell them to go piss up a rope. It's your money. Do what you want with it. But let me make one thing perfectly clear. You know the type who's always saying "When I'm dead, save your money, spend it on something really useful, do me cheaply"? I'm not one of them. Never was. I've always thought that funerals were useful. So do what suits you. It is yours to do. You're entitled to wholesale on most of it.

As for guilt – it's much overrated. Here are the facts in the case at hand: I've known the love of the ones who have loved me. And I've known that they've known that I've loved them, too. Everything else, in the end, seems irrelevant. But if guilt is the thing, forgive yourself, forgive me. And if a little upgrade in the pomp and circumstance makes you feel better, consider it money wisely spent. Compared to shrinks and pharmaceuticals, bartenders or homeopaths, geographical or ecclesiastical cures, even the priciest funeral is a bargain.

I want a mess made in the snow so that the earth looks wounded, forced open, an unwilling participant. Forego the tent. Stand openly to the weather. Get the larger equipment out of sight. It's a distraction. But have the sexton, all dirt and indifference, remain at hand. He and the hearse driver can talk of poker or trade jokes in whispers and straight-face while the clergy tender final commendations. Those who lean on shovels and fill holes, like those who lean on custom and old prayers, are, each of them, experts in the one field.

And you should see it till the very end. Avoid the temptation of tidy leavetaking in a room, a cemetery chapel, at the foot of the altar. None of that. Don't dodge it because of the weather. We've fished and watched football in worse conditions. It won't take long. Go to the hole in the ground. Stand over it. Look into it. Wonder. And be cold. But stay until it's over. Until it is done.

On the subject of pallbearers – my darling sons, my fierce daughter, my grandsons and granddaughters, if I've any. The larger muscles should be involved. The ones we use for the real burdens. If men and their muscles are better at lifting, women and theirs are better at bearing. This is a job for which both may be needed. So work together. It will lighten the load.

Look to my beloved for the best example. She has a mighty heart, a rich internal life, and powerful medicines.

After the words are finished, lower it. Leave the ropes. Toss the gray gloves in on top. Push the dirt in and be done. Watch each other's ankles, stamp your feet in the cold, let your heads sink between your shoulders, keep looking down. That's where what is happening is happening. And when you're done, look up and leave. But not until you're done.

So, if you opt for burning, stand and watch. If you cannot watch it, perhaps you should reconsider. Stand in earshot of the sizzle and the pop. Try to get a whiff of the goings on. Warm your hands to the fire. This might be a good time for a song. Bury the ashes, cinders, and bones. The bits of the box that did not burn.

Put them in something.

Mark the spot.

Feed the hungry. It's good form. Feed them well. This business works up an appetite, like going to the seaside, walking the cliff road. After that, be sober.

This is none of my business. I won't be there. But if you're asking, here is free advice. You know the part where everybody is always saying that you should have a party now? How the dead guy always insisted he wanted everyone to have a good time and toss a few back and laugh and be happy? I'm not one of them. I think the old teacher is right about this one. There *is* a time to dance. And it just may be this isn't one of them. The dead can't tell the living what to feel.

They used to have this year of mourning. Folks wore armbands, black clothes, played no music in the house. Black wreaths were hung at the front doors. The damaged were identified. For a full year you were allowed your grief – the dreams and sleeplessness, the sadness, the rage. The weeping and giggling in all the wrong places. The catch in your breath at the sound of the name. After a year, you would be back to normal. "Time heals" is what was said to explain this. If not, of course, you were pronounced some version of "crazy" and in need of some professional help.

Whatever's there to feel, feel it – the riddance, the relief, the fright and freedom, the fear of forgetting, the dull ache of your own mortality. Go home in pairs. Warm to the flesh that warms you still. Get with someone you can trust with tears, with anger, and wonderment and utter silence. Get that part done – the sooner the better. The only way around these things is through them.

I know I shouldn't be going on like this.

I've had this problem all my life. Directing funerals.

It's yours to do – my funeral – not mine. The death is yours to live with once I'm dead.

So here is a coupon good for Disregard. And here is another marked My Approval. Ignore, with my blessings, whatever I've said beyond Love One Another.

Live Forever.

All I really wanted was a witness. To say I was. To say, daft as it still sounds, maybe I *am*.

To say, if they ask you, it was a sad day after all. It was a cold, gray day.

February.

Of course, any other month you're on your own. Have no fear – you'll know what to do. Go now, I think you are ready.

Summary of Interior Photography

All of the photographs in Lost and Found are the work of Keith Tishken.   Keith teaches film studies and production at Towson University, Baltimore, Maryland. He has been exhibiting his photographs throughout the United States since 1984. Keith can be reached at P.O. Box 22279, Baltimore, Maryland 21203 or at kdtishken@juno.com.

Page 8: A moment of reflection on my honeymoon. Mackinac Island, Michigan.

Page 26: On top of the world above the Arctic Circle. Lapland, Finland.

Page 44: A Saturday excursion with family and friends. Annapolis, Maryland.

Page 60: Refreshing solitude on a brisk February morning walk. Martha's Vineyard, Massachusetts.

Page 76: The day comes to a close and the vacationer's retreat. Cocoa Beach, Florida.

Page 100: The glory of a Spring afternoon in February on a North Atlantic beach. Martha's Vineyard, Massachusetts.

Page 110: Traversing the Straits of Mackinac; my wife at my side. Off Mackinac Island, Michigan.

Page 136: No matter how many times you do it, the chaos that always comes at tax time.

Page 158: A suitable place to begin a family. Baltimore, Maryland.

Page 174: A classic home to which one admires and aspires. Baltimore, Maryland.

Page 190: The incredible adventure of being in love. Annapolis, Maryland.

Page 196: Seeing myself alone along the Thames, feeling even more isolated by the many couples who pass. London, England.

Page 206: Rising above the storm can give way to the most magnificent sights. Somewhere over the Eastern United States.

Page 222: Enjoying the same perspective as Howard Hughes; he resides at my back. Houston, Texas.

Appendix A

Asset Inventory with Values Worksheet						
Asset Type	Ownership					
	Husband	Husband's Trust	Wife	Wife's Trust	Joint w/ spouse	Joint w/ others

Lost and Found Glossary

Adjusted gross estate

The value of all property owned by a decedent (valued on the date of death), less funeral expenses, the expenses of administering the estate, and debts owed by the decedent.

Alternate valuation date

A date, six months after the date of death, used to value property owned by the decedent. The alternate valuation date (sometimes known as the "AVD") may be used for estate tax purposes in cases where the value of the estate has declined in the six months following death.

Annual gift tax exclusion, or "annual exclusion"

The amount (currently $10,000 per donee) that can be excluded each year in computing the gift tax of the donor. Gifts in excess of the annual exclusion are taxable gifts that reduce the donors Unified Credit. Married couples may split gifts. See "Gift splitting" below.

Applicable Exclusion Amount

The total value of lifetime taxable gifts or transfers at death that can be transferred tax-free after application of the unified credit.

Basis

Term used in tax accounting to describe the cost of an asset for purpose of determining gain (or loss) on its sale or transfer. The starting point in calculating an owner's basis in an

	asset is to determine its original cost to the owner.
Beneficiary	A person who has any present or future interest, vested or contingent, under a Will, trust, retirement plan or life insurance policy.
Bond	An instrument of debt. In issuing bonds, a corporation agrees to pay holders a stated rate of interest until the principal is repaid on a specified date.
By operation of law	The automatic change of title when one of multiple owners of property dies, such as joint tenants, P.O.D. or beneficiary designation. No court action is needed to transfer title.
Bypass trust	A trust established when the first spouse in a married couple dies (also called "credit shelter" or "family" trust). It "bypasses" the estate of the second spouse for estate tax purposes.
Capital Gains Tax	A tax on the difference between the sales price and the adjusted basis of a capital asset. Long-term and short-term capital gains taxes are paid depending upon the length of time you have owned the asset.
Capitalization	The total value of a company's bonds and preferred and common stock outstanding. The size of a company can be expressed as Small-Cap (less than one billion dollars), Mid-Cap (between one and ten billion dollars) and large-Cap (over ten billion dollars).

Certified Financial Planner	The designation bestowed on an individual who has completed coursework and passed an examination. A CFP certificate must be maintained by continuing education.
Closely Held Business	A privately held business in which stock is not publicly traded.
COBRA	An acronym for the Consolidated Omnibus Budget Reconciliation Act. It contains provisions, which allow the surviving spouse (as well as laid off workers and a number of other eligible employees defined in the statute) of an employee to continue to be covered by the health insurance previously provided by the employer, to a maximum of 36 months, as long as the surviving spouse pays the premium cost.
Columbarium	A structure consisting of numerous compartments or niches designed to hold the urns containing cremated remains.
Commodities	Investments in staples such as wheat and oranges.
Conservator	A person appointed by the Court to exercise powers over the estate (financial matters) of a protected person.
Cremains	That which remains after a body is cremated.
Crummey notice	A notice sent to an irrevocable trust beneficiary to alert the beneficiary that a contribution has been made to a trust and the beneficiary has a right to obtain some or all of the contribution. Used to

	qualify the contribution as a "present interest" and qualify for the annual gift tax exclusion.
Debenture	A bond not secured by any specific property but backed only by the general credit of the issuing company.
Disclaimer	A decision to not accept a gift or inheritance. Usually done for estate tax saving purposes.
Diversification	The practice of spreading investments among a range of different securities in order to reduce risk.
Divestment	The process of transferring property to reduce your net worth in order to qualify for a means-eligible program like Medicaid.
DNI	Distributable Net Income. An internal tax computation that measures the deductible portion of distributions made from trusts or estates to beneficiaries.
Donee	The recipient of a gift
Donor	One who makes a gift to another.
Durable powers of attorney	A written instrument whereby one person (the "principal"), appoints another person as his agent, with authority to perform certain acts on the principal's behalf. Powers of attorney are usually used to give an agent power to transact personal business if the principal is unable to do so directly. The term "durable" signifies that the power being granted continues to be effective despite the disability of the principal.

Equity Investment	An ownership investment in an entity. The shareholder participates in any profits or loss of the entity.
Family trust	See "Bypass trust".
FICA taxes	Acronym for the Federal Insurance Contributions Act taxes that are withheld from workers' paychecks to fund Social Security.
Fiduciary	A person or institution who manages money or property for another and who is legally required to exercise a standard of care in such management activity. Trust fiduciaries are strictly bound to implement the terms of the trust instrument under which they are appointed.
Fixed Income Investments	Those investments for which a company is committed to paying a specific amount of return to investors.
FTC funeral rule	Rule enacted by the Federal Trade Commission in 1982 to protect funeral consumer rights. The Rule requires funeral directors to provide funeral consumers with a general price list containing the price or price range for all services and merchandise.
General power of appointment	A power given the decedent by a third party to consume, invade or appropriate certain property in favor of the decedent, his estate or his creditors. Property over which the decedent possesses a general power of appointment at death is included in the decedent's gross estate for estate tax purposes.

Grantor	A person making a grant; the transferor of property. The creator of a trust is usually designated as the grantor of the trust. The term "settlor" is often used in the place of "grantor" since the terms are synonymous.
Gross estate	All property in which the decedent had a beneficial interest at the time of death. Examples include cash, stocks, bonds, real estate, business interests, and other tangible property.
Guaranteed investments	Investment entities such as Money Market and Passbook accounts, Certificate of Deposits and Treasury bills, each of which pay specified rates of interest.
Guardian	A person appointed by the court or designated as such in a Will to exercise powers over the person of a minor or legally incapacitated person.
Health Care Finance Administration	The federal agency in charge of the Medicare program.
Heir	Those persons, including the surviving spouse, who are entitled to the property of a decedent under the statutes of intestate succession.
Inflation	An increase in the cost of consumer goods which leads to a decline of the purchasing power of the dollar.
ILIT	Acronym for "Irrevocable Life Insurance Trust." An ILIT is the owner and beneficiary of life insurance on the life of the grantor. Proceeds of the policy are not includ-

ed in the estate of the grantor, and such trusts cannot be revoked or amended once created. See "Irrevocable Trust."

Incidents of ownership

Rights a person may have in a life insurance policy such as the right to name or change the beneficiary of the policy or the right to borrow from the policy.

Intestate

Term used to describe one who dies without leaving a valid Will.

IRD

Items of income earned by a decedent before death but paid to his or her estate after death. Such income is includible in the decedent's gross estate and is taxable income to the recipient. Examples of IRD include the decedent's last paycheck, interest on U.S. savings bonds, royalties, as well as IRA, 401(k) and other retirement income paid after death.

Irrevocable trust

A Trust (see "Trust" definition) created during the life of the grantor, under which the grantor gives up the right to amend or revoke the Trust, so that once created, the Trust cannot be altered. See "ILIT."

Joint tenants with rights of survivorship

A form of ownership that automically vests ownership of a deceased joint owner's share in the surviving joint tenant(s).

Joint Trust

A joint trust is a revocable grantor trust with two grantors-typically a husband and wife. Both spouses create the trust and transfer their assets to the trust. The trust normally provides that both spouses are the initial co-trustees and that the surviving spouse continues as the sole trustee, and retains the power to amend the trust after the first spouse's death.

Last Will and Testament   A legal declaration setting forth one's desires concerning the disposition of his or her property after death. Often simply referred to as a "Will."

Letters of authority   A document issued by the Probate Court giving the Personal Representative legal authority to transact the estate's business.

Limited Liability Company (LLC)   An entity created under state law which (like a corporation) limits the potential legal liability of its owners to the amount they have invested in the LLC. Like partnerships LLCs pay no income tax, instead items of income and loss flow through to "members" who pay tax at their marginal income tax rate.

Limited Partnerships   A partnership consisting of at least one general partner who has unlimited liability and at least one limited partner who is liable for only the amount of his or her investment.

Marital trust   Trust into which trust assets in excess of the Applicable Exclusion Amount are allocated after the death of one spouse. All income and principal of the marital trust is available to the surviving spouse for her use. The surviving spouse may be permitted to designate the beneficiary of the balance of the Marital Trust (a "general power of appointment"), or may not ("QTIP" Trust).

Medicaid

A state-run health care program for individuals with low income and little or no resources. Eligibility is determined based on state guidelines. The state also determines which health care services are covered.

Medicare

The federal government's health insurance program for seniors (over the age of 65), the disabled (under age 65), and individuals of any age who have permanent kidney failure. The Health Care Finance Administration manages Medicare.

Medigap insurance

A private health insurance policy covering services not covered by Medicare.

Mutual Funds

Close-ended: A fund that has a relatively fixed number of shares that are bought or sold through broker/dealers on the stock exchange.

Open-ended: A fund that is able to redeem or issue new shares for cash and deals directly with its investors.

Notice to creditors

The notice published in a legal newspaper notifying any and all potential creditors of the decedent's death and the time frame in which they must file their claims against the estate

Notice to known creditors

The notice sent directly to the decedent's known creditors to inform them of the death and the time frame for making claims against the estate

Pay-on-death	A type of beneficiary designation; pay-on-death (also, "P.O.D.") accounts are payable to the named beneficiary immediate on the account owner's death. Also known as "transfer-on-death," or "T.O.D." Typically used on brokerage accounts. Allows the account to pass by operation of law at the death of the primary owner to the beneficiaries named on the account. Only the owner can access the P.O.D or T.O.D. account while alive.
Personal property memorandum	A writing indicating the individuals who are to inherit particular items of the decedent's personal property, such as jewelry, collectibles and other family heirlooms.
Personal representative	A person, or committee of individuals, or a corporate fiduciary like a bank, appointed by the probate court, to administer the probate estate of a decedent. Sometimes also known as an "executor" or "executrix." The person named in the decedent's Will has first priority to be appointed as personal representative. If that individual is unable or unwilling to serve, or if the decedent died without a Will, the surviving spouse has first priority.
Pick-up tax	A type of state inheritance tax where the state receives a portion of the federal estate tax equal to the maximum state death tax credit available on the federal estate tax return.
Postnuptial agreement	An agreement entered into after mar-

riage concerning the division of marital assets in the event of divorce or death; the agreement overrides state law with respect to such division.

Pour Over Will

A Will used in conjunction with a Revocable Living Trust, which serves as a safety net to transfer probatable assets into trust at death.

Prenuptial agreement

An agreement entered into before marriage concerning the division of marital assets in the event of divorce or death; the agreement overrides state law with respect to such division.

Present interest

The current right of a gift recipient (donee) to the unrestricted enjoyment of the gifted asset. To qualify for the annual gift tax exclusion, a gift must be of a present interest. A Crummey Notice is used to convert a future interest transfer to an irrevocable trust to a transfer of a present interest.

Probate

Generally, the process by which assets owned individually at death are transferred to the decedent's heirs; specifically, probate is court proceeding to authenticate the decedent's Will, appoint the personal representative, pay debts and taxes, identify heirs and distribute assets. A Will does not avoid probate; only a fully funded trust will obviate the necessity of probate.

Publication period

The period of time (usually four months) during which the decedent's creditors must file their claim against the estate, or else the claim is

	forever barred.
QTIP trust	Acronym for "Qualified Terminable Interest Property" Trust. A QTIP trust qualifies for the unlimited marital deduction if the surviving spouse has the exclusive right to income and principal from the trust during his/her lifetime. The surviving spouse cannot direct the disbursement of the balance of the QTIP Trust at his or her death.
Qualified pension and profit sharing plans	Retirement plans that comply with the federal Employee Retirement Income Security Act ("ERISA"); usually employer sponsored plans. Examples include company pension, profit sharing, and 401k plans.
Required minimum distribution	The minimum amount you must take annually from your retirement plan(s) beginning at age 70 ½ ; the amount is calculated by dividing your retirement plan account balance (as of the previous December 31) by the Applicable Divisor from the IRS Uniform Table that corresponds to your age. If you have more than one IRA, 403(b), 401(k) or qualified plan, all like plans must be aggregated for purposes of meeting the RMD requirement.
Revocable Trust	A Trust (see "Trust") created during the Settlor/Grantor's life, under which the Settlor/Grantor retains the right to amend or revoke the Trust during his or her lifetime.
Rollover	A complete distribution taken from an IRA, 401k or other retirement plan

which is then completely deposited into another IRA, 401k, etc.

Special needs trust

A trust established for a beneficiary who is receiving means tested benefits like Medicaid or SSI, restricting transfers for the beneficiary's primary care so as to not disqualify the beneficiary from government benefits.

Specific bequest

A gift in a Will of particular items to a particular person. The gift must be of the item, not its value.

State death tax credit

A credit allowed by the Federal estate tax for estate or inheritance tax paid to a state.

Stepped up basis

An increase in the income tax basis of property held at death. Inherited property receives an income tax basis equal to its fair market value as of the date of the decedent's death. Items of IRD do not receive a stepped up basis.

Tangible Investment

Investments that have physical properties, such as gold and silver, stamps, coins and collectibles (e.g. artwork and sports memorabilia).

Tenancy by the entirety

A form of ownership of real property by a husband and wife, which is not recognized in all states. Unlike a joint tenant, one tenant's interest in a tenancy by the entireties cannot be separated from the interest of the other. If the parties divorce, they become tenants in common. Upon the death of the husband or wife, title goes to the survivor by operation of law.

Term insurance	A type of life insurance policy that does not build up any cash value and whose coverage ends when its term expires or when premiums are no longer paid.
Testate	Term used to describe one who dies leaving a valid Will.
Testator	One who makes a Will; one who dies leaving a Will.
Transfer-on-death	See "Pay-on-death."
Trust	A legal arrangement created under state law with three essential elements: 1) A Settlor/Grantor who establishes the Trust and who supplies the property for the Trust, 2) a Trustee who manages the property in the Trust, and 3) a Beneficiary, for whose benefit Trust property is held. A single person may occupy of these roles
Unified credit	A $211,300 credit against the federal Unified Transfer Tax that allows a person to make up to $675,000 (2001) of taxable gifts during life, or at death, with no tax liability.
Uniform Probate Code	A set of laws dealing with Wills, trusts, and probate, drafted by the National Conference of Commissioners on Uniform State Laws, to serve as a model for states that want to modernize their own laws on these subjects. In Lost and Found, we have used the Uniform Probate Code as the basis of our discussion.
Universal life insurance	A type of whole life insurance that

combines term insurance with a side fund invested in interest bearing instruments.

Unlimited marital deduction	This deduction allows spouses to make unlimited gifts or unlimited transfers to each other at death. Not available if the recipient spouse is not a U.S. citizen.
Variable life insurance	A type of whole life insurance that combines term insurance with a side fund invested in mutual funds.

Index

G

H

I

J

L

Directory of Resources

"I measure every Grief I meet
With narrow, probing eyes—
I wonder if It weighs like Mine
Or has an Easier size."
-Emily Dickinson

Grief and Bereavement

ORGANIZATIONS

Centre for Living with Dying
554 Mansion Park Drive
Santa Clara, CA 95054
(408) 980 9801
http://www.thecentre.org
This agency is devoted to those dealing with the life issues of loss and grief. The goal of the agency is to provide an organization that would actively reach out to individuals, families and professionals living with the reality of loss. Over the years, the Centre has developed specialized programs to facilitate the natural human process of bereavement in a safe, nonjudgmental atmosphere.

Hospice Foundation of America
2001 S St. NW #300
Washington DC 20009
(800) 854-3402
http://www.hospicefoundation.org
The Hospice Foundation is a not-for-profit organization that assists those who deal either personally or professionally with terminal illness, death and the process of grief. Hospice offers a variety of bereavement and counseling services to families before and after a patient's death.

National Association of Military Widows
4023 25th Road North
Arlington, VA 22207
(703) 527-4565
Provides referral service, social outings and support groups for the newly widowed. The association acts as lobby for legislation beneficial to military widows and surviving children.

National Hospice and Palliative Care Organization
1700 Diagonal Road, Suite 300
Alexandria, VA 22314
(800) 658-8898
(703) 837-1500
http://www.stepstn.com/
The National Hospice and Palliative Care Organization is the largest association and leading resource for professionals and volunteers committed to and providing service to patients and their families during end of life. NHPCO provides educational programs and technical assistance, and works to influence health programs and public policies related to end of life care. The National Hospice Help line (800) 658-8898 provides hospice care information for terminally ill persons and referrals to hospice programs nationwide.

National Mental Health Association
1021 Prince Street
Alexandria, VA 22314
(800) 969-NMHA

http://www.nmha.org
The National Mental Health Association is dedicated to the treatment, diagnosis and prevention of mental illness. Widows who experience signs of depression or anxiety can contact NMHA for counseling, referrals and treatment options.

Sena Foundation
USA Central Office
108 South Main Street
Bowling Green, VA 22427
(804) 633-7575
http://www.sena.org
The Sena Foundation has been a direct force in the grief and loss field for over a decade. This non-profit organization provides substantial support for death/dying/hospice movements. Offers free support for those going through catastrophic loss. Provides hands-on support (one on one, peer support, practical in-home and assistive living support) as well as educational programs (workshops, seminars, retreats and training programs.)

The Shiva Foundation
551 Cordova Rd. #709
Santa Fe, NM 87501
(800) 720-9544
http://goodgrief.org
E-mail: shiva@goodgrief.org
The Shiva Foundation is a not-for-profit, non-sectarian organization committed to developing resources and offering support in the grieving process. These programs are offered to individuals, families and communities. Shiva Foundation offers counseling, seminars, educational programs and referrals for grieving families.

THEOS Foundation, Inc. (They Help Each Other Spiritually)
1301 Clark Building
717 Liberty Avenue
Pittsburgh, PA 15222
(412) 471-7779
Publishes THEOS Magazine, books, printed materials for both men

and women of any age who have lost a spouse. Additionally, THEOS organizes local support groups in both the United States and Canada. THEOS helps persons whose spouses have died, providing educational materials and emotional support for the newly widowed. Chapters offer ongoing self-help support groups. THEOS also publishes and hosts an annual national conference, open to both professionals and those who are recently widowed.

Widowed Persons Services
American Association for Retired Persons
601 E Street, N.W.
Washington, DC 20049
(800) 424-2277
(202) 434-2260
http://www.aarp.org/griefandloss
The American Association for Retired Persons provides outreach, referral, support, education and printed material for retirees. Widowed Persons Services is an outreach program, sponsored by AARP, in which trained widowed volunteers offer support to newly widowed persons of any age. AARP/WPS assists local community organizations and regional chapters of national organizations to coordinate, maintain and develop programming and support services.

HOTLINES AND TOLL-FREE NUMBERS

Grief Recovery Institute
P.O. Box 6061- 382
Sherman Oaks, CA 91413
(800) 445-4808 (hotline hours: 8:00 a.m. - 5:00 p.m.)
(818) 907-9600
http://www.grief-recovery.com/
The National Grief Recovery Hotline seeks to ease the isolation of those suffering from a loss and assists them in coping with their grief. Offers information, handbooks, resources and news to help individuals deal with grief.

National Institute of Mental Health
Anxiety Disorder Education Program
1021 Prince Street

Alexandria, VA 22314
(888) 8-ANXIETY
http://www.nmha.org
Trained counselors can give referrals and information to callers. The National Mental Health Association is dedicated to improving mental health and diagnosing mental disorders and diseases.

INTERNET SITES AND WEB RESOURCES

Bereavement Magazine Online offers an extensive links area at http://www.bereavementmag.com/resources/default.asp. The magazine itself is available to subscribers only. Subscriptions can be ordered on-line.

Death and Dying Support Online offers a safe haven to those who have lost a loved one to death, are anticipating the loss of a loved one or who are facing their own death in the near future. Death and Dying provides comfort, support and education about issues surrounding death at a time when people are confused, apprehensive and dealing with shock and sorrow.
http://www.death-dying.com/

At Grief Recovery Online, others who have experienced the pain of losing a loved one share their experience and strength. There are message boards, resource listings and secure chat rooms for all who are grieving.
http://www.groww.com

Grief Share is a national organization to help grieving friends, families and partners through the loss of a spouse. The national organization trains and supports local support groups in the recovery process. This website gives information on how to start or find a local Grief Share group and begin healing.
http://www.griefshare.com

GriefNet, created by a non-profit organization, is a resource for people experiencing bereavement. It includes a memorial garden, sup-

port groups, bulletin boards, and links to other resources on the Internet. There is also a library of articles and poetry, and a "bookstore" for purchasing special publications.
http://www.rivendell.org

Growth House is an international gateway to resources for life-threatening illness and end of life care. Their primary mission is to improve the quality of compassionate care for people who are dying through public education and global professional collaboration. The site offers an extensive bookstore, chatrooms and many resource guides.
http://www.growthhouse.org

The Layman's Guide to Death and Dying is an 'e-book' - an electronic book created to help those who grieve and those who provide support for the bereaved. Its purpose is to foster an understanding of the human response to the phenomena of death, dying and bereavement.
http://www.bereavement.org/

WidowNet is consistently referred to as the foremost web authority on widowhood. The site includes information and self-help resources for, and by, widows and widowers. Topics covered include grief, bereavement, recovery, and other information helpful to people, of all ages, religious backgrounds and sexual orientations, who have suffered the death of a spouse or life partner.
http://www.fortnet.org/WidowNet/index.html

Suggested Reading

Beresford, Laryy. **The Hospice Handbook : A Complete Guide.** Little, Brown & Co. 1993.
Presents a definitive guide to hospice care. Discusses how to find the right one and how to get the best care for the money.

Brothers, Joyce. **Widowed.** Ballantine Books. 1992.
In her personal, comforting way, Dr. Joyce Brothers describes the very real incidents and feelings that every woman who has lived through the death of a spouse will immediately recognize.

Fairview Hospice. **The Family Handbook of Hospice Care.**
Fairview Press. 1999.
Answers basic questions about hospice services.

Felber, Marta. **Grief Expressed: When a Mate Dies.** Lifewords. 1997.
Emphasizes the importance of having a reactive mindset and suggests specific steps to dealing with loss. Empowering and optimistic, from somebody who knows what she is writing about.

Gates, Philomene. **Suddenly Alone: A Woman's Guide to Widowhood, Divorce and Loneliness.** Gridiron Publishers. 1998.
A valuable guide for people facing any kind of loss, especially that of a significant other.

James, John W. **The Grief Recovery Handbook : The Action Program for Moving Beyond Death Divorce, and Other Losses.**
Harper Collins. 1998.
Illustrates what grief is and how it is possible to recover and regain energy and spontaneity. Offers grievers the specific actions needed to complete the grieving process and accept loss.

Jones, Jane Griz. **From Grief to Gladness: Coming Back from Widowhood.** Recovery Communications. 2000.
Frankly describes the process of beginning a totally different kind of life. Those experiencing a loss either through death or divorce will find helpful and insightful advice.

Jowell, Barbara Tom. **After He's Gone: a Guide for Widowed and Divorced Women.** Birch Lane Press. 1997.
Articulates the emotions specific to newly widowed and newly divorced women—as well as the emotions they have in common—and provides realistic advice on getting through the first weeks, plus a useful list of simple things women can do to feel better immediately.

Kubler-Ross, Elizabeth. **On Death and Dying.** Collier Press. 1997.
Explores the five stages of death and the impact felt on the patient, professionals and family.

Kushner, Harold. **When Bad Things Happen to Good People**. Avon Books. 1983.
Offers a moving and humane approach to understanding life's tragedies.

Lynn, JoAnne. **Handbook for Mortals: Guidance for People Facing Serious Illness**. Oxford University Press. 1999.
Provides practical information on caregiving options and decisions.

McLeod, Beth Witrogen. **Caregiving: The Spiritual Journey of Love, Loss and Renewal**. John Wiley & Sons. 1999.
Presents a view of caregiving that is both practical and spiritual.

Neeld, Elizabeth Harper. **Seven Choices : Taking the Steps to New Life After Losing Someone You Love**. Centerpoint Press. 1997.
Contains personal narratives, medical and scientific research, and suggestions and advice on the subject of change, loss, and grief. Identifies the unexplainable myriad of emotions that one experiences when losing someone, not only to death, but to divorce and other losses as well.

Rando, Therese. **How to Go on Living When Someone You Love Dies**. Bantam Books. 1991.
Presents comprehensive guidance including an extensive resource listing. Offers the solace, comfort, and guidance to help you accept your loss and move into a new life without forgetting your treasured past.

Wolfelt, Alan. **The Journey Through Grief: Reflection on Healing**. Companion Press. 1997.
This spiritual guide to those grieving the death of someone loved explores the mourner's journey through grief, in particular the six needs that all mourners must meet to heal and grow.

Social Security and Government Benefits

ORGANIZATIONS

Department of Veterans Affairs (VA)
810 Vermont Ave. NW
Washington, D.C. 20420
(800) 827-1000
(202) 273-5400
http://www.va.gov/
The VA Web site is a worldwide resource that provides information on VA programs, benefits and facilities worldwide. The "Facilities Directory" at **http://www.va.gov/stations97/guide/home.asp?DIVI-SION=ALL** allows visitors to locate VA centers in their state. Many benefit application and information forms are available from this site.

Department of Veterans Affairs
National Cemetery Administration
810 Vermont Avenue, N.W.
Washington, D.C. 20420
(800) 827-1000
http://www.cem.va.gov/index.htm
The National Cemetery Administration (NCA) honors Veterans with a final resting place and lasting memorials that commemorate their service to our nation. Maintains national cemeteries and provides a headstone or marker and Presidential Memorial Certificates in recognition of veteran's service to their nation.

Pension and Welfare Benefits Administration (PWBA)
U.S. Department of Labor
200 Constitution Ave., N.W.
Washington, DC 20210
(202) 219-8776
http://www.dol.gov/dol/pwba/
Protects the integrity of pensions, health plans, and other employee benefits for more than 150 million people. The Division of Technical Assistance and Inquiries assists members of the public with technical questions relating to pension, health, or other benefits offered by employers.

Pension Benefit Guaranty Corporation (PBGC)
1200 K Street N.W.
Washington, D.C. 20005-4026
(800) 400-PBGC
www.pbgc.gov
PBGC is a federal corporation created under the Employee
Retirement Income Security Act of 1974 to guarantee payment of
basic pension benefits earned by about 43 million American workers
and retirees participating in nearly 40,000 private-sector defined
benefit pension plans.

Social Security Administration (SSA)
Office of Public Inquiries
6401 Security Blvd.
Room 4-C-5 Annex
Baltimore, MD 21235-6401
(800) 772-1213
www.ssa.gov
The SSA's OnLine website provides a wealth of information including benefit information publications, how to apply for retirement
benefits, and how to locate and contact your local office. A search-
able Q&A database provides answers to the most commonly asked
questions regarding Social Security Benefits. A new feature of the
website is an on-line "Social Security Retirement Planner" at:
http://www.ssa.gov/retire/ which will help Americans better prepare
for their financial future. The planner lets individuals compute esti-
mates of their future Social Security retirement benefits online. Also
new, **http://www.ssa.gov/women**, provides basic social security
information on retirement, survivors benefits, disability, and Supplemental Security Income pertinent to women.

Veterans of Foreign Wars (VFW)
406 West 34th Street
Kansas City, Missouri 64111
(816)756-3390
http://www.vfw.org/home.shtml
VFW administers a host of programs and pursues issues of national
importance to veterans. The VFW has more than 15,750 trained ser-

vice officers to assist any veteran or their dependents in gaining federal or state entitlements.

HOTLINES AND TOLL-FREE NUMBERS

Social Security Administration's hotline provides recorded public information on benefits 24 hours a day. Other direct customer services are available at this toll-free number from 7 a.m. to 7 p.m. on business days.
(800) 772-1213.

INTERNET SITES AND WEB RESOURCES

Access America for Seniors believes that members of the public should be able to go to one comprehensive website to help them find the particular agency(ies) to satisfy their needs. The "Federal Retirement Benefits" section of this site provides a one-stop information center on Social Security and Veteran and Railroad Retirement Board benefits.
http://www.seniors.gov/retirementplanner/federal_retirement_benefits.html

The Pension and Welfare Benefits Administration website contains several consumer articles on pensions.
http://www.dol.gov/dol/pwba/public/pension.htm

SUGGESTED READING

Cash, Connacht. **The Medicare Answer Book**. Race Point Press, 1999.
Provides definitions of commonly misunderstood terms, useful addresses and phone numbers and extremely practical advice about how to keep from being overwhelmed by the paperwork.

Dickens, Thomas. **Keys to Understanding Social Security Benefits (Barron's Keys to Retirement Planning**. Barron's Educational Series. 1992.
An easy-to-read summary of how each of us contributes to the pro-

gram and the various ways in which we're entitled to benefit.
Jehle, Faustin. **The Complete & Easy Guide to Social Security, Health Care.** Williamson Publishing. 2000.*Discusses medical, hospice and drug expenses and explains which programs provide coverage for them. An extensive directory provides telephone numbers for the organizations and people who can help.*

Landis, Andy. **Social Security : The Inside Story : An Expert Explains Your Rights and Benefits.** Crisp Publications. 1997.
A comprehensive, easy-to-read guide to the Social Security and Medicare systems, outlining benefits and special provisions. Discusses the organizations and their histories, eligibility requirements, payment computations, the claim process, family and survivors benefits.

Matthews, Joseph L. **Social Security, Medicare & Pensions.** Nolo Press. 1999.
An essential handbook that shows everyone over the age of 55 how to maximize benefits and cut through the bureaucracy to get what they're entitled to.

Tomkiel, Stanley. **Social Security Benefits Handbook.** Sourcebooks. 1998.
For those looking for accessible, understandable assistance. The author has distilled details about how Social Security is administered and what benefits are available for whom into clearly presented, easy-to-locate explanations.

Treanor, J. Robert. **Mercer Guide to Social Security and Medicare 2000.** Wm. M. Mercer Publishing. 2000.
A simple explanation with easy-reference benefit tables.

Insurance

ORGANIZATIONS

American Association for Retired Persons (AARP)
601 E. Street, N.W.
Washington, D.C. 20049
(800) 424-2277
(202) 434-2260
http://www.aarp.org/hcchoices/medicare/makechoice/home.html
The "Making Medicare Choices" section of the AARP website provides invaluable information, referral agencies and an extensive glossary of terms regarding Medicare coverage.

American Council of Life Insurers (ACLI)
1001 Pennsylvania Avenue, N.W.
Washington, D.C. 20004-2599
(800) 589-2254.
http://www.acli.com/public/consumer/mainframe_cons.htm
Gives tips on buying insurance products online and answers commonly asked questions regarding life insurers and the Internet.
Explains the best way to shop for long-term care insurance.

Center for Medicare Advocacy, Inc.
P.O. Box 350
Willimantic, CT 06226
(860) 456-7790
http://www.medicareadvocacy.org/index.html
The Center for Medicare Advocacy, Inc. is a private, non-profit organization which provides education, advocacy, and legal assistance to
help elders and people with disabilities obtain necessary healthcare.
Provides a summary of Medicare benefits and current rate information.

Health Care Financing Administration (HCFA)
7500 Security Boulevard
Baltimore, MD 21244, USA
(800) MEDICARE (800) 633-4227)
(410) 786-3000

http://www.medicare.gov/
The HCFA is a federal agency within the U.S. Department of Health
and Human Services. HCFA runs the Medicare and Medicaid programs — two national health care programs that benefit about 75
million Americans. The website allows visitors to search for information on health plans, nursing homes, Medigap policies, contacts,
and Medicare activities in their area.

Health Insurance Association of America (HIAA)
P.O. Box 753
Waldorf, MD 20604-0753
(800) 828-0111
(301) 374-6711
http://www.hiaa.org/cons/cons.htm
Provides various insurance guides for consumers and a state-by-state
directory to insurance bureaus at
http://www.hiaa.org/cons/state_insurance.html

Independent Insurance Agents of America, Inc. (IIAA)
127 South Peyton Street
Alexandria, VA 22314
(800) 221-7917
(703) 683-4422
http://www.iiaa.org/
The IIAA is committed to providing consumers with the most up-to-
date information about trends in the insurance industry as well as
independent advice about shopping for insurance. IIAA is the
nation's oldest and largest national association of independent insurance agents, representing a network of more than 300,000 agents
and agency employees nationwide. Discusses what to look for when
selecting an agent.

Insurance Information Institute (III)
110 William Street
New York, NY 10038
(212) 669-9200
http://www.iii.org/home.html
Founded in 1960, the III is recognized by the media, governments,

regulatory organizations, universities and the public as a primary source of information, analysis and referral concerning insurance. The III also answers nearly 50,000 questions through the National Insurance Consumer Helpline, a toll free telephone service. Their site provides links to various state insurance departments.

Life and Health Insurance Foundation for Education (LIFE)
2175 K Street, NW
Suite 250
Washington, DC 20037
(202) 464-5000
http://www.life-line.org/
The Life and Health Insurance Foundation for Education (LIFE) is a non-profit organization designed to address the public's growing need for information and education on life, health, and disability insurance. On-line information is provided on a variety of insurance topics and extensive glossaries are available.

Medicare Rights Center (MRC)
1460 Broadway, 11th Floor
New York, NY 10036
(212) 869-3850
http://www.medicarerights.org/Index.html
MRC is a national, not-for-profit organization that helps ensure that older adults and people with disabilities get good affordable health care. MRC works to teach people with Medicare and those who counsel them—healthcare providers, social service workers, family members, and others—about Medicare benefits and rights. Provides easy-to-understand information on various Medicare benefits and how to solve problems.

National Center for Assisted Living (NCAL)
1201 "L" Street, N.W.
Washington, D.C. 20005
(202) 842.4444
 http://www.ncal.org/consumer/ltcneeds.htm
The National Center for Assisted Living (NCAL) is the assisted living voice of the American Health Care Assn. (AHCA), the nation's

largest organization representing long term care providers. The "Consumer Information" section of their website provides extensive information about Long Term Care insurance including costs and how to select a good policy.

United Seniors Health Cooperative (USHC)
409 Third Street, SW, Second Floor
Washington, D.C. 20024
(202) 479-6973
http://www.unitedseniorshealth.org/
USHC helps older adults achieve health, independence and financial security through a wide range of programs and services. They have developed publications on topics of vital concern to older consumers, including managed care, financial planning, home care, long-term insurance, Medicare and Medigap insurance.

Hotlines and Toll-Free Numbers

Insurance Information Institute (III)
110 William Street
New York, NY 10038
(800) 942-4242
Insurance experts can give information about auto, home, business or life insurance problems. Hours of operation are 8:00 a.m. - 8:00 p.m., ET Monday - Friday.

Medicare Rights Center (MRC)
1460 Broadway, 11th Floor
New York, NY 10036
(888) HMO-9050

MRC operates a national Medicare HMO Appeals hotline (1-888-HMO-9050) to assist Medicare HMO members who are appealing HMO denials of care or coverage.

National Insurance Crime Bureau (NICB)
901 N. Stuart St., Suite 1150

Arlington, VA. 22203
(888) 241-7159
(703) 469-2200
The NICB partners with insurers and law enforcement agencies to facilitate the identification, detection and prosecution of insurance criminals. Provides a hotline at (800) TEL-NICB (835-6422).

INTERNET SITES AND WEB RESOURCES

A. M. Best - The Insurance Information Source is the world's oldest and most authoritative source of insurance company ratings and information. Its Best's Ratings are the industry's standard measure of insurer financial performance and ability to meet ongoing obligations to policyholders. Free registration is required to access ratings. http://www.ambest.com/

Agenet.com This site provides links to various resources on Medicare and other insurance programs. It also offers information on long term care insurance, nursing homes and other health care choices. http://www.agenet.com

The Coalition Against Insurance Fraud's website provides consumer tips on how to avoid being victimized by insurance fraud. http://www.insurancefraud.org/

A Glossary of Insurance and Financial Planning terms is provided by Norma L. Nielson, Ph.D. of the University of Calgary, Canada. http://www.ucalgary.ca/MG/inrm/glossary/index.htm

HealthInsuranceInfo.Net provided by Georgetown University Institute for Health Care Research and Policy has written "A Consumer Guide for Getting and Keeping Health Insurance" for each state and the District of Columbia. The guides can be found at http://www.healthinsuranceinfo.net/

Insurancecorner.com features a consumer information page that provides

easy-to-understand explanations of various insurance related topics.
http://www.insurancecorner.com/Consumer%20Info/consinfo.htm
Insure.com provides consumers and insurance professionals with the
most comprehensive and current insurance information. Insure.com also
produces interactive tools to assist users in their insurance decisions. An
"Insurance Company Complaint Finder" feature allows visitors to view
complaint rankings as compiled by state insurance departments.
http://www.insure.com/

SUGGESTED READING

Abromovitz, Les. **Long-Term Care Insurance Made Simple**.
Login Brothers Book Company. 1999.
Offers practical advice for consumers on long-term care insurance
and how to buy the best one for the money.

Baldwin, Ben G. **The Complete Book of Insurance : The Consumer's**
Guide to Insuring Your Life, Health, Property and Income
Probus Pub Co. 1996.
In easy-to-understand language, the book explains everything from
variable annuities to disability insurance. Shows how to determine
the right insurance for consumers of different incomes, age group
and family responsibilities.

Brownlie, William. **Life Insurance Boot Camp Buyer's Guide**. Life
Insurance Book Camp. 2000.
This buyer's guide provides the information you need to make rea-
sonable, comprehensive financial planning decisions pertaining to
life, disability, and long term health care insurance,

Davidson, Cynthia. **The Over 50 Insurance Survival Guide : How to**
Know What You Need, Get What You Want and Avoid Rip-Offs.
Silver Lake Publishing. 1995.
Takes older consumers through the maze of insurance products and
helps them determine what's available and what's advisable.

Enteen, Robert. Health Insurance : **How to Get It, Keep It, or**

Improve What You've Got. Demos Vermande. 1996.
Shows how to locate and evaluate coverage, compare costs, and obtain the maximum benefits — even from your existing insurance plan. Discusses long-term care coverage and Medicare.

Godin, Seth. **If You're Clueless About Insurance and Want to Know More.** Dearborn Trade. 1997.
Outlines how insurance needs change over a lifetime as well as how to take an intelligent, comprehensive approach to insurance.

Inlander, Charles. **Medicare Made Easy.** Peoples Medical Society. 1999.
This comprehensive guidebook offers the most current information on Medicare, explaining eligibility requirements, coverage, hospital information, long-term care, doctor fees, treatment options, and more.

Knaus, Denise. **Medicare Made Simple : A Consumer's Guide to the Medicare Program.** Health Information Press. 1996.
Presents a basic guide to Medicare. Covers entitlement, enrollment, coverage of services, payment methods, and requirements.

Shelton, Phyllis. **Long Term Care Planning Guide.** Shelton Marketing Services. 1999
Provides families with a sense of urgency to plan ahead for long-term care and the necessary information to do so. Discusses how long-term care works and why it's needed as an essential part of financial planning.

Silver Lake Editors. **How to Insure Your Income : A Step by Step Guide to Buying the Coverage You Need at Prices You Can Afford (How to Insure...Series)** Silver Lake Publishing. 1997.
Tells consumers what they need to know about disability insurance—the least known yet most often needed coverage.

Wilson, Reg. **How to Insure Your Life : A Step by Step Guide to Buying the Coverage You Need at Prices You Can Afford.** Silver Lake Publishing. 1996.
Offers protection guidelines to safeguard against misleading information when purchasing life insurance.

Fincancial Planning

Organizations

American Association of Individual Investors (AAII)
625 N. Michigan Ave.
Chicago, IL 60611
(800) 428-2244
(312) 280-0170
http://www.aaii.org/
Specializes in providing education in the area of stock investing, mutual funds, portfolio management and retirement planning. AAII is a non-profit organization that arms members with the knowledge and tools needed to manage their finances effectively and profitably.

American Savings Education Council (ASEC)
2121 K Street NW, Suite 600
Washington, DC 20037-1896
(202) 659-0670
http://www.asec.org
The ASEC, in an effort to create a better understanding of savings issues, is developing user-friendly educational materials to educate Americans on the need to save, assist individuals in setting their savings goals, provide basic steps to follow to achieve savings goals, answer frequently asked questions, and direct individuals to other sources of information. Selected materials are available in hard copy as well as online.

Certified Financial Planner Board of Standards (CFP Board)
1700 Broadway, Suite 2100
Denver, CO 80290
(888) 237-6275
(303) 830-7500
http://cfp-board.org
The "Consumers" section of the CFP Board's website discusses questions to consider when selecting a financial planner. Tells how to file a complaint and welcomes visitors to order their free *Financial Planning Resource Kit*.

Forum for Investor Advice
7200 Wisconsin Avenue, Suite 709
Bethesda, Maryland 20814
(301) 656-7998
http://investoradvice.org
Provides a glossary of investment advice and an interactive pop-quiz for testing your knowledge of investing. Includes articles about investing and links to organizations offering information to investors at little or no charge.

National Association of Investors Corporation (NAIC)
P.O. Box 220
Royal Oak, MI. 48068
(877) ASK-NAIC
(248) 583-NAIC
http://www.better-investing.org/
NAIC is a non-profit, largely volunteer organization dedicated to investment education. NAIC offers many unique products, services and professional support to help you become an informed investor. Most of the investment analysis forms and guides are easy to learn and use and provide a sound, proven method for investment analysis. Explains how to start an "Investment Club" in your area.

HOTLINES AND TOLL-FREE NUMBERS

Federal Consumer Education Center
Pueblo, CO 81009
(800) 688-9889
http://www.pueblo.gsa.gov
Federal Consumer Information Center serves as a single point of contact for individuals with questions about Federal agencies, programs and services. Their website provides on-line brochures on investing, saving, estate planning and other money management topics. The toll-free Call Center staff can answer questions about all aspects of the Federal government or direct callers to an appropriate contact.

U.S. Securities and Exchange Commission Headquarters (SEC)
450 Fifth Street, NW
Washington, DC 20549
(800) SEC-0330
Office of Investor Education and Assistance:
(202) 942-7040
e-mail: help@sec.gov
http://www.sec.gov/
Contact the SEC to obtain free publications, investor alerts, learn how to file a complaint, and how to contact the SEC.

INTERNET SITES AND WEB RESOURCES

About Money is AARPs guide to finance and work. It contains consumer information on financial planning, retirement, career choices, and tips on books and websites.
http://www.aarp.org/moneyguide/

Investment Company Institute's webpage entitled "Online Resources for Retirement Investors" is a one-stop link area to many sites offering retirement planning information.
http://www.ici.org/aboutfunds/addl_resources_retir.html

Investor Protection Trust's website serves as an independent source of non-commercial investor education materials and assists in the prosecution of securities fraud. Provides independent, objective information needed by consumers to make informed investment decisions.
http://www.investorprotection.org/

Investorama provides a wealth of information on all investment topics for the novice as well as the experienced investor. Offers links to thousands of investment sites, financial guides, interactive calculators and an extensive glossary of investment terms. Membership is free and includes access to their chatrooms and message boards.
http://www.investorama.com/

Investorwords.com is the most comprehensive financial glossary you'll find online. Provides over 5,000 definitions of investment terms.

http://www.investorwords.com/

Money-minded brings you up-to-the-minute advice and news. One of the few websites dedicated to women's financial goals, it helps you find the smartest, easiest ways to obtain the best deals and secure your future.
http://www.moneyminded.com/

MsMoney.com is a financial services Internet company offering commerce and community to empower and educate women to be financially healthy.
Women require a trusted arena in which to receive high quality, relevant financial information and services to meet their unique needs.
http://www.msmoney.com/index.asp

Principles of Retirement Planning presented by accounting firm Deloitte and Touche discusses how to gather data and develop goals for a financially secure retirement.
http://www.dtonline.com/prptoc/prptoc.htm

SEC's Investor Education and Assistance website contains a wealth of information for investors including many interactive investment tools and an online complaint form.
http://www.sec.gov/oiea1.htm

Smartmoney.com is the Wall Street Journal's magazine of personal business. This section of their website deals exclusively with financial planning for retirement topics.
http://www.smartmoney.com/ac/retirement/

SUGGESTED READING

Bach, David. **Smart Women Finish Rich**. Broadway Books. 1999.
Discusses the seven steps to achieving financial security.

Berger, Lisa. **Feathering Your Nest**. Workman Publishing. 1993.
An extensive planner for those who want to invest for the future.

Brenner, Lynn. **Smart Questions to Ask Your Financial Advisors.** Berkley Books. 1997.
A guide for people who are serious about managing their money and want to work with their advisors as partners.

Brostoff, Phyllis. **Old Talk, New Conversations: A Planning Guide for Seniors and Their Families.** Elton-Wolf Publishing. 2000.
A planning guide for seniors and their families. Discusses how to make decisions about the financial, legal, medical, and lifestyle issues that arise as a loved one grows older.

Hoffman, Ellen. **The Retirement Catch-Up Guide: 54 Real-Life Lessons to Boost Your Retirement Resources Now!** Newmarket Press. 2000.
Gives easy-to-read, easy-to-follow successful strategies that seniors have taken to get their retirement saving and planning up to speed, so that you too can catch-up.

Holzer, Bambi. **Set for Life: A Financial Planning Guide for People Over 50.** John Wiley and sons. 2000.
Discusses how to assess your needs, manage your investments, cope with taxes and insurance, stay ahead of inflation, prepare your estate, and develop realistic financial goals, no matter what your situation or how financially savvy you are.

King, Al. Suddenly Alone: **A Financial Guide for Widows.** Maple Leaf Press. 1997.
An essential book for every woman who has ever wondered about how, and what she will do with her assets when her husband is gone. It is an uncomplicated, sincere and friendly book of survivor success stories, financial facts, practical money strategies, investment counsel, and retirement planning.

Morris, Kenneth M. **The Wall Street Journal Guide to Planning Your Financial Future.** Lightbulb Press. 1998.
Provides clear explanations of the things you'll need to know and guidelines for the decisions you have to make to enjoy a comfortable retirement.

Estate Planning

ORGANIZATIONS

National Charities Information Bureau (NCIB)
19 Union Square West
New York, NY 10003
(212) 929-6300
http://www.give.org/index.cfm
NCIB's mission is to promote informed giving and to enable more contributors to make sound giving decisions. NCIB believes that donors are entitled to accurate information about the charitable organizations that seek their support. *A Quick Reference Guide* provides a handy way of determining whether a charity NCIB evaluates meets all of established standards in philanthropy.

INTERNET SITES AND WEB RESOURCES

Big Charts features an easy to use Historical Quotes tool which allows users to look up a security's exact closing price on any date since 1985. Simply type in the symbol and a historical date to view a quote for that security. Useful for determining "date of death" values for income and estate tax purposes.
http://www.bigcharts.com

California Estate Planning, Probate and Trust Law's website features a useful checklist of questions to ask to help determine if an attorney is qualified to handle estate planning matters and a list of documents to be brought to a first meeting with an estate planning attorney. An extensive "Links" page refers to other sites on estate planning. The site also allows users to search for U.S. Estate Planning, Probate and Trust Attorneys with websites by entering their home state.
http://www.ca-probate.com/

Colorado Bar Association's website explains estate planning in simple terms and gives examples of questions to ask an estate planning attorney.
http://www.cobar.org/estateplanning.htm

Martindale-Hubbell Lawyer Locator provides basic practice profile data on virtually every attorney in the U.S. The search feature allows the user to designate "Probate, Trusts & Estates" as a practice area to find an estate planning attorney in any city or state.
http://lawyers.martindale.com/marhub/form/by.html

Moneycentral discusses the important steps in planning an estate. Provides various estate planning questions and answers and a message board allows visitors to ask their own specific questions.
http://moneycentral.msn.com/articles/retire/estate/contents.asp?p=1

Smartmoney.com is the Wall Street Journal's magazine of personal business. This section of their website deals exclusively with estate planning topics.
http://www.smartmoney.com/ac/estate/

U.S. General Services Administration has prepared life advice pamphlets called *Making A Will, Planning Your Estate and Being An Executor* in conjunction with the MetLife Consumer Education Center and the Division for Public Education of the American Bar Association. They are available on-line at:
http://www.pueblo.gsa.gov/cic_text/money/will/makewill.htm
http://www.pueblo.gsa.gov/cic_text/money/estate/estate.htm
http://www.pueblo.gsa.gov/cic_text/money/executor/executor.htm

SUGGESTED READING

Accettura, P. Mark. **The Michigan Estate Planning Guide: The Twenty Most Commonly Asked Estate Planning Questions.** Collinwood Press. 1999.
A complete estate planning guide organized in question and answer form.

Adams, Kathleen. **The Complete Estate Planning Guide.** Penguin-Putnam. 1998.
A complete and authoritative guide to building maximum financial security for you and your heirs.

American Bar Association. **Guide to Wills and Estates: Everything You need to Know About Wills, Trusts, Estates and Taxes.** Times Books. 1995.
Written by a group of America's top lawyers, this book provides expert legal counsel. Among the topics covered are living wills and how to avoid inheritance taxes.

Bennett, Jarratt. **Maximize Your Inheritance for Widows, Widowers and Heirs.** Dearborn. 1999.
Explains how to manage your assets, invest for the future and make the money last.

Berry, Dawn Bradley. **The Estate Planning Sourcebook.** Lowell House. 1999.
Explains how to get expert help, minimize costs, and maximize the amount of property you can bestow on others or favorite charities.

Bove, Alexander. **The Medicaid Planning Handbook.** Little, Brown & Co. 1996.
A guide to protecting your family's assets from catastrophic nursing home costs.

Condon, Gerald. **Beyond the Grave: The Right Way and the Wrong Way of Leaving Money to Your Children (And Others).** Harper Business. 1996.
With good sense, humor, and authority, the author provides a thorough look at inheritance planning with an eye toward maintaining good, stable family relations well after the estate has been settled.

Doane, Randell C. **Death and Taxes: The Complete Guide to Family Inheritance Planning.** Swallow Press. 1998.
Wills, trusts, probate, life insurance, taxes and many other estate planning concerns are discussed in detail. Over a hundred of the most commonly asked questions are answered in simple, straightforward terms.

Esperti, Robert. **The Living Trust Workbook: How You and Your**

Legal Advisors Can Design, Fund, and Maintain Your Living Trust Plan. Penguin USA. 1995.
A useful guidebook for safe financial planning for those who wish to keep their assets probate-free and private. Provides money-saving tips, checklists, and information on choosing a lawyer.

Esperti, Robert. **Protect Your Estate: A Personal Guide to Intelligent Estate Planning.** McGraw-Hill Books. 1993.
Presents innovative strategies with practical, easy-to-implement tips on working with wills, federal estate taxes, and the other hows and whys of estate planning.

Hawley, Thomas Hart. **The Artful Dodger's Guide to Planning Your Estate, Revised Edition: The Only Book on Estate Planning Guaranteed to Keep You Entertained.** Linthincum Press. 2000.
Gives practical, straightforward and lighthearted advice crucial to anyone who has acquired even modest wealth.

Trusty, Sharon. **Widowed: Beginning Again Personally and Financially.** August House Publishers. 1999.
Offers practical help with the personal and financial concerns after the loss of a spouse.

Ormon, Suze. **The 9 Steps to Financial Freedom.** Crown Publishing. 1997.
Explains how to master the practical elements of financial life: investments, credit, insurance, and estate and retirement planning. This books tells you everything to need to know to provide for yourself and your family - not abstract principles but specific, concrete and easy-to-follow procedures.

Rosenberg, Stephen. **Last Minute Retirement Planning.** Career Press. 1998.
Maybe there's only a few more years to retirement, or perhaps early retirement may be an option. Readers need to know what strategies can put them over the top and make their retirement years more comfortable.

Funeral Arrangements

ORGANIZATIONS

American Association for Retired Persons (AARP)
601 E. Street, N.W.
Washington, D.C. 20049
(800) 424-2277
(202) 434-2260
http://www.aarp.org/confacts/money/funeral.html
The "Funeral and Burial Costs" section of the AARP website provides invaluable information and referral agencies for funeral and burial costs.

Cremation Association of North America (CANA)
401 North Michigan Avenue
Chicago, Illinois 60611
(312) 644-6610
http://www.cremationassociation.org/html/for_consumers.html
The "Consumer" section of this website provides brochures answering the most commonly asked questions about cremation as a memorial option.

Funeral and Memorial Societies of America (FAMSA)
P.O. Box 10
Hinesburg, VT. 05461
(800) 458-5563
(802) 482-3437
http://www.funerals.org
FAMSA monitors the funeral industry for consumers and is dedicated to a consumer's right to choose a meaningful, dignified, affordable funeral. Lobbies to reduce unjustifiable costs of burial and other funeral services. Provides extensive information about veteran's funeral and burial benefits, organ and body donation and cremation.

International Cemetery and Funeral Association (ICFA)
1895 Preston White Drive
Reston, VA. 20191
(800) 645-7770

(703) 391-8400
http://icfa.org
Presents straight answers to real questions about funerals, cemeteries, cremation, grief and other issues related to the end of life. Dedicated to the belief that no family should have to face the loss of a loved one uninformed and unprepared.

Jewish Funeral Directors of America (JFDA)
150 Lynway, Suite 506
Lynn, MA. 01902
(781) 477-9300
http://www.jfda.org
The JFDA was organized in 1932 and since that time has been assisting people of the Jewish faith arrange meaningful and affordable funerals in the Jewish tradition. Within the Jewish community, the JFDA works closely with the Conservative, Reform, and Orthodox religious movements. Users can search the site for a funeral home in their state. Guides on the site include Jewish funeral information and Jewish funeral etiquette.

Monument Builders of North America (MBNA)
3158 S. River Rd., Suite 224
Des Plaines, IL. 60173
(800) 827-1000
(847) 803-8800
http://www.monumentbuilders.org
MBNA members are actively engaged in the design, production, installation and maintenance of monuments/memorials, both personal and civic. While maintaining a broad range of programs and services for its members, MBNA also actively encourages public interest, knowledge, and appreciation of the art of memorialization. Their website contains information on purchasing a monument and presents examples of creative and unique memorials.

National Funeral Directors Association (NFDA)
13625 Bishop's Drive
Brookfield, WI 53005
(800) 228-6332

(262) 789-1880
http://nfda.org/resources/index.html
The mission of NFDA is to enhance the funeral service profession and promote quality service to the consumer. The "Consumer Resources" page of their website features links providing extensive information on funeral costs, state funeral director associations, and funeral service organizations.

U.S. Department of Veterans Affairs
National Cemetery Administration
810 Vermont Avenue, N.W.
Washington, D.C. 20420
800-827-1000
http://www.cem.va.gov/index.htm
The National Cemetery Administration (NCA) honors Veterans with a final resting place and lasting memorials that commemorate their service to our nation. Maintains national cemeteries and provides a headstone or marker and Presidential Memorial Certificates in recognition of veterans service to a their nation.

HOTLINES AND TOLL-FREE NUMBERS

Federal Trade Commission
Consumer Response Center
Washington, D.C. 20580
(877) FTC-HELP
http://ftc.gov/ftc/complaint.htm
Contact the Federal Trade Commission to file a complaint against a funeral home.

Funeral Service Consumer Assistance Program (FSCAP)
P.O. Box 486
Elm Grove, WI. 53122-0486
(800) 662-7666
(708) 827-6337
FSCAP is a nonprofit consumer service designed to help people understand funeral service and related topics and to help them resolve funeral service concerns. FSCAP service representatives offer

consumers recommendations to steer them in the right direction and to the right resources to identify needs, address complaints, and resolve problems.

INTERNET SITES AND WEB RESOURCES

eGroup provides an e-mail discussion forum for consumers with comments about funeral and cemetery purchases. Members are invited to share their experiences or post questions.
http://www.egroups.com/list/funeral/consumers/

Federal Trade Commission Consumer Response Center presents useful information on making funeral and burial arrangements.
http://www.ftc.gov/bcp/conline/pubs/services/funeral.htm

Funeralnet is a comprehensive online resource for obituary, funeral, cremation and cemetery information. Has a section on bereavement travel.
http://www.funeralnet.com/info_guide/index.html

University of Florida College of Medicine Anatomical Board's website provides a state-by-state directory of medical schools that accept organ donations.
http://www.med.ufl.edu/anatbd/usprograms.html

SUGGESTED READING

AARP's Product Report on Funerals and Burials: Goods and Services
For a free copy of the report, send an e-mail to member@aarp.org. Include the title, your name and your postal mailing address.
You can also call AARP at (800) 424-2277 to obtain a copy
This product report offers more information on these topics. It can be a resource when you prearrange a funeral and burial (whether or not you prepay) or when you make arrangements at the time of death for someone.

Carlson, Lisa. **Caring for the Dead: Your Final Act of Love.** Upper

Access Book Publishers. 1998.
This is a comprehensive guide for consumers making funeral arrangements with or without a funeral director.

Fatteh, Abdullah. **At Journey's End: A Complete Guide To Funerals And Funeral Planning.** Health Information Press, 1999.
An invaluable guide, reference and resource for planning one's own funeral and/or the funeral of a loved one.

Kerr, Margaret. **Facing a Death in the Family: Caring for Someone Through Illness and Dying, Arranging the Funeral, Dealing with the Will and Estate.** John Wiley & Sons. 1999.
An easy-to-understand guide to the difficult task of caring for ailing loved ones.

Lynch, Thomas. **The Undertaking: Life Studies From the Dismal Trade.** Penguin USA. 1998.
Ostensibly about death and its attendant rituals. The Undertaking is in the end about life. In each case Mr. Lynch writes, it is the one that gives meaning to the other. Mr. Lynch is a poet, an author and a funeral director in Milford, Michigan.

Lynch, Thomas. **Bodies in Motion and at Rest: On Metaphor and Mortality.** W.W. Norton & Company. 2000.
A collection of essays in search of the meaning of our lives and times, between birth and death.

Martin, Sheila. **Saying Goodbye with Love: A Step-by-Step Guide Through the Details of Death.** Crossroad Publishing Co. 1999.
A handbook for overcoming the challenges of the newly bereaved. Includes information on estate planning.

Miller, Clarence. **The Funeral Book.** Robert D. Reed Publishing. 1994.
Gives insider's advice for saving money and reducing stress while planning a funeral.

Moderow, Karen. **The Parting: Celebrate a Life by Planning a**

Meaningful, Creative Funeral. Jordon West Publications. 1996.
Offers encouragement and step-by-step instructions for creating a memorial that will reflect the special life and personality of a loved one.

Polen, Dallas. **Funeral Arrangement Choice Guide: A Workbook for Arrangements at the Time of a Death.** Servant Publications. 1996.
This workbook is a step-by-step guide to asking questions, delegating duties and evaluating funeral options.

Young, Gregory. **The High Cost of Dying: A Guide to Funeral Planning.** Prometheus Books. 1994.
This comprehensive overview of the funeral home business provides valuable inside information needed by thoughtful consumers.

HOW TO ORDER

Copies of *Lost and Found: Finding Self-Reliance After the Loss of a Spouse* can be ordered directly through our website www.lostandfoundspouse.com or by sending $24.95 plus $1.50 Michigan Sales Tax to:

Collinwood Press, LLC
35055 W. Twelve Mile, Suite 132
Farmington Hills, Michigan 48331

Please provide the address to which book(s) are to be sent.
Also provide a phone number or email address in the event we have any questions about your order.
Allow 7 days for shipping.

SHIPPING COSTS ARE INCLUDED IN THE PRICE OF THE BOOK.

QUANTITY DISCOUNTS AVAILABLE UPON REQUEST

A portion of the proceeds donated to
Hospice of Michigan

HOW TO ORDER

Copies of *Lost and Found: Finding Self-Reliance After the Loss of a Spouse* can be ordered directly through our website www.lostand-foundspouse.com or by sending $24.95 plus $1.50 Michigan Sales Tax to:

Collinwood Press, LLC
35055 W. Twelve Mile, Suite 132
Farmington Hills, Michigan 48331

Please provide the address to which book(s) are to be sent.
Also provide a phone number or email address in the event we have any questions about your order.
Allow 7 days for shipping.

SHIPPING COSTS ARE INCLUDED IN THE PRICE OF THE BOOK.

QUANTITY DISCOUNTS AVAILABLE UPON REQUEST

A portion of the proceeds donated to
Hospice of Michigan